D0163071

Bloom's Modern Critical Views

African American
Poets: Wheatley-
Tolson
African American
Poets:
Hayden-Dove
Edward Albee
American and
Canadian Women
Poets, 1930–present
American Women
Poets, 1650–1950
Maya Angelou
Asian-American
Writers
Margaret Atwood
Jane Austen
James Baldwin
Honoré de Balzac
Samuel Beckett
Saul Bellow
The Bible
William Blake
Jorge Luis Borges
Ray Bradbury
The Brontës
Gwendolyn Brooks
Elizabeth Barrett
Browning
Robert Browning
Italo Calvino
Albert Camus
Truman Capote
Lewis Carroll
Willa Cather
Cervantes
Geoffrey Chaucer
Anton Chekhov
Kate Chopin
Agatha Christie
Samuel Taylor
Coleridge
Joseph Conrad

Contemporary Poets
Stephen Crane
Dante
Daniel Defoe
Don DeLillo
Charles Dickens
Emily Dickinson
John Donne and the
17th-Century Poets
Fyodor Dostoevsky
W.E.B. DuBois
George Eliot
T. S. Eliot
Ralph Ellison
Ralph Waldo Emerson
William Faulkner
F. Scott Fitzgerald
Sigmund Freud
Robert Frost
Johann Wolfgang
von Goethe
George Gordon, Lord
Byron
Graham Greene
Thomas Hardy
Nathaniel Hawthorne
Ernest Hemingway
Hermann Hesse
Hispanic-American
Writers
Homer
Langston Hughes
Zora Neale Hurston
Aldous Huxley
Henrik Ibsen
John Irving
Henry James
James Joyce
Franz Kafka
John Keats
Jamaica Kincaid
Stephen King
Rudyard Kipling

Milan Kundera
D. H. Lawrence
Doris Lessing
Ursula K. Le Guin
Sinclair Lewis
Norman Mailer
Bernard Malamud
Christopher Marlowe
Gabriel García
Márquez
Cormac McCarthy
Carson McCullers
Herman Melville
Arthur Miller
John Milton
Molière
Toni Morrison
Native-American
Writers
Joyce Carol Oates
Flannery O'Connor
Eugene O'Neill
George Orwell
Octavio Paz
Sylvia Plath
Edgar Allan Poe
Katherine Anne
Porter
Thomas Pynchon
Philip Roth
Salman Rushdie
J. D. Salinger
Jean-Paul Sartre
William Shakespeare:
Histories and
Poems
William Shakespeare:
Romances
William Shakespeare:
The Comedies
William Shakespeare:
The Tragedies
George Bernard Shaw

Bloom's Modern Critical Views

Bloom's Modern Critical Views

IVAN TURGENEV

Edited and with an introduction by
Harold Bloom
Sterling Professor of the Humanities
Yale University

CHELSEA HOUSE
PUBLISHERS
A Haights Cross Communications Company
Philadelphia

Library of Congress Cataloging-in-Publication Data

Ivan Turgenev / edited and with an introduction by Harold Bloom.
   p. cm. -- (Bloom's modern critical views)
Includes bibliographical references and index.
  ISBN: 0-7910-7399-8
 1. Turgenev, Ivan Sergeevich, 1818–1883--Criticism and
interpretation. I. Bloom, Harold. II. Series.
   PG3443.I925 2002
   891.73'3--dc21
                                          2002152673

Chelsea House Publishers
1974 Sproul Road, Suite 400
Broomall, PA 19008-0914

http://www.chelseahouse.com

Contributing Editor: Janyce Marson

Cover designed by Terry Mallon

Cover photo © Bettman/CORBIS

Layout by EJB Publishing Services

Contents

Editor's Note

My introduction centers upon "Forest and Steppe," the last of the *Sportsman's Sketches*, which I interpret as an emblem of the deliberate limitations of Turgenev's art in his first major work.

Richard Freeborn, translator of the *Sketches*, begins this volume with Turgenev's early apprenticeship to Pushkin, founder of Russian literature.

Fathers and Sons is read by Kathryn Feuer as the doomed saga of Bazarov the nihilist, which she speculates that Dostoevsky admired.

Turgenev's realistic insight that love is a momentary illusion is shown by Edgar L. Frost to dominate the "love story," "Mumu."

The influence of Turgenev upon Hemingway is traced by Robert Coltrane, who shows that Hemingway's novella, *The Torrents of Spring*, takes more than its title from Turgenev's novella, *The Torrents of Spring*.

In another influence-study, Richard C. Harris shows the effect of Turgenev's "First Love" upon Willa Cather's *A Lost Lady*.

Fathers and Sons returns with Harold K. Schefski's analysis of the Parable of the Prodigal Son (Luke 15:17-22) and its relation to Turgenev's novel.

Patrick Waddington attempts to rescue Turgenev's *Dym* (*Smoke*) from its neglect, while Irene Masing-Delic sees the *Notes of a Hunter* (or *Sportsman's Sketches*) as a quest for the Russian universal man.

Henry James regarded Turgenev as "the novelist's novelist," and Glyn Turton describes the role of Turgenev in helping James to formulate his critical stance.

Fathers and Sons receives contrasting interpretations from Dennis Walder, Glyn Turton, and Pam Morris, after which Richard Gregg usefully juxtaposes Turgenev and Hawthorne, Henry James's unacknowledged precursor.

In this volume's final essay, Turgenev's pervasive American influence returns in Paul W. Miller's account of the debt of Willa Cather and Sherwood Anderson to the Russian master.

Introduction

My favorites among the *Sportsman's Sketches* are "Bezhin Lea" and "Kasyan from the Beautiful Lands," but as I have written about them in *How to Read and Why* (2000), I turn here to "Forest and Steppe," the last of the *Sketches*.

With Chekhov, Turgenev invented one prevalent mode of the modern short story, challenged later by the irreality of what could be called the Kafka-Borges tradition. The aesthetic splendor of Turgenev's *Sketches* partly depends upon the writer's apprehension of natural beauty: this hunter's quarry is not so much game as vista.

"Forest and Steppe" begins by emphasizing the hunter's solitary joy:

> By the time you've travelled two miles or so the rim of the sky is beginning to crimson; in the birches jackdaws are awakening and clumsily fluttering from branch to branch; sparrows twitter about the dark hayricks. The air grows brighter, the road clearer, the sky lightens, suffusing the clouds with whiteness and the fields with green. Lights burn red in the cottages and sleepy voices can be heard beyond the gates. In the meantime dawn has burst into flame; stripes of gold have risen across the sky and wreaths of mist form in the ravines; to the loud singing of skylarks and the soughing of the wind before dawn the sun rises, silent and purple, above the horizon. Light floods over the world and your heart trembles within you like a bird. Everything is so fresh, gay and lovely! You can see for miles. Here a village glimmers beyond the woodland; there, farther away, is another village with a white church and then a hill with a birchwood; beyond it is the marsh

1

to which you are driving ... Step lively there, horses! Forward at a brisk trot! ... No more than two miles to go now. The sun is rising quickly, the sky is clear ... The weather will be perfect. You meet a herd of cattle coming in a long line from the village. Then you ascend the hill ... What a view! The river winds away for seven miles or more, a faint blue glimmer through the mist; beyond it are the water-green meadows: beyond them, low-lying hills; in the distance lapwings veer and cry above the marsh; through the gleaming moisture which pervades the air the distance emerges clearly ... there is no summer haze. How freely one breathes the air into one's lungs, how buoyant are one's limbs, how strong one feels in the grip of this fresh springtime atmosphere!

The line of descent to Hemingway's Nick Adams stories is clear: the issue is solitary freedom, Hemingway's "living your life all the way up." You and your dog are at last alone together in the forest, and you behold a totality of vision:

You walk along the edge of the forest, keeping your eyes on the dog, but in the meantime there come to mind beloved images, beloved faces, the living and the dead, and long-since dormant impressions unexpectedly awaken; the imagination soars and dwells on the air like a bird, and everything springs into movement with such clarity and stands before the eyes. Your heart either suddenly quivers and starts beating fast, passionately racing forward, or drowns irretrievably in recollections. The whole of life unrolls easily and swiftly like a scroll; a man has possession of his whole past, all his feelings, all his powers, his entire soul. And nothing in his surroundings can disturb him— there is no sun, no wind, no noise ...

This vision, however individually total, knows its own limits. Yours is the freedom of the forest, and not the dismaying sublime of the steppe:

Farther, farther! The steppelands are approaching. You look down from a hill—what a view! Round, low hillocks, ploughed waves; ravines overgrown with bushes weave among them; small woods are scattered here and there like elongated islands; from village to village run narrow tracks; churches gleam white;

between thickets of willow glitters a small river, its flow staunched in four places by dams; far off in the field wild cranes stick out as they waddle in file; an antiquated landowner's mansion with its outbuildings, orchard and threshing floor is settled comfortably beside a small pond. But you go on travelling, farther and farther. The hillocks grow shallower and shallower and there is hardly a tree to be seen. Finally, there it is—the limitless, enormous steppe no eye can encompass!

The *Sketches* confine themselves deliberately to what the eye can encompass. For confronting the steppe, you need to be Tolstoy, yourself a sublime nature, as strong as what you might behold. With remarkable, nuanced control, Turgenev subtly implies his own limits, and shows us again why his *Sketches* are so modulated a masterpiece.

RICHARD FREEBORN

The Literary Apprenticeship:
Pushkin—A Sportsman's Sketches

Turgenev underwent his literary apprenticeship in the forties, but in any discussion of his literary development it is necessary to begin a decade earlier. In fact, in any study of the major Russian writers of the nineteenth century one has to begin with Pushkin. Pushkin was an artistic example and a literary determinant of the utmost value. His many merits cannot be described in so many words, but his influence is undeniable, and his influence on Turgenev is particularly important because it was from Pushkin that Turgenev was to take his literary example, especially in the case of the novel. Before Pushkin there was no Russian literature to speak of and there was certainly no indigenous Russian novel. It is probably in respect of the novel that Pushkin made his greatest contribution to the development of nineteenth-century Russian literature, since it was in the novel—specifically in the *realistic* novel—that nineteenth-century Russian literature was to be so outstanding.

In 1846, in a review of *The Death of Lyapunov*, a play by Gedeonov, who was a rival for Pauline Viardot's affections—and this, among other things, accounts for the unfavourable tone of the review—Turgenev offered a brief summary of the kind of development that had occurred in Russian literature during the first half of the nineteenth century:

From *Turgenev: The Novelist's Novelist*. © 1960 by Oxford University Press.

The history of art and literature in Russia is remarkable for its special dual growth. We began with imitation of foreign models; writers with a purely superficial talent, garrulous and prolific, presented in their works, which were entirely devoid of any living connection with the people, nothing more than reflections of other people's talents and other people's ideas.... 0Meanwhile, a revolution was quietly occurring in society; the foreign elements were being remoulded, were being assimilated into our blood-stream; the receptive Russian nature, just as if it had been awaiting this influence, developed and grew not day by day but hour by hour, and developed along its own path....[1]

In the context of the review Turgenev is referring to the importance of Gogol and in this he is following Belinsky (the review was in fact first thought to have been written by Belinsky). But in the emphasis which he lays upon the increasing realism and the extraordinary rapid development of Russian literature Turgenev is remarking something that is common to Russian literature as a whole during the nineteenth century and is particularly true of the novel. In 1830, for instance, Russian literature could boast of no novel of importance, whereas in 1880 Russian literature could boast of a tradition of the realistic novel equal to, if not superior to, that of any other European literature. For the beginnings of this extraordinarily rapid growth one has to look to Pushkin. Before Pushkin, in the work of Karamzin (*Poor Liza, A Knight of Our Time*) at the turn of the century or in the later work of such writers as Polevoy, Marlinsky, Vel'tman and Zagoskin, certain tentative beginnings had been made. Their work, meeting the demand for pseudo-historical novels on the lines of Walter Scott or romances on the French model, had the effect of gradually awakening the Russian reader to the importance of literature as an educative and social force. No one could have called the work of these writers—with the exception of Karamzin's short prose works—specifically Russian. Despite the fact that the settings and the names might be Russian, their works were imitative of models in Western European literature. To this extent their stories were quite simply not 'real', not directly related to the experience of the Russian reader. Yet this consideration of 'reality' is very important, for the Russian novel as we know it is the Russian *realistic* novel which set out to portray, and by inference to expose, the realities of Russian social life, its virtues and its vices. The first work of this kind to appear was Pushkin's *Eugene Onegin*, completed in 1831.

The work was an oddity in formal terms, being a 'novel in verse', as Pushkin subtitled it, and it had no successors in this particular genre. However, it was a work which presented to the Russian reader a picture of his own society in unmistakable clarity and detail, and it illuminated one of the most important problems of the day: the problem of the 'superfluous man'. In concentrating on this problem Pushkin was drawing an important distinction between the 'imitative' elements in Russian society and the elements in Russian society which might be called 'indigenous', represented in the novel by the contrast between the metropolitan civilization of St. Petersburg and the traditional life of the Russian countryside, though this contrast is chiefly apparent in the relationship between hero and heroine. Pushkin's hero, Onegin, was a 'superfluous man', a product of those Western influences which had penetrated Russian society after the Napoleonic campaign. He was Byronic, both in inspiration and in manner, but he was a Russian Byronic hero who adopted the pose of Byronism as a form of protest against prevalent conditions. It is in the social sense that he must be regarded as 'superfluous'—as a man who by virtue of his upbringing, his undisciplined and tragically inadequate education and the adoption of the Western pose of Byronism in Russian circumstances finds himself indifferent to those circumstances, intolerable of their norms and proprieties and, as a consequence, 'superfluous' in the social conditions of his time. Naturally, there is here an implied criticism of Russian society itself. This 'superfluous man' is not unintelligent or without talent. Indeed, he represents new ideas, however poorly assimilated they may be, and a new social force, a new generation with new aspirations. Such aspirations, however, have been stifled by society, with the result that the 'superfluous man' has become a divided character, in which the head and the heart are mutually antagonistic; he betrays signs of disillusionment and emotional indifference, a mind that prides itself on cynicism and a precosity that cloaks itself in haughtiness. Such are the inner symptoms of the 'superfluous man', the living embodiment of the sickness at the heart of Russian society, which Pushkin exposes in his psychological portrait of Eugene Onegin, and in so doing he created a prototype figure for several generations of similar heroes in the Russian realistic novel. But of equal importance is the figure of the heroine, Tat'yana, whose emotional spontaneity and 'naturalness' are contrasted with the egotistical preoccupations of Onegin. It is in the relationship between Tat'yana and Onegin that the contrasting issues in the fiction—the opposition of imitative and indigenous, of town and country, of new and old—are not only made clear, but interact upon each other, revealing the social, psychological and—what is most important—the moral dilemma at the root both of Russian society and of all human relationships in general.

This relationship establishes a formula which is to be followed by several subsequent Russian novelists, though especially by Turgenev. The relationship only begins when the hero finds himself in a milieu that is unfamiliar to him, either through long dissociation or simply because he has had no previous knowledge of it, and the result is that the hero appears in this milieu as a relative stranger, whose very strangeness and newness are a source of fascination to the heroine. The contrast afforded by the presence of the hero in this strange milieu is at once both social and psychological. His social attributes contrast with the social characteristics of the strange milieu and his psychological attributes contrast with the psychological characteristics of the heroine, who is always an integral part of the milieu in which he finds himself. When the heroine falls in love with him, as is usually the case, the love is represented as a challenge to his character, which he can either accept or fail to live up to, and the extent to which he succeeds or fails reveals the extent of his moral worth.

In Pushkin's novel Tat'yana falls in love with the stranger-hero, Onegin, imagining him to be the very image of the romantic heroes whom she had learned to admire from her reading, but he coldly dismisses her challenge and lectures her on the need to control her youthful feelings. Haughtily disdainful of her love for him and scornful of the provincial society in which he finds himself at her nameday ball, he asserts his egoism by deliberately paying his attentions to her sister, Ol'ga. This immediately provokes the young romantic, Lensky, who is in love with Ol'ga, and he challenges Onegin to a duel. Onegin has no wish to fight a duel with his romantic young friend, but honour must be satisfied. As a result of the duel Lensky is killed and Onegin leaves the district. After lengthy travels Onegin eventually returns to St. Petersburg, the world that is familiar to him, where he once more meets Tat'yana, who is now married, and he falls desperately in love with her. But it is already too late: she has vowed to remain faithful to her husband. On this note the superficial action of the novel ends, leaving the moral in the air for many other Russian writers to grasp and make into a recurring theme in Russian literature. This recurring theme is one of happiness, its meaning and the extent to which it is imperilled either by human necessity or by superhuman agencies which rule over man's destiny. In Pushkin's novel there is a law of fate which orders the destinies of his hero and heroine. Their mutual happiness may have been precluded at the beginning of their relationship by the mutual disparity in social background and psychological attributes which divided them, but in their final meeting they face each other as equals—Onegin stripped of his social *hauteur* and his Byronic pretence, Tat'yana of her earlier naivety and her illusions about him. It is only the law of fate that now seems to divide them. The unspoken moral of the novel is simply that the relationship is doomed, that neither hero nor heroine is fated to enjoy happiness. It seems that the social disparity which divides them, the differences in psychological attitude revealed during the course of the relationship, the moral calumny visited on Onegin by the killing of his best friend and the marital responsibility which Tat'yana has incurred in her marriage to the old general have the nature of inevitable laws which blend to circumscribe their lives in their final tragic meeting.

The 'realism' of this novel is not due simply to the fact that it presents a 'realistic'—that is to say, recognizable—picture of Russian life. Its 'realism' also resides in the emphasis laid upon psychological analysis and contrast in the characterization of the hero and the heroine. Finally, the impression of 'realism' is due as much as anything to the objective, uncommitted attitude of Pushkin towards his fiction. By presenting his fiction in this realistic manner Pushkin is both implying social criticism, without overtly offering any comment that could be offensive to the censorship, and professing a realistic view of life in which fate is as much of a reality as any other aspect of life. The action of the novel is set down much in the form of a documentary record, for which, as it were, Pushkin scarcely regards himself as being responsible. He is only the dispassionate chronicler, relating all the necessary facts culled from the lives of his hero and heroine with the required deference and Olympian magnanimity. The ribald, wry, slightly ironical passages of commentary that accompany the action of the novel do not, in fact, impair the objectivity of the way it is presented. They lend the work an air of topicality, of immediate reference to the period being described. This very topicality is to be a great feature of the Russian nineteenth-century realistic novel. On the example of Pushkin's *Eugene Onegin*, the Russian realistic novel was to become a fusion of *belles-lettres* and journalism, of art and social criticism, which was to comprise a committed literature of a far more pointed, dedicated variety than its equivalent in Western Europe.

Turgenev's novels owe much to the pattern established by *Eugene Onegin*. But when Turgenev began writing, Pushkin's reputation, so strong in the twenties, was already beginning to decline. In the thirties Turgenev became heir to the Byronic romanticism of the decade, expressed most fully in the poetry of Pushkin's successor, Lermontov. Turgenev's first known literary work dates from 1834 when he was sixteen years old. In December of this year he completed a poetical drama, *Steno*, modelled on Byron's *Manfred*. It is a work of little intrinsic merit, though it naturally claims our attention as the first surviving work and because it contains portents of his later development. The hero, Steno, is a typical product of the romanticism of the period, the intellectual crossed in love who loses faith in life and yearns for death as a means of escape from his spiritual torment. He is represented as a man divided against himself, whose heart has been oppressed and atrophied by experience of life and whose mind, always searching to discover a meaning to existence, works in a vacuum, unwilling to admit anything beyond itself. If the *leit-motif* of the dramatic monologues put into his mouth is primarily despairing and cynical, there is the compensating factor that he is portrayed as one who is not afraid to exercise his intellect nor afraid to assert his human rights in face of life's apparent purposelessness. In this respect he is in embryo the first of Turgenev's 'superfluous men', to be compared, if only as a result of the Byronic inspiration common to both, and not in any realistic social sense, with the Pushkinian model. Similarly, the formula which is to form the basis for so many of Turgenev's studies of this type of intellectual hero is expressed here for the first time in the contrast which is drawn between Steno, the intellectual divided against himself, and the girl, Dzhuliya (Julia), whose simple expression of emotion in her love for him is a challenge to his complicated heartsearchings. It is in the monologues that the interest of the work resides; they betray a concern for philosophical questions, for the meaning of life and man's attitude to God, which is striking evidence of Turgenev's intellectual maturity. But the melodramatic story betrays the fact that this is a romantic work written by an impressionable author of tender years. Dzhuliya, having befriended Steno and fallen in love with him, eventually dies of love with the hero's name upon her lips. Steno's fate is no less disquieting. Unable to reconcile himself to the sincere love that has been offered him, he seizes a loaded pistol and shoots himself before retribution, in the shape of Dzhuliya's brother, can overtake him.

    Steno was not an isolated work in this early period. In 1835 he wrote an unfinished poem called *The Old Man's Story*. In 1836 he translated parts of *Othello* and *King Lear* (with which he was very dissatisfied and later destroyed) and he also translated *Manfred*, but as he remarked in a letter to his friend, Nikitenko: 'I am quite unfitted to be a translator.'[2] It was in this same year that he published a lengthy review of a book by A. Muravyov on Russia's holy places in the journal of the Ministry of Education. In 1837, before leaving for Germany, he was preoccupied with a large work to be entitled *Our Age*. In addition, he admitted to having written about a hundred short poems and three other works—*Calm at Sea, Phantasmagoria on a Summer Night and Dream*. Of all these only *Steno* and one or two short poems have survived.

Between 1838 and 1843 several of his poems appeared in *The Contemporary* and *Annals of the Fatherland* and he busied himself with other short poems, some short dramas, and a longer work, *The Temptation of St. Anthony*. All his poems betray a remarkable poetic competence and an obvious lyrical vein. He drew on his knowledge of Shakespeare and Goethe, especially the latter, for some of his themes, but these poems are chiefly revealing for their lucid, classical form, despite the romantic tinges in their subject-matter, and in this they owe much to Pushkin's example. But such poems are necessarily slight and often very personal in their content. It is with the publication of *Parasha* in 1843 that Turgenev's work shows signs of a new maturity.

Parasha, 'A Story in Verse', as it is subtitled, composed of sixty-nine stanzas, is important for the extent to which it falls directly into the Russian tradition. It owes much to Pushkin, betraying the influence of *Eugene Onegin* in its evocation of the Russian scene, in its portrayal of the hero and heroine, especially the latter, and in its lighthearted, fluent manner. Its story is so slight as scarcely to bear examination: Parasha, the heroine, typical of the many provincial young ladies who are to be encountered in fictional works of the time and obviously modelled on Pushkin's Tat'yana, falls in love with a certain Viktor Alekseich and finally marries him. It is the background scene, the bantering commentary and the characterization which supply the interest of the work. Here Turgenev reveals himself, if only sketchily and in certain set passages, as an incomparable master of nature description. However, it is Parasha herself who is of greatest interest, for here for the first time in Turgenev's work we find a full-length portrait of a heroine, artless but capable of deep emotion, innocent but not insipid, awakened to life through her love but not sentimentalized, who is to be the archetype of so many future Turgenevan studies. She is the unified personality, responsive to her natural feelings and inclinations, to whom is contrasted the figure of Viktor Alekseich, the haughty and indifferent hero, reminiscent of the disillusioned heroes of Byron, though of more markedly Russian derivation and character.

Although in its theme and form *Parasha* is largely derivative in inspiration, for Turgenev's development as a writer it is significant because it marks his first attempt to come to terms with the Russian scene. *Steno* had been set in Italy, although it might have been set anywhere. The same can be said of *The Conversation* (1844), a dialogue in verse, which, like *Parasha*, was also highly praised by Belinsky. It is notable for the way in which the question of the romantic hero's disillusionment and lack of will is given an unmistakable social slant in the young man's censure upon his own generation. This shows the direction in which Turgenev's thought is moving, but neither *Steno* nor *The Conversation* betray any attempt at depicting the particular malaise of Turgenev's generation—the atrophying of the passions and the will, the morbid preoccupation with 'ego' and intellect, which are the marks of a divided personality—in the circumstances of Russian society. These works define and analyse this malaise in general terms. It is only in *Parasha*, particularly in the figure of the hero, Viktor Alekseich, that Turgenev attempts to define this malaise in social terms.

Subsequently this sociological slant, clearly inspired by the teaching of Belinsky, was to form the basis of all Turgenev's character studies in this type of disillusioned, divided intellectual. Much later he was to give it a universal inference in his comparison between the types of Hamlet and Don Quixote (in his lecture of 1860). Evidence, however, of the increasing maturity of Turgenev's thought on this subject is to be seen in his review of Vronchenko's translation of Goethe's *Faust* (*Annals of the Fatherland*, February 1845), where he writes:

> We have called *Faust* an egotistical work.... But could it be otherwise? Goethe, the champion of all that is human and terrestrial, the enemy of every spurious ideal and everything supernatural, was the first to defend the rights—not of man in general, no—but of individual, passionate, limited man; he showed that an indestructible force is secreted in him, that he can live without any external support, and that with all the insolubility of his personal doubts, with all the poverty of his beliefs and convictions, man still has the right and the opportunity to be happy and not to be ashamed of his happiness.[3]

Although this refers to Goethe's view of man, it might also refer to the view of the problem held by Turgenev himself. He was also to become champion of 'individual, passionate, limited man' who has 'the right and the opportunity to be happy and not be ashamed of his happiness'. But Turgenev's view, as he explains a sentence later, has undergone the modification demanded of it by the sociological ideas of the time. 'For we know', he writes, 'that human development cannot stop at such a result; we know that the cornerstone for man is not man himself, as an indivisible unit, but humanity, society, which has its own eternal, unshakable laws....'[4] Two distinct problems are discernible here. There is the problem of man with his right to individual happiness and the larger issue of humanity and society with their own eternal laws. The inference of this opposition of man and society, of the indivisible unit and the greater law of humanity, is to be projected into the contrast between egoism and altruism which is at the root of practically all the relationships in Turgenev's novels. Man, the egotistical being, has to abandon his purely egotistical rights in order to be of service to the higher laws of humanity and society. It is in this connection that Turgenev offers a striking conclusion:

> ... any 'reconciliation' of Faust outside the sphere of human activity is unnatural, but of any other kind of reconciliation we can at present only dream.... We will be told: such a conclusion is joyless; but, firstly, we are not concerned about the pleasantness but about the truth of our views; secondly, those who argue that unresolved doubts leave behind them an appalling emptiness in the human soul have never sincerely and passionately surrendered themselves to a secret struggle with their inner selves; if they had done, they would know that on the ruins of systems and theories there remains one things, indestructible and imperishable: our human I, which is immortal, because it, it alone, can destroy itself.... So let *Faust* remain incomplete, fragmentary, like the time of which it is an expression—a time for which the sufferings and joys of Faust were the highest sufferings and joys, while the irony of Mephistopheles was the most pitiless irony! It is in the incompleteness of this tragedy that its greatness lies. In the life of every one of us there is an epoch when *Faust* seems to us the most remarkable achievement of the human intellect, when it satisfies all our demands to the full; but there comes another time when without ceasing to recognise *Faust* as a great and beautiful work, we journey forwards following others, perhaps lesser talents, but the strongest of characters, towards another aim.... We repeat that, as a poet, Goethe had no equal; but it is not only poets that we need now....[5]

In this conclusion Turgenev touches on several issues that are to have a prominent part in his later career as a realistic writer. Man for Turgenev will always be the apotheosis of reality, its single criterion, and there will be no 'reconciliation' of man outside reality. 'Our human *I*', as he says, is 'immortal, because it, it alone, can destroy itself ...' and there is to be no other kind of immortality for man in Turgenev's fiction. This totally realistic and unsentimental view has to be accepted without reservations, for Turgenev does not offer any palliatives to the human soul that are not consistent with the reality of man's existence. Such a conclusion may be 'joyless'—we may like to think of it as pessimistic—but, as Turgenev notes, he is concerned only with truth. Accepting this and the great importance which Turgenev ascribes to *Faust* and its creator, whose influence is to be felt throughout Turgenev's work, it is the 'other aim' which must also be taken into account. This other aim is his concern not simply for 'our human I'— though single man, alone, isolated, denying God and any convictions save those which he can justify to himself as a rational being, will always be at the centre of Turgenev's fiction—but the social context and the social purpose of the intellectual of his day. This is to be Turgenev's main aim in the future.

This concern for man, 'the indivisible unit', 'our human I', coincides with Turgenev's real forte as a writer, which was portraiture. All the other components of his fiction were made subservient to the aim of providing a portrait of one or another person. As an aid to such portraiture Turgenev made use of the Pushkinian formula of contrast between hero and heroine— as, for example, in such early works as *Steno* and *Parasha*—in which the role of the heroine was that of a yardstick of all that is natural and emotionally unaffected, against which the hero's falseness was to be judged. But in several of the stories which he published at the beginning of his career the problem of portraiture itself is the main feature. In *Andrey Kolosov*, for instance, the first story in prose that Turgenev published (1844), the contrast is drawn between the emotional 'realism' of the central figure, Andrey Kolosov, and the emotional 'romanticism' of the narrator of the story. Kolosov fell in love with a girl, afterwards ceased to love her and abandoned her. The moral is drawn by the narrator:

> 'This has happened to everyone,' [he remarks] '... but which one of us has been able to break with the past at the right moment? ... Gentlemen, the man who parts with a woman, his former love, at that bitter and all-important moment when he unwillingly acknowledges that his heart is no longer entirely consumed by love for her, such a man, believe me, understands the sacred nature of love better and more profoundly than all those petty people who from boredom and weakness continue to play on the broken strings of their drooping and sensitive hearts.'

Here is one of the most important themes in Turgenev's work, already presented with the realism of manner and psychological percipience which are to be characteristic of Turgenev's later studies. And just like Steno, or like the narrator of *Andrey Kolosov*, so many of Turgenev's later heroes are to play on the broken strings of their drooping and sensitive hearts with a morbid, introspective relish. But Turgenev is often to accompany this kind of portrait with a tone of satire and implicit censure. It is the un-Byronic, the 'natural' hero who is to gain Turgenev's approval in such essays in contrasting portraiture as *The Duellist* (1846) or *Khor' and Kalinych* (1847), the first of his *A Sportsman's Sketches*. The tendency in all his stories of the mid-forties can be seen as a movement away from preoccupation with romanticism, whether it be the romanticism of the hero-figure or the melodramatic terms in which such stories as *The Duellist* or *Three Portraits* are couched, towards a naturalness in both characterization and form. As one might expect, the influence of Gogol is to be detected in this trend towards greater realism, to be seen especially clearly in *Petushkov* (1847). The major influence, however, though not of a literary variety but just as important, was Belinsky.

Apart from all other political considerations, Belinsky insisted on the sacred importance of the individual. Although he thought of the individual as primarily valuable for his intelligence and thus always upheld the importance of the Russian intelligentsia, his thinking was pervaded by a spirit of Christian humanism—best expressed in his famous *Letter to Gogol* of 1847—which viewed all men as equal. It was this that made him pay particular attention to the social untouchables in Russia, the oppressed city-dwellers such as those depicted in Gogol's *The Greatcoat* or in Dostoyevsky's *Poor Folk* and the peasants, first depicted in the forties by Grigorovich in his *Anton the Unfortunate* and *The Village*, works which Belinsky seriously over-estimated simply because he was so anxious to see Russian literature live up to the humanistic ideal that he had conceived for it. Moreover, serfdom was an injustice, and Russian literature had therefore to expose it, in Belinsky's opinion. The influence of Belinsky's humanism could not fail to have its effect on Turgenev and it was to be this influence of the spirit of the forties, as fostered by Belinsky, which inspired him to write the work that first brought him literary fame, *A Sportsman's Sketches*. Here Turgenev, the painter of portraits, reached maturity. Between 1847 and 1851 twenty-one such *Sketches* appeared in *The Contemporary*—*Sketches* which mirrored the new mood of social awareness and responsibility which *The Contemporary* had been designed by Belinsky to create. It was not a new Turgenev who emerged in these works, simply a Turgenev who was applying his artistic talents as a painter of portraits to a purposeful social end. Here the other aim, of which he spoke in his review of Goethe's *Faust*, comes into its own, and the aim consisted in presenting to educated, upper-class Russian society portraits from rural life, especially life among the peasants, just as Gogol and Dostoyevsky had provided pictures from urban life or George Sand had provided pictures from rural life in France or, more aptly, Harriet Beecher Stowe pictures of negro slavery in America.

This does not mean that the purposefulness or tendentiousness of Turgenev's portraits was accompanied by an excessive beating on the old sociological drums. The beating is very muted—considerations of censorship, apart from anything else, were bound to make it so. These *Sketches* are simply an album of pictures from Russian rural life, unified very loosely by the presence of a common narrator, the *Sportsman*. In the majority of cases they are brief episodes taken from the narrator's experience and the narrator's part in the narrative is scarcely more than that of observer. It is, in fact, only the compassionate, frank observation which suggests that these are pictures having the social purpose of exposing the injustice of serfdom. Overt tendentiousness is to be detected more readily in those *Sketches* which portray the land-owning classes. Turgenev's squirearchal background naturally cast him in the role of critic of the gentry and their tyrannical disregard of their peasants' lives. But several of the *Sketches* which are set among the land-owning classes have definite story interest (*Pyotr Petrovich Karatayev, My Neighbour Radilov, The Provincial Apothecary*, for instance) and are frequently little more than love-stories with a rural background that have nothing substantially important to tell us of the problem of serfdom. In other words, *A Sportsman's Sketches* is by no means a homogeneous work, being diverse and experimental in form as in content, although it is the studies of peasant life which give its unity of theme and its importance as a sociological document.

In examining this theme one may draw certain conclusions about Turgenev's development as a writer between 1847 and 1851. Accepting that it is the observation which is the most important feature of those *Sketches* that deal with peasant life, and that such observation derives as much from Turgenev's personal experience as from the experience which he may impute to his narrator, then one can trace the way in which Turgenev's attitude to the content of his fiction and his literary method undergo significant changes, maturing and deepening as his understanding of the Russian scene and of human nature grows more profound. The first *Sketch* betrays a frankly Westernist approach to the peasants. Khor' and Kalinych are recognizable types, equatable with the European literary types of Don Quixote and Hamlet. In his original version of the *Sketch* Turgenev compared them rather grandiloquently to Goethe and Schiller.[6] But the inference of this method is clear. Turgenev was attempting to humanize his peasants, to project their images on the public mind in universal terms and thus to make them more acceptable. The result may have produced 'idealized' portraits, figures who are observed and wondered at rather than profoundly understood and appreciated, but there is no denying that this method was effective in its sociological intent. The same proselytizing, Westernist approach can be seen in the contrast between the natural, universally human characteristics of the peasants and the 'inhumanity' which is suggested in the portraits of the landowners in such stories of 1847 and 1848 as *Yermolay and the Miller's Wife*, *L'gov*, *The Bailiff* and *Raspberry Water*. The influence of Belinsky's ideas on the importance of the individual and his rights lies behind the morality of these pictures from peasant life, and it is significant that *The Bailiff*, the most outspoken of these, was written while Turgenev was at Salzbrunn with Belinsky in July 1847. But in 1848 a change occurs. The spirit of the forties had begun to die; Turgenev's earlier buoyant Westernism could not survive the shock of Belinsky's death and the failure of the Paris Revolution. In 1849 he does not publish any *Sketches* dealing with the peasantry. Instead, he returns to the problem of the 'superfluous man', in this case the faded, provincial *Hamlet of Shchigrovsky Province*, offering a touching but merciless exposure of this man's inadequacy and spinelessness. It is followed in the next year by a further examination of the same type (although this study was not included among his *Sketches*) in the figure of Chulkaturin in *The Diary of a Superfluous Man*. In both cases it is the lack of will, the humiliating self-pity and emotional weakness of such intellectuals which are emphasized, although these portraits are marked by a profounder psychological insight into the complexity and extent of their spiritual dilemma. It is this greater maturity of understanding and outlook that is also to become apparent in Turgenev's subsequent studies of peasant life. In 1850, for instance, two *Sketches* appear—*The Singers* and *The Meeting*—which deal exclusively with the peasants and not with the peasant-master relationship. Turgenev's attitude has obviously undergone an important change. The peasants are no longer studied as object lessons in a tendentious tract; they are studied as people possessing a culture and interests which are worthy of attention for their own sake. *The Singers* is a brilliant genre-picture of a singing competition between local peasant bards. The detailed observation of background and character, the astonishing manner in which the effect of the singing is conveyed without unnecessary grandiloquence or bathos and the frank depiction of the ensuing revelry make the work a snapshot from life that needs no sociological embellishment for it to be effective both as literature and as propaganda for the peasant cause. *The Meeting* is less striking artistically, although it is of interest for two reasons: firstly, in that it is an isolated attempt among these studies of the peasantry to illustrate a love-relationship. Turgenev had usually restricted himself to the role of observer in portraying the peasants, in the sense, at least, that he had never attempted to describe any kind of emotional relationship between them (although he had not hesitated to use love-stories as the basis for several of his *Sketches* with upper-class settings). Secondly, *The Meeting* illustrates a device of which Turgenev is to make considerable use in his novels: the use of the natural scene to highlight the emotions of the figures in the foreground (in this case, of the peasant girl's feelings as she awaits the arrival of her beloved and then witnesses his departure). In 1851 two more *Sketches* of this kind—*Bezhin Meadow* and *Kas'yan from Krasivaya Mech'*—make their appearance. Indeed, these two *Sketches* are among the finest that he wrote, betraying all the careful observation of his earlier ones but with an increased understanding of, and sympathy for, the peasants as Russians and as individuals, as human types with specific national characteristics and not as generalized types—as were Khor' and Kalinych, for example—endowed with literary or other traits to make them universally acceptable. There is a 'humanity' about the portraits of the peasant boys in *Bezhin Meadow* or the picture of the peasant-philosopher, Kas'yan, which raises these works into minor masterpieces. But this change of attitude in these later *Sketches* should not be taken as indicating any change of heart on Turgenev's part. These works may have appealed to the Slavophils and may give the impression that Turgenev has modified his Westernist views, although it was not so much a modifying of his views as a maturing of his talent and his profounder understanding of the Russian scene after 1848 that gave rise to such a change and set the seal on his fame as a champion of the serfs.

Between 1843 and 1852 Turgenev had revealed himself, firstly, as an incomparable painter of portraits and, secondly, as a master of the love-story. During this period, however, these talents are separate, two distinct veins running side by side through his work but never combining with any marked success. His most outstanding work of the period is, naturally, the portraits of individual peasants or episodes from peasant life which he offers us in his *Sketches*. In considering Turgenev's subsequent development as a writer, however, it is such stories as *Hamlet of Shchigrovsky Province* or *The Diary of a Superfluous Man*, in which an emotional relationship is studied, that are of greater interest, although even in these cases the element of pure portraiture ultimately outweighs the importance of these works as love-stories. It is in a different medium that Turgenev first succeeded in combining his talent as a portraitist with his talent as an analyst of the subtleties of feeling involved in the relationship between hero and heroine. This was his 'Comedy in Five Acts', *A Month in the Country* (1850), and the only full-length play that he wrote.

Apart from the stock device of comedy which demands that the characters should be intentionally ignorant of, should intentionally misunderstand or should intentionally overlook, the motives and feelings of other characters—and there is a great deal of this in *A Month in the Country*—this work is a comedy only in the Chekhovian sense. In fact, it was to form the basis of Chekhov's dramaturgy. The two main relationships in the play are essentially serious. The relationship, in the first instance, between Rakitin and the heroine, Natal'ya Petrovna Islayeva, is commonly supposed to be an oblique reflection of the kind of relations which existed between Turgenev and Pauline Viardot at this time. Rakitin is in love with Natal'ya Petrovna, but his love is not reciprocated. In the words of the narrator of *Andrey Kolosov*, he is one of those who 'continue to play on the broken strings of their drooping and sensitive hearts' long after there is any need to do so. Over a period of four years Rakitin has indulged this melancholy passion for Natal'ya Petrovna and their talk has become, as she puts it, like 'weaving fine lace'. This emotional lace-making, so claustrophobic and so relentlessly analysed by Turgenev, forms the basis of their relationship. What Natal'ya Petrovna looks for, however, is 'a glass of cold water on a hot day'—a passionate involvement that will recapture the ardour of her youth. She is to experience this in her feelings for the young tutor, Belyayev, and it is this second relationship which provides the central theme of the play. Since her feelings for Belyayev are just as incommunicable in the last resort and just as likely to remain unreciprocated as Rakitin's love for her, the result is an ironic commentary on the absurdity of human passions. The consequences are just as ironically tragic and pathetically comic as they are in the plays of Chekhov. But it is the nuances of dialogue, the incongruities of personal relationship and the characteristic, atmospheric flavour, which distinguish the work. Turgenev's experience from writing this five-act comedy was to prove invaluable to him in matters of construction and dialogue when he came to write his novels.

By the time of his arrest for his obituary notice on Gogol in 1852, Turgenev had reached a turning point in his career. In the eyes of the reading public he had acquired fame; in the eyes of officialdom—notoriety. But seen in the perspective of his life as a whole, until this moment he had simply been undergoing the apprenticeship which was to lead to his work as a novelist. Viewed in this light, *A Sportsman's Sketches* are no more nor less than the notebook of the future novelist, the trial sketches for the larger and more complex portraits, while *A Month in the Country* is the essay in theatrical construction which was to be such an important feature of the form of so many of his novels. Turgenev was already aware of the need to abandon what he called his 'old manner'.[7] But what form was his new manner to take? The choice was to be governed largely by the state of the Russian novel at this time.

Pushkin in his *Eugene Onegin* had established the pattern of future developments in the novel, but his novel was in verse and the tradition of the Russian novel was to be a prose tradition. Pushkin, in such short prose works as he wrote before his death in 1837, pared down the language and refined it to serve as an efficient vehicle for narrative devoid of unnecessary embellishment. His two successors—Lermontov and Gogol—were to adopt a less disciplined or classical approach to the question of prose language. The former was primarily a poet and his greatest contribution to the development of the prose language is limited to *A Hero of Our Time* which appeared in its completed form in 1840. Lermontov's prose is a remarkable blend of the poetic and the prosaic, extremely supple and lucid, capable at once of sustaining lyrical flow and colloquial nuance without the least strain. But in point of form *A Hero of Our Time* is more of interest as a vehicle for the characterization of the hero, Pechorin, than as a novel. It is a concatenation of stories, an amalgam of different genres in the short-story form—the travelogue, the 'atmospheric' *conte* (*Taman*'), the diary form (*Princess Mary*)—and its content reflects the influence of such European writers as Constant and de Musset. The resulting portrait is another variation on the type of 'superfluous man' on the Byronic pattern, but the psychological characterization is more penetrating than was Pushkin's in *Eugene Onegin*. If *Eugene Onegin* was a documentary record, then *A Hero of Our Time* is a psychological casebook which points the way to the manner of Dostoyevsky. Gogol's contribution to the development of the Russian novel, on the other hand, had greater originality and greater enduring influence than Lermontov's. His *Dead Souls*, the first part of which appeared in 1842, bears little relationship to European literary tradition except in the sense that its picaresque form shows traces of the influence of Cervantes. It is a work so idiosyncratic and rich, so undisciplined and diffuse, such a mixture of *Kleinmalerei* and high-flown eloquence that interpretations of it have been as capricious and miscellaneous as its variegated elements. In its language and its characterization it marks a departure from all previous styles: the ornate richness of Gogol's devious sentence-structure, his protracted metaphors, his proneness to digression in the narrative are paralleled by the infinite variety of unrelated facts which he uses as embellishments to characterization. Yet it is a work poured out 'all of a piece' despite its profuseness; it is 'a poem', as Gogol called it, which is unmistakably stamped with all the intricacies and crudities of his personality. But, most important, it is the first generically Russian prose novel. It is at one and the same time a personal statement by Gogol and a social indictment, a satire on Russia's present and a profession of faith in Russia's future. With the appearance of the first part of *Dead Souls* Russian prose literature achieved maturity.

The works by Lermontov and Gogol initiated a decade of prose literature that was to see the emergence of such important writers as Dostoyevsky, Herzen, Goncharov, and Grigorovich—in addition, of course, to Turgenev. Of these only Herzen and Goncharov wrote what can, strictly speaking, be called novels. Dostoyevsky began his career in 1846 with the publication of his *Poor Folk* in Nekrasov's *Petersburg Almanac* and thereafter published such stories as *The Double*, *Mr. Prokharchin*, and *The Landlady*, but his only attempt at a novel was the curious, fragmentary *Netochka the Unnamed* and it was only after his return from exile in 1859 that his large novels were to appear. Similarly, Grigorovich wrote what can only be termed stories during this period, of which his studies of peasant life are the most famous. But Herzen's *Who is Guilty?* and Goncharov's *An Ordinary Story*, which appeared together in completed form in 1847, are both novels. Belinsky immediately recognized this and singled them out for comment and comparison as examples of the way in which 'the novel and the story (*povest'*)[8] give complete freedom to the writer as regards the predominant features of his talent, character, tastes, tendencies, and so on'.[9] Herzen's novel is a further study in the 'superfluous man', but its interrogative title indicates that it is more overtly publicistic and less exclusively literary than the previous studies. It is the social and the political problem, rather than the psychological problem, of the 'superfluous man' which is examined here. For this reason Herzen's novel cannot claim the purely literary merit which is a feature of Goncharov's *An Ordinary Story*. This latter work harks back to the pattern of *Eugene Onegin* in some respects, particularly in its emphasis upon the love-story, but its primary interest lies in its contrast between the rural and the urban scene, between the romantic ideas of the young nephew and the hard common sense of the uncle—an interplay of contrasts which is to preoccupy Goncharov in all his novels. Neither of these novels, however, can be regarded as good examples of artistic form. They give the impression of being media for the portrayal of different types of person and their concomitant problems with little attempt at the development of a consecutive plot or intrigue. The major feature, in fact, of the best work during the forties is portraiture rather than plot, so that the Russian novels to appear during the forties resemble extended short stories designed to provide extended portraits rather than novels designed—as Dickens's novels, for instance, which were rapidly becoming popular—to develop a particular intrigue. Moreover, there is an undisciplined and experimental air about all these novels; they represent the very beginnings of a tradition. But, for all their inadequacies, the novels of the forties have a character and flavour which are unmistakably Russian. By the time he was writing in 1846, Turgenev could rightly claim that the foreign elements had been remoulded and assimilated into the blood stream of Russian literature. This meant that there was a basis upon which to build. It now remained for Turgenev himself to turn the Russian novel into a work of art.

NOTES

1. *Sobr. soch.* (1956), xi. 56.

2. Letter to A. V. Nikitenko, 26 March/7 April 1837, in *Sobr. soch.* (1958), xii. 12.

3. *Sobr. soch.* (1956), xi. 33.

4. Ibid.

5. Ibid., 35-6. For an extended study of Turgenev's attitude to *Faust* and of this article on Vronchenko's translation in particular, see Dr. Katharina Schütz, *Das Goethebild Turgeniews* (Bern, 1952).

6. Annenkov notes: 'He enjoyed any kind of discussion of his works, listened to it with the submissiveness of a schoolboy and displayed a willingness to make changes. One remark about the inappropriateness of the comparison which he had made between Khor' and Kalinych and Goethe and Schiller was sufficient to ensure that the comparison remained only in the pages of *The Contemporary* of 1847 where it first appeared and was not transferred to subsequent editions.' P. V. Annenkov, *Lit. vosp.* (SPB., 1909), 480.

7. Letter to K. S. Aksakov, 16 October (O.S.) 1852. *Sobr. soch.* (1958), xii. 120.

8. There is no direct English equivalent of this word. It describes a work that stands midway between a short story and a novel, corresponding to what the Germans call a *Novelle*. I have preferred to translate it simply as 'story'.

9. V. G. Belinsky, 'Vzglyad na russkuyu literaturu 1847 goda; stat'ya vtoraya', *Sobr. soch.* (1948), iii. 120.

KATHRYN FEUER

Fathers and Sons: *Fathers and Children*

That *Fathers and Sons* (*Ottsy i deti*) is a novel about the conflict between Russia's liberal, idealistic "men of the 1840s" and the radical, materialist "men of the 1860s" hardly needs demonstration. Most impressive in this respect is the delicacy and subtlety with which Turgenev has introduced many of the key signata of that debate into his fiction: the Pushkin—Gogol quarrel is there because Kirsanov senior loves to read Pushkin; Büchner's *Kraft und Stoff* is there as a "popularization" which Bazarov recommends for the elder Kirsanov's first step toward enlightenment (though nothing that we hear from Bazarov suggests that his own scientific sophistication extends beyond Büchner); even the seminarists are there—Bazarov's grandfather; we learn in a side remark, was a sexton, while Pavel Kirsanov refers to Bazarov as a "dirty seminarist." Many more instances could be cited of beautifully integrated specific references to Russian intellectual life in the late 1850s and anticipatory of the early sixties. As D. S. Mirsky has observed, "*Fathers and Sons* is Turgenev's only novel where the social problem is distilled without residue into art...." It is even prophetic, in its clash between the force of nihilistic destruction (Bazarov) and reverence for created beauty (Nikolai and Pavel Kirsanov), of three great future novels of revolution: Dostoevsky's *The Possessed* (*Besy*), Joseph Conrad's *Under Western Eyes*, and Henry James's *The Princess Casamassima*. Perhaps the most decisive argument for the novel's

From *The Russian Novel from Pushkin to Pasternak.* © 1983 by Yale University Press.

topicality, if any is needed, can be derived from the characters not included
in its cast. In *Fathers and Sons* there are no reactionaries, not even any
conservatives (except Nikolai Kirsanov's coachman, "who didn't share the
latest views");[2] in a novel set in 1859, on the eve of the emancipation of the
serfs, there is not one landowner who regrets, let alone opposes, this measure
which, as Tolstoy wrote at the time, "deprived them of half their property."
Here then is no panorama or even slice of Russian country gentry life but
rather a selective representation of one small part.

The social-political interpretation of *Fathers and Sons* has been
widespread. It was most recently articulated by Isaiah Berlin in his Romanes
Lectures, published as *Fathers and Children*, where he calls the "central topic
of the novel ... the confrontation of the old and the young, of liberals and
radicals, traditional civilization and the new, harsh positivism which has no
use for anything except what is needed by a rational man."[3] Ralph Matlaw,
in his preface to the valuable Norton Critical Edition, explains that he has
chosen the widely used English title "Fathers and Sons" rather than the
literal "Fathers and Children" because "'Sons' in English better implies the
notions of spiritual and intellectual generations conveyed by the Russian
deti." Matlaw, with the majority of non-Soviet critics, sees Turgenev as
having drawn on the specific details and data of the debate between Russian
liberals and radicals for the portrayal of a not merely political but universal
theme, the eternal conflict of generations.

Yet can our interpretation of the novel stop here? Only, I believe, at the
cost of ignoring its deepest layer of meaning and thus missing its
consummate achievement. The most perceptive discussion of *Fathers and
Sons* that I have read is also, regrettably, very brief, an "introduction" to the
novel by René Wellek. Wellek begins by explaining and paying tribute to the
admirable "concrete social picture" of an era and its disputes which Turgenev
presents. Calling "the eternal conflict between the old and the young ... one
of the main themes of the book," nevertheless, he asserts, *Fathers and Sons*
"goes beyond the temporal issues and enacts a far greater drama: man's
deliverance to fate and chance, the defeat of man's calculating reason by the
greater powers of love, honor, and death."[4] "Man's deliverance to fate and
chance" is indeed, I would submit, one central theme of the novel, but to see
this clearly we must go a step further in the rejection of traditional
interpretations. We must dispense with the notion that the novel portrays
the conflict of generations and recognize that instead it portrays love
between generations, the triumph of love over tension and conflict; that its
essential core is the intertwining of two great themes, affectionate continuity
from parent to child and child to parent and "man's deliverance to fate and

chance," that is, man's knowledge of his own mortality. It is to this novel that Turgenev gave the title *Fathers and Children*, which is, moreover, a novel far more profound in its political implications than we have heretofore realized.[5]

This reading of the book can best be elucidated by beginning at its conclusion, at the almost unbearable closing picture of Bazarov's aged parents kneeling and weeping at his grave. Waste, futility, and anguish are overwhelming, but then comes a dramatic reversal, and the novel ends with a declaration of hope:

> Can it be that their prayers, their tears, will be fruitless? Can it be that love, sacred, dedicated love will not be all-powerful? Oh no! However passionate, guilty, rebellious the heart concealed in the grave, the flowers growing over it gaze at us serenely with their innocent eyes: not only of eternal peace do they speak to us, of that great peace of "indifferent" nature; they speak also of eternal reconciliation and of life without end.... [chap. 28]

This passage is remarkable, almost incomprehensible as a conclusion to all that has gone before it in the novel; the incongruity has been described best by Wellek: "Turgenev puts here 'indifferent nature' in quotation marks, but as early as in *A Sportsman's Sketches (Zapiski okhotnika)* he had said: 'From the depths of the age-old forests, from the everlasting bosom of waters the same voice is heard: "You are no concern of mine," says Nature to Man.'" And he adds, with reference to *Fathers and Sons*: "There is no personal immortality, no God who cares for man; nature is even a disease beyond reason—this seems the message Turgenev wants to convey."[6] The contradictory quality of the last sentence of the novel has been noted by many readers, yet Wellek alone has commented on the particular peculiarity of Turgenev's having written "'indifferent' nature" with the adjective in quotation marks, seeming to imply rejection of the idea of nature's indifference, an implication almost insulting to the reader, so opposite is it to the text of *Fathers and Sons* and to the major body of Turgenev's writings over the preceding quarter of a century.

The quotation marks can be read another way, however, as meaning not "so called" or "not really" but denoting—literally—a quotation, in this case a quotation from Pushkin, from the last lines of one of his best-known poems, "Whether I wander along noisy streets" ("Brozhu li Ya vdol ulits shumnykh"):

> And let indifferent nature
> Shine in her eternal beauty.

That Turgenev could have had the poem in mind is not difficult to suppose. For most writers there are other writers whose lines, paragraphs, works, exist as part of their consciousness, touchstones which may only occasionally be specified but whose presence is constant. For Turgenev, Pushkin was such a writer. The last stanza of the poem, indeed, is a major passage in the conclusion of one of Turgenev's most important early works, "Diary of a Superfluous Man" ("Dnevnik lishnego cheloveka"). Moreover, Pushkin's poetry is an important presence in *Fathers and Sons*: as a thematic element, as an emotional vector, as an emblem for the existence of beauty.

The significance for the novel of the proposed allusion to "Whether I wander ..." emerges only from the entire poem:

> Whether I wander along noisy streets,
> Or go into a crowded temple,
> Or sit among carefree young men,
> I give myself up to revery.   4
>
> I say: the years will pass,
> And though so many of us are here today,
> We shall all reassemble beneath the
> Eternal vaults—And for some one
> Of us the hour is already near.   8
>
> if ! gaze at a solitary oak tree
> I think: this patriarch of the forest
> Will outlive my transitory age,
> As it has outlived that of my fathers.   12
>
> As I caress a sweet little child,
> Already I think: farewell!
> I yield place to you:
> It's time for me to decay, for you to flower.   16
>
> Every day, every season
> It's become my habit to accompany with the thought
> Of the anniversary of my approaching death
> Trying to guess what day it will be.   20
>
> And where will fate send death to me?
> In battle? On the road? On the sea?

Or will a near-by valley	
Receive my cold ashes?	24

And although to my lifeless body
It can make no difference where it will molder,
Still I would wish to rest
Close to a dear familiar place.   28

And at the entrance to my tomb
Let there be young life at play.
And let indifferent nature
Shine in her eternal beauty.[7]   32

Pushkin's poem is about death and about the poet's morbidly haunted awareness of the random uncertainty of the time when it will come and the utter certainty of its coming. What we find in *Fathers and Sons*, I suggest, is the onset of Pushkin's malady in Bazarov, as a direct consequence of his love for Odintsova. Once this love has infected him, he becomes haunted by the knowledge of his own mortality. It has always been recognized that Bazarov's love crippled him, although some readers see Odintsova's rejection as the decisive event. I am proposing here that the effect of love on Bazarov was not some sort of general demoralization coming from a recognition that his nature does not correspond with his ideology, but a specific effect, the one I have called Pushkin's malady: an obsession with the knowledge of his own mortality.[8]

Throughout the first fourteen chapters of the novel Bazarov is a triumphant expression of the life-force, a man exuberantly intelligent and supremely self-confident, caring for no one's good opinion but his own. He is liked by the peasants, works assiduously, takes pride in being Russian, exhibits a zest for life in a variety of ways: his pleasure in Fenichka's "splendid" baby, his eagerness for a visit to town, his appreciation of pretty women. His serious concerns are positive. He scorns upbringing or the "age we live in" as excuses for weakness: "As for our times—why should I depend on that? Let my times depend on me" (chap. 7).

In chapter 15 the crucial transition occurs. When Bazarov and Arkadi first call on Odintsova, Arkadi sees that "contrary to his habit Bazarov was talking a good deal and obviously trying to interest" Odintsova. Then, as they leave, when Odintsova expresses the polite hope that they may visit her estate: "Bazarov only bowed and—a last surprise for Arkadi; he noticed that his friend was blushing." Shortly after, when Arkadi comments on

Odintsova's beauty, Bazarov agrees: "A splendid body! Perfect for the
dissection table." And three days later, as the friends are driving to
Odintsova's estate: "'Congratulate me,' Bazarov suddenly exclaimed, 'today
is June 22nd, my guardian angel's day. Well, we'll see how he'll take care of
me.'"

What has happened here? Bazarov has called on his "guardian angel";
whether he realizes it or not he is aware for the first time of his vulnerability
to death; he is subconsciously asking Pushkin's question. "Is the hour already
near?" He will continue to ask the question until he dies and his
preoccupation, usually just below the surface though sometimes bursting
forth in bitter outrage, will be expressed in the imagery of disease or death,
which first enters his consciousness and conversation in the moment we have
witnessed: "A splendid body! Perfect for the dissection table."

In chapter 16 he illustrates a nonmedical argument to Odintsova by an
analogy with "the lungs of a consumptive." In chapter 17, when he has
acknowledged his passion to himself, this love "tortured and possessed him,"
for he regarded such feelings "as something like deformity or disease." In
chapter 18, when Odintsova asks whether happiness exists, Bazarov can
answer only: "You know the proverb: it's always better where we don't exist."
A little later, when she tries to question him about his plans and ambitions,
he answers ominously: "What's the point of talking or thinking about the
future, which for the most part doesn't depend on us?"

Immediately after this exchange come Bazarov's declaration of his love
and Odintsova's refusal. Now the images of disease increase: in Bazarov's
speech there is a movement from the sense of vulnerability to that of fatality.
Moreover, new motifs appear: insecure megalomania supersedes self-
confidence, hostility to Arkadi replaces condescending but genuine
friendship. In chapter 19 he agrees to Arkadi's accusation of elitism: "'Is it
that *you're* a god while I'm just one of the blockheads?' 'Yes,' Bazarov
repeated weightily, 'you're still stupid.'" Besides increasing in number,
Bazarov's images of disease and death are now applied to himself: "The
machine's become unstuck." Then, still in chapter 19, Bazarov articulates the
first unequivocal statement of his intimation: "Every man hangs on a thread;
the abyss can open up beneath him at any moment...."

Soon after, his preoccupation with his "approaching ... anniversary"
breaks forth more explicitly:

"I think, here I am, lying under a haystack ... the tiny, cramped
spot I occupy is so minute in comparison with the rest of the
universe, where I don't exist and where I don't matter; and the

space of time allotted for me to live in is a mere moment in that eternity of time where I was not and will not be.... And in this atom, in this mathematical dot, the blood circulates, the brain works, there's even a desire for something.... How outrageous it is! How petty!" [chap. 21]

Bazarov now gives way to impotent fury, vindictiveness, malice:

"Ha! There's a fine fellow of an ant, dragging off a half-dead fly. Take her, brother, take her. It doesn't matter that she resists, make use of her as you will."

When Bazarov lauds hatred, "How strange!" Arkadi observes, "why I don't hate anyone." "And I hate so many," Bazarov replies:

"Hatred! Well, for example take yesterday—as we were passing our bailiff, Phillip's cottage—and you said that Russia will attain perfection when every last muzhik has such a place to live, and that every one of us ought to work to bring that about.... And I felt such a hatred for your every last muzhik.... Yes, he'll be living in a white cottage, while the nettles are growing out of me...."
    "Ah, Arkadi, do me a favor, let's have a fight, a real fight, till we're laid out in our coffins, till we destroy each other."

This attack on Arkadi has been triggered by his comment on a dead leaf falling to earth, fluttering like a butterfly: "Gloom and death," he remarks, "and at the same time gaiety and life!" What seems to enrage Bazarov is that Arkadi can accept the unity of life and death, can see death as a part of life rather than as its negation.

Bazarov's bravery during the duel with Pavel Kirsanov only underlines the depth and inner intensity of his preoccupation with death. It is not the concrete incident in which his life is endangered which obsesses the death-haunted man; it is the subliminal question, when and where, which accompanies him whether wandering noisy streets or lounging beneath a haystack.

After his departure from the Kirsanovs Bazarov pays a brief visit to Odintsova; once again the imagery of death is related to himself. When Odintsova tells him that he is a "good man," he replies: "That's the same as laying a wreath of flowers on the head of a corpse" (chap. 26). Is there also a presentiment of fatality in Bazarov's parting words to her? When she tells him she is sure they will meet again (as of course they do, at Bazarov's deathbed), he answers: "In this world, anything may happen!" Such an interpretation of his words is prepared by the grim pun with which he has just before informed Arkadi that he is stopping by at Odintsova's on his way home: "Well, so I've set off 'to the fathers.'" As Matlaw points out, Bazarov here "mockingly (and ominously) recalls the '*ad patres*' used by Bazarov's father earlier [in chap. 20] as an expression for death."

Bazarov goes home for six weeks to settle down to work. Are the lethargy and melancholy that soon overtake him further evidence of his morbid preoccupation? It hardly matters. Soon, whether by accident or suicide, he *is* dying and, as when he faced death in the duel, his behavior is calm and courageous. The fear has dissolved, once it has become recognized reality. On one occasion he does rebel: he takes hold of a heavy table and manages to swing it around: "'Strength, real strength,' he murmured. 'It's all still here, and yet I must die! ... Well, go and try to refute death. She'll refute you, and that's that!'" (chap. 27). Bazarov is no longer haunted by wondering: the question of the date of the "approaching ... anniversary" has been answered and we have come to the scene of Bazarov's grave, to the grieving parents, to Turgenev's assertion that the flowers speak of eternal reconciliation and not just of "'indifferent' nature," and so back to Pushkin's poem.

The poet is haunted by the question of when death will come and then proceeds to a corollary question; *where* will it come? But this question is not obsessive; rather it provides a transition to the one consideration which can make the question of "when" bearable, for it allows him to imagine the grave in which—since there must be one—he would choose to lie. He has spoken of "moldering" or "decaying," but now he writes of "the place where I shall rest." It is, he hopes, a nearby valley, radiant with the beauty of "indifferent nature" but also alive with "young life at play." Death is bearable because life goes on. Pushkin has prepared this final statement in stanza 4: "As I caress a sweet little child." He speaks, moreover, of the continuity of generations not only for the future but from the past; in stanza 3 he writes of the oak tree which will outlive his age as it has outlived those of his fathers. (The force of the juxtaposition is vitiated in translation; in the original, "fathers" is the last word of stanza 3 and "child" is the first word of stanza 4.)

Once again the poem sheds light on *Fathers and Sons*. At Bazarov's grave are only his aged parents, grieving for the worst thing that can happen to parents, for the most unnatural pain which Nature can inflict, to outlive one's own child. Despite the birds and flowers and young pine trees there is no "young life at play;" Bazarov has been denied the single solace Pushkin offers to the man beset by the knowledge of his own mortality. This solace not only sheds light on the novel's closing scene but also states its second, inextricably related theme: love and continuity between generations.

Sharp conflict in the novel there is, but it is not between fathers and sons: it is between two men who dislike each other because they are fundamentally so much alike, Pavel Kirsanov and Bazarov. Were they contemporaries they might find different things to quarrel and duel over, but quarrel and duel they would. The father–son and son–father relationships are, on the other hand, respectful, affectionate, and deeply loving, despite the faint note of menace at the very outset, on the ride home after Arkadi's father has met him and Bazarov at the station. Arkadi and his father, riding together in the carriage, are renewing their acquaintance with affectionate sympathy when Bazarov, from the other coach, interrupts to give Arkadi a cigar. Arkadi lights the cigar, and it emits "such a strong and sour smell of stale tobacco that Nikolai Petrovich … could not avoid averting his face, though he did so stealthily so as not to offend his son" (chap. 3). But the threat of estrangement dissipates; it is never more substantial than cigar smoke in the breeze.

Arkadi's father defers to him on occasion after occasion and tries hard to adopt his attitudes and opinions. When he cannot, it is himself he considers inferior, as, when musing in the garden, he reflects:

> "My brother says that we are right, and putting aside any element of vanity, it does seem to me that they are farther from the truth than we are, but at the same time I feel that behind them there is something that we don't possess, a kind of superiority over us.… Is it youth? No, it's not just youth. That's not the source of their superiority; isn't it that in them there are fewer traces of the slave owner than in us?" [chap. 11]

At the end of this remarkable scene Kirsanov is called by Fenichka, and he answers her more offhandedly than he would a woman of his own class: "I'm coming—run along!" And yet throughout the novel, although she is the housekeeper's daughter, both Nikolai and his brother treat her with perfect courtesy: Pavel Kirsanov, for example, always addresses her formally. It is only Bazarov who, having no right to do so, uses the familiar form of her name. And it is only Bazarov who flirts with her as with a servant girl, who behaves as he does not and would not behave with Odintsova. It is only Bazarov, in fact, who displays "the slave owner's mentality."

Bazarov's mother beatifically adores him, while his father does not merely defer to his son's views, he suppresses some of his own deepest feelings. The love of the fathers for the sons, however, hardly needs demonstration; instances can be found in every scene in which they appear together. The interpretation of the novel as a depiction of the conflict of generations rests rather on the attitudes of the sons toward the fathers. Where are these conflicts to be found? In a few moments of condescension or irritation or even unkindness by the sons, in Nikolai Kirsanov's hour of melancholy in the garden, in the disappointment of Bazarov's parents that his visit is so short. One can apply the term *conflict* to such moments only under the assumption that gentle condescension, slight irritation, unkindness, sorrow, and disappointment are not normal components of all human relations, under the assumption that we are living on the planet of Dostoevsky's Ridiculous Man before he visited it.

From the outset Arkadi is glad to be hugged and kissed by his father and hugs and kisses him in return, calling him "daddy" (*papasha*); even Bazarov's presence is only faintly inhibiting. The one feeling Arkadi has toward his father that could be called critical is that of condescension; it occurs on three occasions. First, when Arkadi, smiling "affectionately," tells him that his shame at his relationship with Fenichka is "nonsense" … "and his heart was filled with a feeling of condescending tenderness toward his good and soft-hearted father, combined with a sense of a certain secret superiority" (chap. 3). Second, when he displays conscious magnanimity in paying a formal call on Fenichka. Third, when Arkadi agrees to give his father *Kraft und Stoff* to read, approving this choice because it is a "popularization" (chap. 10). Not only does Arkadi never once manifest hostility or irritation toward his father, there is even no friction between them. On the three occasions when he condescends to him he does so tenderly, with affectionate respect, with embraces, with loving compassion and gentleness.

Perhaps even more significant is Arkadi's behavior to his uncle. Their mutual affection is open, and for a man of Pavel Petrovich's deep reserve, even demonstrative. When Pavel criticizes Bazarov (and on this occasion unjustly) Arkadi's response is the one with which we are acquainted—a silent look of compassion for his uncle's noncomprehension. When Bazarov criticizes Pavel (both wittily and aptly) Arkadi attempts a weak rejoinder, then deflects the attack: "Maybe so, only truly, he's a fine, good person" (chap. 4). Most important is that, despite his imitation of Bazarov's opinions, awe of his powers, and fear of his disapproval, despite, in short, Arkadi's schoolboy crush on Bazarov, he never wavers in his defense of his uncle.

Bazarov can be brusque to his parents but never treats them with the rudeness with which he treats everyone else. He submits to their repeated embraces ("Just let me hug you once more, Yenyushechka"), and he willingly kisses his mother (chap. 20). He is perfectly good-humored about having the priest to dinner, understanding what this means to his mother and father. When he decides to leave—abruptly and even cruelly after a visit home of only three days—part of his motivation is, in fact, love for his parents:

> "While I'm here, my father keeps assuring me: 'My study is all yours; no one will bother you there'; and he can't keep a foot away from me. And it makes me feel guilty to shut myself away from him. And it's the same with mother. I hear through the wall how she's sighing—and so I go out to her—and then I have nothing to say to her." [chap. 21]

Though he tells himself, "never mind, they will get over it," all the same it takes Bazarov a whole day to bring himself to inform his parents that he is leaving, and having gone: "Bazarov was not altogether satisfied with himself" (chap. 22). At the one place in the novel where he exposes his inner feelings with ruthless honesty, the scene beneath the haystack, there is the following solemn exchange:

> "Do you love them, Yevgeni?"
> "I love them, Arkadi."

The supreme expression of Bazarov's love for his parents comes with his ultimate sacrifice for their sake. He is willing to receive extreme unction, though "at the sight of the priest in his robes, of the smoking censer and the candles before the icon something like a shudder of horror passed for a moment over the death-stricken face" (chap. 27). This is for him a final negation of all that his life has meant to him.

May it not even be said that Bazarov, who loves his parents and understands their love for him, has intimations not only of his mortality but also of the despair that will surround his grave, where there will be no "young life at play"? Consider his final parting with Arkadi:

> "There is, Arkadi, there is something else I want to say, only I won't say it because it's romanticism—and that means soggy sentiments. You get married, as soon as you can, and you build your nest, and you have lots of children...."   [chap. 26]

I began with the thesis that *Fathers and Sons* is a novel with two entwined themes: "man's deliverance to fate and chance" and the love between generations, the continuity of generations as man's only consolation for the knowledge of his inevitable mortality. The political details of the debate between the men of the forties and the men of the sixties, I suggested, were only the temporal, particular setting for Turgenev's eternal and universal theme. Yet the implications of this theme are profoundly political, for the good pragmatic reason that it is the continuity of generations which is probably the most counterrevolutionary force in the world. On some level of consciousness, I would suggest, the real import of *Fathers and Sons* was sensed by Chernyshevsky when he set out to reply to Turgenev in his novel *What Is to Be Done? (Chto delat?)*[9] Doubtless there were other contributing factors: his desire to present his social theories in popularized form, his belief that Turgenev had slandered the radicals by portraying Bazarov in an alien environment, his conviction that Bazarov was a deliberate caricature of his recently deceased comrade, Dobrolyubov. Chernyshevsky's novel was indeed a successful manifesto; it recruited countless thousands into the radical movement and led Lenin (who is known to have read it at least five times) to declare, "[it] profoundly transformed me" and "created hundreds of revolutionaries."[10] It played this role not only because of its idyllic prophecies but because of its reply to the affirmation in *Fathers and Sons* of love and continuity between generations.

What, after all, is the usual experience of youthful political idealists? They rebel against their parents and against Society, which they seek to remake, often with a partner. Time passes, children are born to them, and their concern for the future becomes personalized, for it is hard—and abstractly inhuman—to pit one's own child's welfare against humanity's, and these are not always in self-evident accord. Having children of one's own has a further effect, that of placing the young rebels in the role of parents themselves. Other factors enter in: compromises of principle come to be accepted as expansion of experience, as recognition of life's ambiguities; more specifically, those who have created life and come to love what they have created are less willing to contemplate its destruction in the name of some abstract goal.

Chernyshevsky understood this process well; moreover, he knew from his own experience in the radical movement that rebellion against parents (and their surrogate, Society) was in fact a primary factor in many young revolutionaries' act of commitment. Given the widespread phenomenon, in Russia at that time, of youthful departure from parents' homes and ways for progressive activity, it is not difficult to suppose that Chernyshevsky's anger at *Fathers and Sons* was at least partially fueled by Turgenev's portrayal of these relationships as loving and positive. In *What Is to Be Done?* he provides in answer an effective presentation of life which fixes and crystallizes youthful rebellion, a program which substitutes for love between the generations a whole other world of affections and loyalties among peers.

This vision of a future with no bothersome babies or bothersome old folks, of a way of life in which revolutionary commitment can escape transformation into generational continuity reaches its apogee in Vera Pavlovna's "Fourth Dream" in the description of man's life in the Crystal Palace, where all social problems have been rationally solved, where there is prosperity and pleasure for all: "Everywhere there are men and women, old, young, and children all together. *But mostly young people: there are few old men, even fewer old women, there are more children than old men, but still not very many*"[11] (italics added). It is significant, I think, that when Dostoevsky sat down to answer *What Is to Be Done?* in *Notes from Underground (Zapiski iz podpolia)* (begun as a review of the novel), he ended:

> We even find it a burden to be men—men with *our own* real flesh and blood; we are ashamed of it, we consider it a disgrace and strive to be some sort of imaginary men-in-general. We are still-born and indeed not for many years have we been conceived by living fathers, and this pleases us more and more.... Soon we shall contrive somehow to be born of an idea.[12]

We know that Dostoevsky admired *Fathers and Sons*, at least that he wrote to Turgenev about it in terms of appreciation which Turgenev said "made me throw up my hands in amazement—and pleasure."[13] We do not know what Dostoevsky wrote about the novel; we can be sure that he would not have been impressed by the notion of conflict between the men of the forties and the men of the sixties because he argued explicitly, in the first two chapters of *Notes from Underground* and throughout *The Possessed (Besy)*, that the men of the sixties are not the opponents but the direct descendants, the necessary offspring of the men of the forties.

Many speculations are possible, but it seems to me likely that Dostoevsky, the great poet of the "living life," would surely have responded to Turgenev's portrayal of Bazarov the nihilist as a man doomed by his preoccupation with death. And it seems even more likely that Dostoevsky, author of the magnificent birth scene in *The Possessed* and of the unforgettable burial scene in *The Brothers Karamazov (Bratia Karamazovy)*, understood Turgenev's affirmation of the reconciliation and continuity of generations, his affirmation of "young life at play" as that which makes bearable the inevitability of the grave.

NOTES

1. D. S. Mirsky, *A History of Russian Literature: From Its Beginnings to 1900*, ed. Francis K. Whitfield (New York: Alfred A. Knopf, 1958), p. 203.

2. Quotations are from I. S. Turgenev, *Polnoe sobranie sochineny i pisem (Complete Collected Works and Letters)*, 8:193–402. The best English translation, which I have sometimes followed, is by Ralph E. Matlaw (New York: W. W. Norton, 1966). Several studies cited in this essay are included in Matlaw's valuable critical apparatus.

3. Isaiah Berlin, *Fathers and Children* (Oxford: Clarendon, 1972), p. 25.

4. René Wellek, "Realism and Naturalism: Turgenev, *Fathers and Sons*," in *World Masterpieces*, vol. 2, ed. Maynard Mack (New York: W. W. Norton, 1956), p. 502.

5. I consider a literal translation of the Russian title to be significant and to have a bearing on my argument, but I will continue to use the generally accepted translation for convenience.

6. Wellek, "Realism and Naturalism." I think the pronouncement of Potugin, in Turgenev's *Smoke*, best expresses the author's essential message: "Man is weak, woman is strong, chance is all-powerful...." And in Turgenev's writing, all-powerful indifferent chance is represented again and again, through imagery or fact, as nature.

7. Translated from A. S. Pushkin, "Brozhu li Ya vdo! ulits shumnykh," *Polnoe sobranie sochineny v desyati tomakh (Complete Collected Works in Ten Volumes)* (Moscow-Leningrad: Akademia Nauk, 1949), 3:133–34. R. D. B. Thomson has pointed out to me that in the notes to the Russian text of *Fathers and Sons*, A. I. Batyuto mentions that, "'indifferent' nature" is a "concealed citation" from this poem of Pushkin. No commentary is, however, offered. I. S. Turgenev, *Polnoe sobranie sochineny*, 8:621, note to p. 402.

8. Hjalmar Boyeson records Turgenev as saying (originally in *The Galaxy* 17 (1874): 456–66): "I was once out for a walk and thinking about death.... Immediately there rose before me the picture of a dying man. This was Bazarov. The scene produced a strong impression on me and as a consequence the other characters and the action began to take form in my mind." Quoted from the Russian in "K biografii I. S. Turgeneva," *Minuvshie gody* 8 (1908): 70, in Richard Freeborn, *Turgenev, The Novelist's Novelist* (Glasgow: Oxford University Press, 1960), p. 69.

9. N. G. Chernyshevsky, *Chto delat?* (Leningrad: Khudozhestvennaya literatura, 1967). The English translation by Benjamin R. Tucker is both inaccurate and incomplete.

10. Nikolai Valentinov (N. V. Volsky), *Encounters with Lenin*, trans. Paul Rosta and Brian Pearce (London: Oxford University Press, 1968), p. 73.

11. N. G. Chernyshevsky, "Excerpts from *What is to Be Done?*," in *Notes from Underground and the Grand Inquisitor*, ed. Ralph E. Matlaw (New York: E. P. Dutton, 1960), p. 169.

12. Ibid., p. 115.

13. Letters to F. M. Dostoevsky, March 18 (30), 1862. The text may be found in Matlaw, *Notes from Underground*, pp. 182–83. Dostoevsky responded warmly to the work of the philosopher N. F. Fyodorov, *The Philosophy of the Common Task*. Konstantin Mochulsky, Dostoevsky's great biographer, says that according to Fyodorov, "All living sons will direct their forces to a single problem—the resurrection of their dead fathers. 'For the present age,' writes Fyodorov, 'father is the most hateful word and son is the most degrading.'" Konstantin Mochulsky, *Dostoevsky, His Life and Work*, trans. Michael A. Minihan (Princeton: Princeton University Press, 1967), pp. 567–69.

EDGAR L. FROST

Turgenev's "Mumu" and the Absence of Love

T here is only one instance in his story "Mumu" where Turgenev directly and uncompromisingly tells the reader that love exists, and those involved are Mumu and Gerasim. Mumu, we are told, "loved Gerasim alone," while for his part "Gerasim … loved her to distraction" (277; trans. mine—E.F.). In no other scene is the reader shown unquestionable, directly attested mutual love, and it is this simple fact which Turgenev plays upon to structure the entire story and to characterize those who act it out. He does so, for the most part, by focusing on the absence of love rather than its presence. Such an approach is not surprising, since love in Turgenev's œuvre is usually illusory or short-lived. The only two characters that love each other and show their love are the dog and her master, and, while the depths of this relationship are shown, the lone instance of such love is outweighed by all the manifestations of its absence elsewhere.

The major example of one who does not love and is not loved is, of course, the *barynja*, and the primary victim of this negative force on the love scene is Gerasim. But it should be noted that there are several other instances of the absence of love in what is indeed a very sad tale. The unfortunate Tat´jana is loved by Gerasim, but does not return his feelings, at least not until it is too late; her main reaction to him is fear, and her main tactic in dealing with him is to try to stay away from him. The eternally rationalizing

From *Slavic and East European Journal*, vol. 31, no. 2. © 1987 by American Association of Teachers of Slavic and East European Languages.

Kapiton, generally stupefied by drink, can hardly be said to be in love with Tat´jana; he is not opposed to the idea of matrimony, but when he learns that it is the excruciatingly shy laundress who has been chosen for him, he thinks painfully and exclusively of the threat Gerasim represents to him. Family life is also noteworthy by its absence, and the fact that the major characters have no families underscores the degree to which love is missing in their lives.[1] And one more point worth emphasizing about love is Mumu's behavior toward all but Gerasim. Faithful to her favior alone, she only fawns before others: "ko vsem laskalas´" (277).[2]

It was mentioned above that Turgenev uses the Mumu-Gerasim relationship to impart structure to the work. Based on this scheme, the first part extends from the introduction to Tat´jana's departure; the second begins with the discovery of Mumu and ends with Gerasim's departure; the third and concluding section covers Gerasim's life back in his former surroundings and the death of the *barynja*, as well as some final comments about the hero.

The first part of the story develops the ill-fated affair between Gerasim and Tat´jana; when it is finished, the stage is ready for his next love. In like manner, when the second object of his affection no longer exists, the action is again ready for a shift, and Gerasim leaves almost immediately, though he is first seen briefly by another of the serfs. The story develops by moving from one love episode to another, or, more precisely, from zero on the love scale, to fairly high, to the top of the scale, and then back down to zero. The episode with Tatjana is a step up and a preparation for the greater love the hero finds with Mumu.[3] The love element, in its presence, its absence, and its degrees, dominates the narrative. For it to loom so large in the plot it must be a symbol for something very important in the lives of Gerasim and others—something, perhaps, more than just love itself. I would suggest that this something was the human dignity of which the serfs were deprived.

There is general agreement that Turgenev was outraged by the treatment of serfs, in general throughout Russia and in particular on his mother's estate.[4] A sensitive person who felt guilty about the lot of the serfs, Turgenev is remembered as one who wrote feelingly about their great suffering and their qualities as human beings. What is less well remembered is that Turgenev was even moved to take up arms in their defense on one occasion.[5] By all accounts, then, Turgenev felt very strongly that the serfs were human beings and should be treated as such. Thus, whether love stands for freedom, happiness, or something else, one can surmise that in the story it represents much that is denied Gerasim. He is a serf, and therefore his life is made incomplete. In the final section, Gerasim is home again, but he remains alone, loveless. He has no family, and the reader is told that he has no dog and sees no women. He is in familiar surroundings, but the story remains pathetic precisely because he has been cut off from the two beings that gave his life a deeper meaning through love, whether real or imagined.

Some might think it improper to speak of the relationship between Tat´jana and Gerasim as "finished," as I have above, since it never really begins, except on his part. Such an objection might be valid in one sense, but not another. While the love is a one-way affair, from Gerasim to Tat´jana, it is clearly an attempt on his part to deepen his life, and as such it is a foreshadowing of the real joy he finds in the joining of his life with Mumu's. Indeed, there is much evidence to link Tat´jana and Mumu. Both fill a void in the life of the hero, thus illustrating his otherwise empty fate at the hands of his mistress. One can scarcely help noticing the link between Tat´jana and Mumu, because of the way Turgenev structures the tale. As Tat´jana is about to leave for the remote country, to accompany her worthless husband, Gerasim comes out of his room and presents her with a red kerchief, an obvious sign of his affection for her. She responds by crying and by kissing him three times, and although the kisses are described as being "in the Christian manner" (276), they nevertheless convey feeling for him. A few moments later, she is gone, but no sooner has the cart bearing her lurched out of his view than Gerasim turns off along the river and notices the as-yet-unnamed Mumu wriggling helplessly in the mud there, trying to extract herself.

It is, of course, quite a coincidence for Gerasim to stumble onto a new and greater love almost before the one he has lost is out of sight.[6] The suddenness of the transition from Tat´jana to Mumu is such that it draws attention to the obvious and invites comparisons of the two objects of Gerasim's love. The precipitousness of the break also makes one mindful of the structure of the story, conveying the notion that something new and important is about to happen and thus setting up the ascendancy of the Mumu-Gerasim relationship.

The similarities between Tat´jana and Mumu make the work a Freudian delight—beginning with the fact that Mumu is a female and shares Gerasim's bed: "[She] immediately leapt onto the bed with a satisfied air" (277). What is important, however, is not sex, but love and all that it stands for in the tale. And in that connection the links between Tat´jana and Mumu are instructive. Both are orphans of vague or unknown ancestry. Tat´jana has a worthless uncle, banished to the country and thus prefiguring her fate with her equally worthless husband. This and the existence of some other uncles are all we are told of her lineage. The author, in fact, pointedly tells us that "she essentially had no relatives" (268). No mention is made of whence

Mumu has come, and one can only surmise that she is unwanted progeny that someone has cruelly disposed of. Both characters have known hardship. The dog has been left to die in the river, and the woman has been oppressed since her early years. Furthermore, the two resemble each other physically. Tat´jana is described as "small, thin, fair-haired, with moles on her left cheek" (267), while Gerasim spies near the river bank a "small pup, white with black spots" (276). The unwanted whelp is also pictured as trembling with "all its ... thin body" (276). The links established between the two are: *malen´kij–nebol'šoj, xudoj–xuden´kij, belokuryj–belyj,* and *s rodinkami–s černymi pjatnami.*

The root *lask–* is also important in connecting Tat´jana and Mumu. When Turgenev sketches Tat´jana's brief background, he mentions that she "never saw any kindness" ("laski nikakoj nikogda ne vidala"; 268). Twice more the same root crops up in connection with her. First, in describing the scene in which Gerasim frightens Tat´jana by coming up behind her and offering her a sweet in the form of a rooster (beware the Freudians!), the author depicts his hero as "stupidly laughing and affectionately lowing" ("glupo smejas' i laskovo myča"; 268). Tat´jana has known no caresses or kindness, and Gerasim yearns to supply these. It is especially poignant when the root occurs again later, when Gerasim has built his intentions to the point of being almost ready to ask the mistress for permission to wed Tat´jana. Seeing the play-acting Tat´jana, Gerasim looks upon her in the instant before falsely concluding that she is inebriated, nodding at her with "affectionate lowing" ("laskovym myčan'em"; 275).

Earlier we mentioned the phrase "ko vsem laskalas´" (277), used in reference to Mumu. This pregnant wording has two effects. One is to link Mumu and Tat´jana more closely through the emotional flavor attaching to the root.[7] The other is to make a connection between them via the more specialized meaning of 'fawning', usually applied to dogs but transferable in the story to the cringing, timorous Tat´jana.[8] Tat´jana is a cowering type who trembles at the mention of her mistress's name and never talks to anyone if she can avoid it. Her only interest is in finishing her work on time. Turgenev's direct words about her are, "She was of an extremely mild, or, it would be better to say, timorous disposition," and, he adds, she "was deathly afraid of others" (268). There is a clear connection between the frightened woman and the intimidated dog that refuses to be enticed by the *barynja* and her servants.

Just as Tat´jana "trembled at the mere mention of the *barynja*'s name" (268), so Mumu "began to shiver and flattened herself against the wall" (279) upon being brought before the old woman. The words "Disposition ...

extremely mild, … timorous," cited before with reference to Tat´jana, are echoed when one reads "became very frightened and was ready to hurl herself toward the door" (279) in the description of the dog's behavior before her mistress. The actions of Gerasim's two love objects are strikingly similar. Both are terrified of the old woman, and it is further significant that Tat´jana's fear exists, "although the latter hardly knew her by sight" (268). The dread *barynja*, of course, is not acquainted with Mumu either, a fact not particularly noteworthy in itself but important as an added parallel between Tat´jana and Mumu.

The accumulation of such evidence would seem to make it difficult to deny that Turgenev had reason for equating the two—as, indeed, he had. And the reason was that he wanted to call attention to their desperate loneliness, isolation, and need of love, as well as their relationships with Gerasim. In a work so devoid of love, theirs is an eloquent connection, both with each other and with the hero. It is a deft touch in the Tat´jana Mumu relationship that the connection via *lask-* combines the ideas of love and a fawning, cringing attitude, two of the essential ingredients of the tale. And though the work is one of love and its absence, it is also one of the frightful cruelties perpetrated upon human beings and symbolized by the equal tyranny over a dumb beast and her dumb master. Within this scheme, too, Tat´jana serves as a link between Mumu and Gerasim, for she is of the dog's nature and the man's kind.

An avenue by which Turgenev airs the theme of nonlove is, certainly, the corollary of isolation. He begins by focusing on the solitary figure of the dictatorial old *barynja* and concludes by sketching the hero in his lonely hut, without family, with no romantic interest, and with no dog. In between, the author shows us the abandoned mongrel and the timid, then banished and isolated, Tat´jana. The work, as will be demonstrated, is partially organized around the theme of isolation.

The opening words of the story are, "In *one* [my italics—E.F.] of the remote streets of Moscow" (264), and forms of the word *odin* appear twice more in the first eighteen lines, thus quickly linking the two lonely figures of the *barynja* and Gerasim. *Odin*, of course, means not only 'one' in Russian, but also 'alone', and it is the aloneness of the pair that manifests itself early on. They are alone in different ways, to be sure, but ironically enough they share equally the fate of being isolated from their fellow beings. Being thus isolated, they cannot love and be loved, a common bond of loneliness between the two.

For her part, the old woman has been cast off by others because of her age and her disposition, foul and surly. A widow, she is all alone though surrounded by servants and handmaidens. Her children have gone off to live their own lives and left her to the artificial company surrounding but not loving her. Unloved, she chooses to meddle in love and arrange a match between Kapiton and Tat´jana, where there is no love of one for the other. The *barynja*, to gain attention and company, feigns illness and fainting spells, but she never manages to break out of the enchanted circle of her loneliness and is forced to live out her last days in bitter solitude.

Gerasim is just as alone, but for very different reasons. First, he is alone because the cruel old woman has brought him to Moscow, where he plainly does not fit. Inured to the arduous toil of the country, where physical prowess and stamina are valuable, Gerasim scoffs at the tasks of the city. The countryside, where his staggering strength served him especially well and where he did the work of four men, is no preparation for the city environment, where he chafes at his relative inactivity. Clearing the yard of roosters and the walks of drunks is not worthy work for one with the air of a *bogatyr´* about him. While the work he performs in the country is also not of an exalted nature, still one has the feeling that Gerasim fits there. His size and strength are of a singular nature and cause him to stand apart from others, emphasizing his isolation, his loneliness, and, ultimately, his separation from love. This is the case even among his fellow serfs, and both they and Gerasim seem to realize it. His fellow workers keep their distance, and Gerasim "didn't like people to come to see him" (266). The repelling, rather than attracting, qualities of Gerasim become evident when one reads, "Not everyone was willing to jeer … at Gerasim: he didn't like jokes" (268). Tat´jana, however mousy and shrinking she may be, is still one of the crowd and can be teased, but Gerasim is not and cannot. The last paragraph in the tale begins, "I živet do six por Gerasim bobylem v svoej odinokoj izbe" ("And Gerasim still lives all alone in his lonely hut"; 292). The words *bobylem* and *odinokoj* in combination serve to underscore the degree of loneliness in Gerasim's existence and to remind us that, however content he may be in the country rather than in Moscow, he has had to leave both of his loves behind. Embittered, he also cuts himself off from any future love. For Turgenev, isolation is terrible because it is a state in which one can neither give nor receive love, as we see through Gerasim's plight and through that of the *barynja*.

The difference, to an extent, between the *barynja* and Gerasim lies in his being deaf and dumb. His proportions and strength serve to make him heroic, and we are told that if it were not for his ailments, any lass in the village would be happy to link her life with his. But his physical handicaps isolate him completely, for they lend to his towering, imposing physique a frightening aspect that causes others to shun and fear him. Much is, in fact, made of what a wide berth others give him, and not just the timid-souled Tat′jana. "Everyone in the neighborhood began to respect him a great deal; even in the daytime passersby, not swindlers by any means but simply strangers, at the sight of the menacing yard-keeper waved him off and shouted at him as if he could hear their cries" (265). And again, at the end of the narrative, "and a dog—what does he need a dog for? You couldn't drag a thief into his yard with a rope!" (292). The stress here is on the threatening side of the hero, which contributes mightily to his isolation. But the reader is given a mixed portrayal of Gerasim, who is both terrible and wonderful. He is an unrefined manifestation of nature, and we are remiss if we fail to notice either aspect: the terrible, for he has that in him, or the marvelous, for he has that as well.

The terrible side of Gerasim is apparent enough—he cracks heads together, flings wrongdoers about as if they were so much chaff, and thrusts a threatening fist at any who dare to tease Tat′jana.[9] The strength which can dislodge a horse and cart stuck in the mud also petrifies the loutish Kapiton with fear, causing him to refer to Gerasim as "tot-to, lešij, kikimora-to" ("that one, the wood-goblin, the she-devil"; 271). The choice of words, albeit from the unreliable Kapiton, is not without interest, for it functions to focus on the dark side of the hero.[10] Specifically, all three terms used by Kapiton can refer to devils. *Tot* is one of many terms used by superstitious folk desirous of avoiding direct usage of the word *čert*, for fear that the use of the name might elicit its owner and bring misfortune to the speaker.[11] While *lešij* may refer to a supernatural forest spirit, and *kikimora* to one of a ridiculous or funny appearance or mode of dress, each term also has a more serious interpretation. *Lešij* occurs in the expression *k lešemu*, synonymous with *k čertu* (Usakov, 2:54), and *kikimora*, usually reserved for females, designates a *nečistaja sila* (1:1353).[12] Gerasim, as we are made to see very plainly, has a strongly developed negative side. The same can be said of the *barynja*, with the vital difference that there is nothing positive about her. She is terrible and only terrible, while Gerasim's positive attributes outweigh his faults.

Ironically, though, it is what he does to the one he loves most of all that best illustrates the terrible side of Gerasim—he drowns Mumu. There is a sense of fulfillment in the act, for he rescues the dog from a watery grave at one point, only to plunge her into one at another. Russia's serfs were often doomed to unhappiness, and this sequence of events serves to bring home the hopelessness of the existence of Gerasim. "Why bother to save the dog in the first place, if you're going to have to end her life later?" runs the implied question. It is, of course, a terribly poignant device to have the hero destroy the creature he loves. But why have him drown her? Perhaps precisely because it is a painful death, and not a quick one. Turgenev thus manages to elicit more sympathy from his readers—Gerasim has said he will kill the dog, and he does. He could do it another way, but no other way would fit quite so well in this particular tale. It demonstrates the blind, mute fury of a downtrodden people, the unthinking savagery of which they were capable. Yet, at the same time, it demonstrates their sometimes unbending honesty and straightforwardness. The act simultaneously attracts and repels.

In the story there is another dog, an old watchdog named Volčok, which is never taken off its chain. It lies about the yard day and night, firmly fastened to its place. But the most interesting thing about it is that it does not try to leave. Volčok, in Turgenev's words, "didn't demand freedom at all" (278). This freedom—freedom to live and love—is also a central concern of the narrative. What better symbol of the situation of the serfs? Here we have an old dog, beaten down by age and experience, which has accepted its fate to the point of not even trying to change it. It barks quite halfheartedly, merely going through the motions. Obviously, Volčok will never lose his chains.

Mumu stands in the starkest of contrasts to this acceptance of one's fate. Until discovered by the old woman, she runs freely about the property and the city with her master. She enters his room, hops onto the furniture, and is familiar to the owners of the restaurant where Gerasim takes her for her last meal. She is, furthermore, a fighter, a creature with spirit. Even though weak, she is struggling for her life when Gerasim first chances upon her in the mud. Cornered by the *barynja* and her servants, she backs up against a wall and bares her teeth at the old woman. Stolen from her owner, she breaks free and returns to him. Moreover, in contrast to Volčok, she has a purpose in life, which is brought out in her barking (277-78). A good watchdog, she makes it known if there really is an intruder or something suspicious about. One may contrast this with the way Volčok lies curled up in his house, aimlessly emitting, from time to time, a hoarse, almost *silent* sound, "as if sensing all its futility himself" (278). Mutatis mutandis, the Russian people lie silently and submissively in their hovels, living out their days, making no effort to attain freedom. Like Volčok, they bark hoarsely, almost silently, only now and then, and to no real purpose.

Gerasim, linked closely with the freedom-loving Mumu, is restless, and he finally gains some individual freedom by leaving Moscow for his native region. But, being a serf, he also shares some of Volčok's heritage. He, like Volčok, has almost no voice and is capable of making only one sound, an indistinct one at that. The Russian people had no voice in their own affairs, and Gerasim's dumbness—he cannot declare his love—symbolizes their total dependence on their owners.

Turgenev, it should be observed, used the world of sounds—alien to Gerasim—very effectively in his tale. He went far beyond employing it in its absence to represent the mere bondage of the serfs. Primarily, he used it as a link with love, once in connection with Tat´jana and on another occasion in reference to Mumu. In the first instance, Turgenev depicts Gerasim sitting on the side of his bed, "singing" mournfully (275). The scene is reported by the coachman Antipka, who peeps through a crack into Gerasim's room. What he sees is the dumb giant seated, head down and hand on cheek, swaying and shaking his head, now and then softly emitting his lowing sound. His eyes are closed, and no sound comes out except the mooing. The motion of his head is compared to that of coachmen or boat-haulers, "when they drag out their mournful songs" (275), and the effect of what Antipka sees is so strong that he stops looking through the crack, obviously unable to do so any longer. The depiction is made more powerful by Turgenev's actual use of the verb *pet´* before going on to make clear that his hero is not really singing but going through the motions of the act nature has prevented him from being able to perform. The reason for this plaintive portrayal is Gerasim's loss of Tat´jana to Kapiton.

The second instance of sound-related depiction having to do with Gerasim also involves a loss, that of Mumu. There is a heart-rending scene in which she has been stolen from her owner, and he runs pitifully about the yard, asking all present whether they have seen her. A pathetic height is reached when Gerasim "turned away and again murmured [*promyčal*]: 'Mumu!'—Mumu didn't answer" (282). The symbolism of the name "Mumu" itself is, of course, quite rich, and it is manifested tellingly here. The name, chosen by Gerasim, is an animal sound, specifically a bovine sound. Thus, it not only reinforces the animal imagery connected with the hero, but also reminds us in particular of his being compared with a young bull taken away by a train. Beyond this, however, it has another function, namely that of calling to mind again for the reader the fact of Gerasim's inarticulateness—literally his inability to speak and figuratively his inability to speak out in protest. We are told of Gerasim's "speech" (*myčan´e*), which Ožegov defines first as the lowing or mooing of cattle (or the bellowing of a bull) and second as speaking indistinctly or inarticulately. This overlapping of meanings thus makes "Mumu" the perfect name for the title character, and the scene in question especially pathos-filled. In sum, the two scenes of Gerasim's using sounds—one in which he "sings," and another in which he calls his dog—are directly love-related, each having to do with the loss of a loved one.

Mumu, the supreme symbol of unselfish, loyal love in the story, values Gerasim highly, and she is the force which changes his life. A willing sacrifice offered up by her master's hands, she becomes the symbol for the coming emancipation of the serfs in Russia. Simply put, she replaces Volčok in Gerasim's (i.e., the people's) life. Not indefinitely would the *mužiki* lie passively chained to the land owned by their masters. Gerasim remains a symbol of potential energy waiting to be unleashed, rather than one of a force roaming unchecked over the land, but he is a powerful symbol whose explosiveness is hinted at in his terrible strength and in the fear and respect he inspires in others.

Gerasim has something of the paradoxical about him. He represents the Russian peasantry as a whole, and yet he is, after all, a very singular individual who stands out from the crowd in ways already enumerated. There is much that is heroic about Gerasim, and heroes by their nature stand above the masses. It is, however, a point well taken that figures like Sten'ka Razin and Robin Hood are beloved by the people and that they are, in the final analysis, of the people. C. M. Bowra, commenting on the nature of the hero, sheds light on the reason common folk feel at one with those greater than they are. "Even when the hero has supernatural powers and is all the more formidable because of them, they do little more than supplement his essentially human gifts." The hero, Bowra continues, "awakes admiration primarily because he has in rich abundance qualities which other men have to a much less extent" (91). Gerasim is heroic because of his strength and because of his actions. But others can relate to him because of his human qualities, which Turgenev insisted on. In short, Gerasim becomes a folk hero very closely identified with the *narod*. He is already such a figure in the introduction to the tale, and his stature as such has grown and is re-emphasized by its end. We should therefore consider how the author paints such a picture and integrates it into the work.

In establishing his protagonist as both heroic and common, Turgenev uses two kinds of descriptive material, both positive in nature. On the one hand, he makes Gerasim *bogatyr'*-like; on the other, he gives him balance by reminding us that this same Gerasim is a common Russian peasant, no matter how big and strong he may be. The result is an aura of positiveness emanating from the humble values of the *mužik* and the legendary qualities of the *bogatyri*. The first mention of Gerasim includes the phrase "složennyj *bogatyrem*" (264), a detail that adds more than strength to his image for the Russian reader. Saying of Gerasim that he was "built like a *bogatyr'*" introduces a whole complex of associations. We do not find in the text references to the hero's "white hands" or "good steed," as one likely would in a *bylina*. But the term *molodec*, familiar from folk poetry, is used to describe Gerasim as he strides determinedly homeward, and he is said to do so "strongly and briskly" ("sil'no i bodro"; 291), a phrase solidly in the *bylina* tradition. The combined effect makes Gerasim a positive figure, despite any shortcomings he may have. We learn, as already mentioned, that the girls do not want to marry him because of his misfortune, and the picture which emerges is not one of an elegant or refined hero. It may even, unquestionably, be said to be one of a crude peasant who scarcely knows his own brute strength, but still the positive traits outweigh the negative.

Some of the words which remind us of his positive nature are those that echo the aura of the *bogatyr'* and establish him as being heroic. Such descriptions as "blessed with extraordinary strength," "it was cheerful to look at him," and "imparted a solemn importance to his tireless labor" (264) paint a strikingly positive picture. And when we read near the end of this opening description of him the statement "Slavnyj on byl mužik" (264), little doubt can remain as to how the author wants us to feel about him.

The author reminds us again of the nature of his hero when he proceeds to describe Gerasim's surroundings, and in so doing informs the reader that the mighty *mužik* has fixed himself "a truly *bogatyr'*-like bed" (266) on which to sleep. Thus we have a second, re-enforcing use of a form of the word *bogatyr'*. So vital was the image to the tale that Turgenev chose to end it with a third, concluding use of the term. The last words of the story are "This is what they say of the *bogatyr'*-like strength of the mute" (292). Also important in the tale's ending is the choice of the word "mute" (*nemoj*) rather than "Gerasim" or "*mužik*." By referring to him as "mute" or "silent," Turgenev adds a great deal to the conclusion. Gerasim's pent-up, mute fury at the fate of first Tat'jana and then Mumu is a symbol of the situation of Russia's repressed peasantry. It has long been silent, like Gerasim, but his flight back to his country home is a form of speaking out and as such serves as a thinly veiled hint that the peasantry cannot be bound to its human masters forever.[13]

The other essential part of Gerasim's portrayal stresses his humble station in life and his oneness with his fellow Russian peasants. With regard to the other servants in the household of the *barynja*, the narrator informs us that Gerasim "considered them his own" (266), a necessary point if Gerasim is to serve as a symbol of his fellows. Not overly friendly with them, he nevertheless knows that his place is among them, and he gets along with them well unless they threaten Tat'jana or Mumu or misbehave in the

territory where he has been assigned to keep order. Significantly, a host of
other details ties him to the peasantry. In his pre-Moscow existence, he lives
in an *izbuška* (266), and upon returning to the country, he resides in an
izbenka (291). In the *traktir* where he orders Mumu's last meal, it is the
peasant fare of *šči* (288) that he sets before his beloved pet, and one thinks
involuntarily of the common people characterizing their diet with the folksy
"Šči da kaša—piščia naša." The weight of similar characterizations mounts
to considerable proportions.

Truly, there are numerous elements which link Gerasim with the
peasant masses from which he has sprung, with the traditions of *Rus'*.
Ironically, his opposite, the *barynja*, is also linked with this old world, but in
a significantly different way: "The old *barynja*...followed the old customs in
everything and kept numerous servants" (266). This passage relating to the
old woman also concerns the peasantry: it pointedly goes on to list the many
different categories of such people she owns. One of the major points of the
work is the inhumaneness of serf owners like the *barynja*, and the quote cited
is used as an introduction to the person of Kapiton Klimov, already
mentioned as the drunken husband of Tat'jana. The author goes to some
lengths to demonstrate the worth of individuals such as Gerasim, then turns
immediately around to document the extent to which they count for naught
in the eyes of those like the *barynja*: she has dozens of them around and
thinks of them primarily in terms of the type and amount of work they do,
not of their value as human beings. Much of the balance of the narrative is
achieved by the author's focusing on the similar, yet dissimilar, isolation of
the *barynja* and Gerasim. The effect is heightened by the device mentioned
here: by again demonstrating a sameness (the connections with the world of
old *Rus'*) and then pointedly showing the gap that exists between serf and
owner. Gerasim yearns for Tat'jana, for the linking of his life with hers. But
the old woman, who has already removed the hero from his native element,
now goes a step further, creating a match between Tat'jana and Kapiton. Her
cruel capriciousness shatters Gerasim's dream, terrifies Kapiton, and saddles
Tat'jana with a less than useless mate.

Still other details, such as the work he performs, identify Gerasim as a
member of his class in society. Now hefting a whole load of firewood, now
effortlessly handling a cumbersome barrel of water, Gerasim toils so
energetically and efficiently that one involuntarily marvels at him, at the very
nature of his prodigiosity. At the same time, one must agree with Ivan
Aksakov that Gerasim as symbol of the people mirrors not only its "terrifying
strength," but also its "inscrutable humility," of which we are reminded by

Mumu's death (Schapiro, 88). Disturbed enough to leave Moscow, Gerasim is still submissive enough to kill the thing he loves and to remain a serf, bound to the soil and working for its owner.

Isolation, the imagery of folklore, and the silence of the hero—who has no voice in either a literal or a figurative sense—have all been shown to play a role in the development of the story. In the end, however, the story comes back to the nullification of love, and it is in leading up to the turning point of Mumu's death that the author makes this plain. He does so by introducing a character named Ljubov' Ljubimovna, the senior "companion" of the old woman. The person in charge of carrying out the *barynja's* orders and kept forever off balance by her whims is Gavrila Andreevič, the chief domestic servant of the household. It is this Gavrila who informs Kapiton of his impending marriage to Tat´jana. He also is put in charge of getting rid of Mumu after she has offended the mistress. The unhappy Gavrila ponders the situation and tries to anticipate how he should act in accordance with the capriciousness of the *barynja*. As he prepares for the final assault upon the barricaded Gerasim and Mumu, Gavrila turns to this "companion" with the transparent name. He speaks to her because she has been sent to him directly from the old woman. And who is this Ljubov´ Ljubimovna? She, it turns out, is Gavrila's partner in crime, guilty of nothing very serious, perhaps, but certainly not manifesting any great love for her mistress by joining Gavrila in stealing tea, sugar, and the like from the household larder (285). And so, just before the climatic incident, Ljubov' Ljubimovna's name is mentioned several times, stressing the emptiness of the *barynja's* life—there is no love in it, neither on the part of this appropriately misnamed servant nor on that of anyone else near the mistress. Servants can be employed, but the life they must shore up is artificial, involving no genuine love. The very opposite, to be sure, of the situation involving Mumu and her master.

These last two, the dog and the dumb peasant, are brought ever closer together in a demonstration of real love, before it is shattered by the cruelty of the aged tyrant. As Gavrila and his helpers cluster about Gerasim's door endeavoring to get him to open it, Mumu barks: "Here again sounded a hollow barking" (286). In the phrase "hollow barking" ("gluxoj laj") one can scarcely keep from noticing the associations with deafness or indistinctness of sound inherent in the first word, the result of which is to unite man and dog more closely and poignantly. The man's "voice" and that of the dog are linked by the combination of words used by the author.

As the final severing of the relationship draws ever nearer, another connection suggests itself. After Gerasim has been deceived with regard to Tat´jana's drinking, we read of Tat´jana and Kapiton that "that same evening they ... set out for the *barynja*'s with geese under their arms, and a week later they got married" (275). If we compare this with the wording of a passage a few pages later, we find a strange echo pertaining to Mumu and Gerasim: stopping on the way to the boat, Gerasim "carried off two bricks...under his arm" (288-89). The bricks will serve Gerasim's purpose, and the words "pod myškoj," repeated from the earlier instance, seem oddly coincidental. In other words, they suggest a "wedding" between Gerasim and Mumu, foreshadowed by the actual but meaningless one between Kapiton and Tat´jana. It is another "couple," but what is borne under the arm this time is not geese, but bricks. Yet the parallel is tempting, for we see two twosomes formalizing their relationships. Neither pair constitutes a normal "couple"; yet each is setting out, clearly embarking on the process of linking themselves more closely, and the parallelism is reinforced by the repetition of "pod myškoj" at key points. It is, furthermore, confirmed by what follows. Gerasim has put on his festive *kaftan* as befits a groom, and Mumu's coat "shone spendidly" (288), as one would expect of a bride's garment. At an earlier stage, Gerasim has been seen partaking of *šči* (269), and now he offers Mumu the same fare, "salting" what he gives her with one of his own tears, which falls into the bowl she is eating politely from (288). Finally, just before he straightens up and drops Mumu into the water, Gerasim remains motionless, as if in prayer, "having crossed his mighty hands on her back" (289). It is appropriate for him to form a cross on her with his hands, for he is playing a dual role, betrothed and priest, the former as indicated above and the latter because it is he who conducts the sacrifice of which she becomes the victim.

When Gerasim opens his hands and Mumu disappears beneath the surface of the water, the "ceremony" ends. Indeed, the whole scene and the preparations for it are carried out ritualistically, as is appropriate for both a wedding and a funeral, which are equally represented. Great love is manifested throughout by both parties: Gerasim displays extreme solemnity and sadness, and Mumu shows complete trust in him, even as he holds her above the waves. The depiction of the love between the two is, of course, what makes the scene so terrible when it has ended, because they are then irreparably separated. The level of love has been brought back to zero, where it was at the outset of the story.

In the beginning, when Gerasim has been brought to the unfamiliar urban environment, we read of his initial unhappiness in the words "he didn't at first like his new life" (265). The straightforward meaning of "ne poljubilos´ emu" has to do with his not liking his life in the new milieu, but it is not difficult a few pages later to find an echo of the wording with a very different emphasis. "He grew fond of her" ("Poljubilas´ ona emu"; 268) occurs in the author's description of how Gerasim falls in love with Tat´jana by stages. This phrase causes us to recall the one that came before it. When we compare the two, it is easy to see that the first refers to the absence of love in the hero's existence. The use of the similar but opposing phrases heightens the tragic nature of the narrative by emphasizing the contrast of his prior life and his new one; so too does the repetition of the key root, *ljub*–.

Gerasim, let it be said, had found no love in his earlier life, a point the introductory material on him makes amply clear. He lived in those days "apart from his brethren" (264), though, as already mentioned, he might have had his pick of the village lasses but for his dual physical afflictions. The key is not merely that he is loveless at beginning and end, but rather that there is a difference because of what has happened in between. There is a finality about his lovelessness in the end that is not there at the outset, and this is a very large and vital difference. What is significant is that his chances for love are taken away by his owner. But for the heartless old woman, he might have found a Tat´jana or a Mumu in the countryside—and his hut might not have been so empty. He might have shared it with a woman or a dog, perhaps both. But, as the author tells us in conclusion, "he has completely quit associating with women, doesn't even glance at them, and doesn't keep a single dog at his place" (292).

The stress in the last paragraph of the story is on the apparent sameness of circumstances surrounding the hero. Three times Turgenev uses the phrase "as before"—first, in reference to Gerasim's strength, which is as great as ever; second, to let us know that Gerasim still does the work of four men, just as he used to; third, to indicate that his staid and sedate nature has remained the same as before (292). It seems clear that the reason for the emphasis on all this sameness is to set up a distinct contrast between it and the one aspect that is not the same: the protagonist's opportunity to love and be loved. Without this opportunity, Gerasim remains less than a man, which is exactly Turgenev's point. Much more than a lachrymose dog story, "Mumu" was at the time of its publication—and remains today—an eloquent statement on the deprivations suffered by the Russian peasants, and its major device was the careful removal of love from Gerasim's sadly limited little world.

NOTES

1. The *barynja*, for example, is a widow. No mention is made of her deceased husband, and even though she has sons and daughters, emphasis is placed on their having left home and no mention is made of grandchildren. It is as though she has no family at all.

2. In the passage cited, Turgenev draws a clear distinction between Gerasim and all the others who come in contact with the dog. The full text is, "All the people in the house grew fond of her and also called her Mumu. She was exceedingly clever, fawned before everyone, but loved Gerasim alone. Gerasim himself loved her to distraction … and he didn't like it when others petted her: whether he feared for her or was jealous on her behalf—God knows!" Readily apparent in this description is the exclusivity of Mumu's love: everyone is fond of her, but she loves only her master. The narrow, intensified love is thus magnified in significance, as becomes apparent when it must be parted with.

3. Geršenzon made clear Turgenev's *modus operandi* in 1919 when he wrote, "One of Turgenev's favorite methods is to juxtapose real love with imagined love in order the more sharply to sketch the nature of the one and the other" (90; trans. mine—E.F.).

4. See, for example, Garnett, 28; Magarshack, 55-56; Freeborn, 39; Yarmolinsky, 23-24 and 110-11; Zhitova, 70-74; Lloyd, 23-25 and 40.

5. Schapiro, 17. The incident concerned Turgenev's intervention on behalf of a serf girl sold by his mother. Police dispatched to fetch the girl were met by a determined Turgenev, armed and threatening to shoot in defense of the girl. The affair ended with Turgenev's mother yielding to her son and negating the sale.

6. See Briggs, 198, which contains a list of the main ways chance meetings function in Turgenev's works. The device is one the author was much given to.

7. *Lask–* is normally connected with the meaning of 'caress'; Patrick, 129, and Wolkonsky and Poltoratzky, 174-75.

8. Patrick, 129, and Wolkonsky and Poltoratzky, 174. See also the related "Sobaka vzlaskalas´, zalaskalas´" (Dal', 4:614).

9. Other examples of Gerasim's precariously restrained murderous strength come readily to mind. We read, for example, in the initial description of his power at work, that "around St. Peter's Day he would wield the scythe so devastatingly as, for example, to uproot a young birch grove" (264). Without going into great detail, it can also be noted that Gerasim threatens Kapiton with a carriage shaft (269), smashes a water barrel (275),

wipes off and cleans a horse, which—as a result of the force used—staggers under his "iron fists" (275), and, finally, looms so menacingly and suddenly in his doorway that all those who had been standing about it are sent reeling head over heels and are referred to as "ljudi?ki" (286-87).

10. Nor is it only Kapiton who holds such an opinion of Gerasim. The same idea is expressed by various other servants in two other instances (269, 270), using *lešij* again and even *čert* (269), leaving little to the imagination.

11. Other euphemistic names used by the Russian folk include but are not limited to *nečist´*, *vrag*, *on*, *lukavyj*, *lukan´ka*, and *rogatyj* (Tokarev, 105).

12. On the other side of the coin, it should be pointed out that Gerasim not only makes a symbolic cross by crossing his hands over Mumu (289), but that he also crosses himself and prays before icons when he leaves Moscow and arrives back in his home village (291).

13. Gerasim's flight to the country constitutes an important element in the narrative, adding much social tension to the plot. It was entirely fabricated by Turgenev, who was well disposed toward the serfs but not toward his own mother. It is well documented that "Mumu" was based on an actual incident at his mother's estate, "with this difference only, that the devotion of Andrew to his mistress remained unchanged" (Zhitova, 87). There was a deaf and dumb giant of incredible strength brought to the Turgenev estate on the whim of Varvara Petrovna Turgeneva, his mother. This serf, whose name was Andrej, did indeed have a little dog named Mumu, and he was forced to dispose of it by his mistress. In real life, Andrej forgave his mistress for the dog's death and continued to serve her faithfully until she died. When he wrote the story, Turgenev changed Andrej's name and added the flight from Moscow (Zhitova, 84-89).

WORKS CITED

Bowra, C. M. *Heroic Poetry*. N.Y.: St. Martin's Press, 1966.

Briggs, Anthony D. "Ivan Turgenev and the Workings of Coincidence." *The Slavonic and East European Review* 58, no.2 (1980):195-211.

Dal´, Vladimir. *Tolkovyj slovar´ živogo velikorusskogo jazyka*. 4 vols. 4th ed., rev. Ed. Jan Baudouin de Courtenay. SPb.-M.: M. O. Wol'f, 1914.

Freeborn, Richard. *Turgenev: The Novelist's Novelist—A Study*. London: Oxford Univ. Press, 1963.

Garnett, Edward. *Turgenev*. Port Washington, NY: Kennikat Press, 1966.

Geršenzon, M. O. *Mečta i mysl' I. S. Turgeneva*. Providence: Brown Univ. Press, 1970.

Lloyd, J. A. T. *Two Russian Reformers: Ivan Turgenev, Leo Tolstoy*. London: Stanley Paul, n.d.

Magarshack, David. *Turgenev: A Life*. N.Y.: Grove Press, 1954.

Ožegov, S. I., comp. *Slovar' russkogo jazyka*. 2nd ed., rev. and suppl. M.: Gos. izd-vo inostrannyx i nacional'nyx slovarej, 1952.

Patrick, George Z. *Roots of the Russian Language: An Elementary Guide to Wordbuilding*. N.Y.: Pitman, 1963.

Schapiro, Leonard. *Turgenev: His Life and Times*. N.Y.: Random House, 1978.

Tokarev, S. A. *Religioznye verovanija vostočnoslavjanskix narodov XIX-načala XX v.* M.-L.: AN SSSR, 1957.

Turgenev, I. S. "Mumu." *Polnoe sobranie sočinenij i pisem v dvadcati vos'mi tomax*, vol. 5, 264-92. M.-L.: AN SSSR, 1960-68.

U?akov, D. N., ed. *Tolkovyj slovar' russkogo jazyka*. M.: Gos. izd-vo inostrannyx i nacional'nyx slovarej, 1935-40.

Wolkonsky, Catherine A. and Marianna A. Poltoratzky, comps. *Handbook of Russian Roots*. N.Y.: Columbia Univ. Press, 1961.

Yarmolinsky, Avrahm. *Turgenev: The Man, His Art, and His Age*. N.Y.: Collier Books, 1961.

Zhitova, Madame V. *The Turgenev Family*. London: The Harvill Press, 1947.

ROBERT COLTRANE

Hemingway and Turgenev:
The Torrents of Spring

*N*ot long after completing "Banal Story," Hemingway undertook a more *extended exercise in literary satire.* The Torrents of Spring, *a novella-length work of short fiction completed in November 1925. Unlike the enduring satire from which it draws its epigraph, Henry Fielding's* Joseph Andrews, The Torrents of Spring *remains largely unread today because its story makes little sense without knowledge of Hemingway's target, Sherwood Anderson's* Dark Laughter, *and because knowledge of* Dark Laughter, *a bestseller in 1925, is today restricted solely to the most conscientious scholars of American literature. Although several studies of* The Torrents of Spring *have examined its parody of* Dark Laughter *in detail, Hemingway's satire continues to suffer the fate of most jokes requiring explanation. Here Robert Coltrane provides a refreshingly different way of reading* The Torrents of Spring, *examining its relationship to the novella by Turgenev from which Hemingway took his title. Not satisfied with merely delineating the many parallels between these two stories of "springtime yearnings" and infidelity, Coltrane goes on to demonstrate how Hemingway used his allusions to Turgenev as a means of disguising his sexual and artistic frustrations, while attacking those who continued to misjudge the nature of his literary ambitions. The resulting informed vision of* The Torrents of Spring *may reopen this work to critical consideration.*

* * *

From *Hemingway's Neglected Short Fiction*, edited by Susan F. Beegel. © 1989 by The University of Alabama Press.

Critical studies of Ernest Hemingway's *The Torrents of Spring* have generally been limited to an examination of the satirical elements, in particular the parody of Sherwood Anderson's *Dark Laughter*. While Hemingway's parody was aimed primarily at Anderson's writing style, the setting, plot, and two female characters were a combination of Hemingway's personal and literary experiences. Although a number of competent studies have been made of Hemingway's satirical technique and his biographical sources, no one has examined the relationship between Hemingway's *Torrents* and the novella by Turgenev from which Hemingway took his title.[1] The primary purpose of *Torrents* was to provide amusement, but it also provided Hemingway a means of fictionalizing his personal frustrations and commenting indirectly on those who insisted on misjudging his literary aspirations. Hemingway is saying satirically that Turgenev's *The Torrents of Spring* is the work Anderson should have tried to emulate but was incapable of emulating. Therefore, Hemingway's only choice was to hold Anderson's work up to ridicule by parodying its stylistic excesses, while pointing to Turgenev—by means of the title—as the proper way to tell the story about springtime yearnings that lead to infidelity. I propose to examine how Turgenev's *Torrents* served as a source for Hemingway's *Torrents*, how these two works are concerned with Hemingway's personal and professional relationships of the mid-1920s, and how they are related to Hemingway's other fiction of that period.[2]

THE MOTIVATION TO PRODUCE A SATIRE

According to Carlos Baker, Hemingway wrote *The Torrents of Spring* in "seven to ten days at the end of November," or approximately from 23 to 30 November 1925. He had likely been sent a copy of *Dark Laughter* by Liveright around the beginning of September and, according to Baker, had finished the first draft of *The Sun Also Rises* by 21 September.[3] Since he did not write *Torrents* until some two months later, one might ask what happened in November to inspire his sudden and rapidly produced parody of Anderson. Many studies suggest that Hemingway's only motivation was to produce a work which would allow him to break his contract with Liveright, so that *The Sun Also Rises* could be published by a more prestigious firm, preferably Scribner's. While this motive no doubt accounts in part for Hemingway's insistence that Liveright publish *Torrents*, Hemingway had other reasons, just as compelling, for writing a satire at this time. I suggest that Hemingway's reading of Constance Garnett's translation of Turgenev's *The Torrents of Spring* sometime between 25 October and 16 November served as the catalyst that fused into a concentrated satirical outburst all the professional and personal frustrations that had been accumulating in him during the latter part of 1925.[4]

For example, the publication of *In Our Time* by Boni & Liveright on 5 October 1925 brought numerous reminders by reviewers of Hemingway's artistic association with Sherwood Anderson. In the omitted preface of *Torrents*, Hemingway sarcastically noted that he had decided from then on to write exclusively like Sherwood Anderson since so many critics had said the only value of *In Our Time* was its resemblance to Anderson's writing.[5] The reviewers did not recognize that Hemingway's study of Turgenev's *Fathers and Sons* and *A Sportsman's Sketches* in the Garnett translations had enabled him by this time to surpass Anderson in craftsmanship.[6] It was from Turgenev rather than Anderson that Hemingway had learned economy of style, especially the revealing of a character's inner turmoil through carefully selected landscape details and description of action. An example from the work under consideration here, Turgenev's *Torrents of Spring*, will serve to demonstrate the effect Hemingway had mastered. When the central character, Sanin, is waiting to risk his life in a duel, Turgenev conveys his agitated mental state both directly and indirectly:

> He walked up and down the path, listened to the birds singing, watched the dragonflies in their flight, and like the majority of Russians in similar circumstances, tried not to think. He only once dropped into reflection; he came across a young lime-tree, broken down, in all probability by the squall of the previous night. It was unmistakably dying ... all the leaves on it were dead. "What is it? an omen?" was the thought that flashed across his mind; but he promptly began whistling, leaped over the very tree, and paced up and down the path.[7]

Hemingway's ability to use physical details and minimum authorial interpretation like Turgenev to convey mental turmoil is already evident in the stories included in *In Our Time*, the best example being "Big Two-Hearted River":

> Ahead the river narrowed and went into a swamp. The river became smooth and deep and the swamp looked solid with cedar trees, their trunks close together, their branches solid. It would not be possible to walk through a swamp like that. The branches grew so low. You would have to keep almost level with the ground

to move at all. You could not crash through the branches. That
must be why the animals that lived in swamps were built the way
they were, Nick thought.... Nick did not want to go in there now.
He felt a reaction against deep wading with the water deepening
up under his armpits, to hook big trout in places impossible to
land them.... In the swamp fishing was a tragic adventure. Nick
did not want it. He did not want to go down the stream any
further today.[8]

Therefore, while many of the reviews would only have been annoying,
one very likely to have aroused Hemingway's wrath was the review published
by the *New York Sun* on 17 October 1925.[9] The reviewer not only noted
Hemingway's stylistic debt to Anderson and to Gertrude Stein but also
concluded that Hemingway's work did not have "the big movement, the rich
content of such a book as *Dark Laughter*," a work Hemingway later described
in *A Moveable Feast* as "terribly bad, silly and affected."[10] After returning
Turgenev's *Torrents of Spring* to Sylvia Beach's bookstore on 16 November,
Hemingway borrowed Donald Ogden Stewart's *A Parody Outline of History*
on 23 November, the date Baker suggests for the start of *Torrents*. The
sequence probably occurred as follows: after reading Anderson's *Dark
Laughter* and finding it a disappointing failure, Hemingway turned to one of
his favorite authors, Turgenev; while reading Turgenev's *Torrents*, he began
to consider writing a satire to relieve the emotional strain imposed by the
discipline of completing his first major novel ("I wrote it after I had finished
the first draft of *The Sun Also Rises*, to cool out").[11] Several days later he
consulted Stewart's book for guidance on the appropriate length for a parody.
A Parody Outline of History is subtitled "a curiously irreverent treatment of
American historical events, imagining them as they would be narrated by
America's most characteristic contemporary authors"; for example, chapter 4
offers "The Courtship of Miles Standish In the Manner of F. Scott
Fitzgerald." In letters to Horace Liveright and Scott Fitzgerald, Hemingway
anticipated objections to the shortness of *Torrents* by suggesting the length
was ideal for a humorous work and pointing out that it was five thousand
words longer than Stewart's book.[12] He may also have derived from Stewart
the idea of using puns on literary works as his chapter titles.

With his primary target, Anderson, already designated by the
reviewers, Hemingway chose for his setting the same Northern Michigan
area that he had earlier used in a number of the stories published in *In Our
Time*. Having read Anderson's *Dark Laughter* and then Turgenev's *Torrents*
around the same time, Hemingway would have noticed the similarities in the

character relationships but would have been annoyed by the differences in writing style. Where Turgenev used a precise choice of words that involve the reader in the scene while also advancing the plot with economy—a technique Hemingway sought to emulate—Anderson's attempts at impressionism and stream-of-consciousness produced monotonous repetition, awkward fragments, and a ponderously slow pace.

Chapter 10 of *Dark Laughter* attempts to convey Bruce Dudley's impressions upon his arrival in New Orleans:

> Consciousness of brown men, brown women, coming more and more into American life—by that token coming into him too.
>
> More willing to come, more avid to come than any Jew, German, Pole, Italian. Standing laughing—coming by the back door—with shuffling feet, a laugh—a dance in the body.
>
> Facts established would have to be recognized sometime—by individuals—when they were on an intellectual jag perhaps—as Bruce was then.[13]

Compared to the precision of Turgenev, Anderson's writing is badly flawed. Given Hemingway's pride of craftsmanship, his reaction to being unfavorably compared with Anderson is not surprising: a parody of the "big movement" and "rich content" of *Dark Laughter*. He also satirized a number of other targets, including his personal relationships in Paris which had served as the emotional basis for several of the stories in *In Our Time*.

SOURCE MATERIAL IN TURGENEV'S *TORRENTS*

Hemingway found in Turgenev's novella more than a title. While Hemingway's two male characters, Scripps O'Neil and Yogi Johnson, are parodies of Bruce Dudley and Sponge Martin in *Dark Laughter*, the source for the two waitresses, Diana and Mandy, is not found in Anderson. Their relationship to Scripps—two women competing for the love of the same man—is a variation on the situation depicted by Turgenev, and also a disguised representation of Hemingway's emotional entanglements in 1925 with his wife Hadley and Pauline Pfeiffer.[14] A brief summary of Turgenev's *Torrents* will demonstrate that the character relationships are similar to those found both in Hemingway's *Torrents* and in Hemingway's personal relations while he was writing his parody.

In Turgenev's story, the young Sanin falls in love, while traveling in Germany, with a beautiful girl called Gemma, who works in a pastry shop. They are betrothed after Sanin rids Gemma of her unsavory fiancé, Herr Klueber. However, a wealthy woman named Maria Nikolaevna seduces Sanin while pretending an interest in purchasing his estate, which he wishes to sell so he can marry Gemma. Sanin becomes emotionally enslaved to Maria and abandons Gemma. We learn the affair was arranged by Maria's husband, Poloznov, merely as a challenge to Maria's ability as a seductress, a challenge made more interesting by Sanin's devotion to Gemma. Maria soon tires of Sanin and sends him away. Sanin has been the victim of an unscrupulous woman and has no one but himself to blame. Ironically, Gemma's happy marriage later to a merchant was made possible by Sanin's freeing her from Herr Klueber. Only the foolish Sanin loses. This tale of "the ultimate degradation of a man enslaved by his passion for a woman" is, according to Turgenev's biographer Leonard Schapiro, "possibly the most forceful statement by Turgenev of this recurrent theme in all his fiction."[15]

Given Hemingway's domineering attitude toward women, he would no doubt have viewed Sanin's submissiveness to Maria with contempt. However, since he was himself in a similar situation of being tempted by a wealthy, attractive woman to abandon an earlier commitment, the attitude of contempt one finds expressed in *Torrents* is directed by Hemingway as much toward his own deceitfulness as toward Sanin's. Turgenev's Sanin has committed himself to a woman he loves, only to be lured away from his commitment by an attractive, wealthy woman who pursues him relentlessly. Similarly, in Hemingway's *Torrents*, no sooner does Scripps marry the elderly waitress Diana than he is attracted to the more vivacious and younger waitress Mandy. After trying unsuccessfully to save her marriage, Diana admits defeat and leaves Scripps to Mandy. This plot situation also reflects Hemingway's personal difficulties of the period: both Hadley and Pauline were trying to please him, a situation he found flattering but emotionally unacceptable. Diana's defeat by Mandy suggests that, subconsciously at least, Hemingway had already made his choice. Hemingway wrote out his frustrations by portraying both women, according to Kenneth S. Lynn, "as waitresses in the most degrading sense of the term," and suggested indirectly the faults that would cause him eventually to leave them both, "Hadley because she was too old, Pauline because she was too talkative."[16]

Hemingway had met Pauline Pfeiffer in March 1925, and by December she had become permanently involved in his life. Hemingway later recalled this period in the last chapter of *A Moveable Feast:* "An unmarried young woman becomes the temporary best friend of another young woman who is married, goes to live with the husband and wife and then unknowingly, innocently, and unrelentingly sets out to marry the husband."[17] The older, matronly Hadley was no match for the vivacious and wealthy Pauline, whose determined pursuit of Hemingway is reminiscent of Maria's seduction of Sanin.[18]

THE THEME OF INFIDELITY IN THE SOURCES

Infidelity permeates both Anderson's novel and Turgenev's novella. In *Dark Laughter*, Bruce Dudley escapes from his unsatisfactory marriage in Chicago by traveling to his boyhood home of Old Harbor, Indiana, where he goes to work for the Grey Wheel Company. Fred Grey, the owner of the company, is married to the sexually restless daughter of a wealthy banker, Aline, who finds Bruce attractive. When spring arrives, bringing emotional yearnings (hence the appropriateness of Hemingway's title), Aline Grey seduces Bruce. At the end of the novel, she deserts her husband and goes off with her lover. Hemingway parodies the Fred and Aline Grey relationship through the naked squaw who attracts Yogi Johnson at the end of *Torrents*. The squaw is married to a little Indian war hero who is a quadruple amputee and is thus equated with Fred Grey, also a war veteran. While playing pool, the squaw's husband admits he does "not shoot so good since the war" (65)—a satirical comment on Fred's virtually nonexistent sexual relations with Aline.

Similarities between Hemingway's two sources can be seen in the wealthy wives, Maria Nikolaevna and Aline Grey, both of whom deliberately pursue and seduce men they find attractive. In both stories the wife is having the extramarital relationship, while the ineffectual husband has no authority in the marriage. Turgenev's Poloznov is tolerated by Maria only as long as he is willing to find new young lovers for her. After long absence, Fred Grey is invited back into Aline's bed only when she discovers Bruce has made her pregnant. Hemingway's story, however, depicts the husband as being unfaithful to the wife, a disguised version of Hemingway's relationship with Hadley. By treating the characters in *Torrents* as a parody of Anderson's fiction, Hemingway obscured the personal relationships that provided the basis not only for this work but also for some of the short fiction he wrote during this period.

SIMILARITIES TO THE SHORTER FICTION

Two of the best examples of Hemingway's use of indirection to disguise the story's intensely personal revelations can be found in "Cat in the Rain" and "Out of Season." Written during the 1923-24 period of Hadley's pregnancy and the birth of their son, these stories reflect Hemingway's discontent about the impending responsibilities of parenthood. They belong to the group Meyers says are concerned with "disintegrating relationships," which also includes two Petoskey stories, "The End of Something" and "The Three-Day Blow."[19] Both "Cat in the Rain" and "Out of Season" are sympathetic portrayals of the woman's point of view and depict the man's attitude unfavorably. Since Nick Adams, as Hemingway's most personalized alter ego, is always portrayed sympathetically, Hemingway presents the man as someone who is not Nick Adams. To promote reader sympathy for the woman, he calls the husband George in "Cat in the Rain" and refers to the man in "Out of Season" only as "the young gentleman." In a letter to Scott Fitzgerald, dated 24 December 1925, Hemingway further disguised the fact that these stories were based on his own marital experiences by giving misleading information to distract Fitzgerald from recognizing the stories' true emotional source, Hemingway's feelings of discontent about Hadley's pregnancy. He writes that "Cat in the Rain wasnt [sic] about Hadley" but about "a harvard kid and his wife that I'd met at Genoa." In the same letter he claims that the most important part of "Out of Season" is what he left out—the drunken guide supposedly hanged himself when he was fired because Hemingway had complained about his conduct. Hemingway tells Fitzgerald, "I meant it to be a tragic about the drunk of a guide."[20] The story, however, is not about the drunken guide, nor has any evidence been found that the man hanged himself.

A third story included in the disintegrating relationships group, "Mr. and Mrs. Elliot," has been considered critically only as a satirical attack on Mr. and Mrs. Chard Powers Smith, due to Carlos Baker's claim that it was "a malicious gossip-story" that makes "fun of the alleged sexual ineptitudes" of the Smiths. Baker based his interpretation on the story's having been originally titled "Mr. and Mrs. Smith" and on an exchange of unfriendly letters between Smith and Hemingway.[21] "Mr. and Mrs. Elliot," also written in 1924, offers a variation on the antipaternity theme of "Cat in the Rain" and "Out of Season." It not only satirizes the Elliots' sexual ineptitudes but also ridicules their desire to have a baby, another disguised expression of Hemingway's discontent about Hadley's desire to become a mother. Much is made in the story of the fact that Mrs. Elliot, like Hadley, is older than her husband, who is the same age as Hemingway. Hemingway may well have been projecting his own feelings of helpless frustration about impending fatherhood into his creation of the Prufrock-like Mr. Elliot. When Mrs. Elliot's older girlfriend arrives to take over the running of their lives (besides being "very neat and efficient" she "was now typing practically all of the manuscripts"), we are reminded of the relationship between Gertrude Stein and her friend, Alice B. Toklas, which Hemingway was later to portray more viciously in *A Moveable Feast*. Mr. Elliot's sterility is a variation on the impotency motif recurrent in the fiction of this period, including *Torrents*.

THE PETOSKEY SETTING

More closely related to *Torrents* is the disguised presentation of Hemingway's marital difficulties with Hadley in two of the Petoskey stories written the previous year. They depict the breakup of Nick Adams's teenage romance, supposedly based on Hemingway's relationship in 1919 with a young girl named Marjorie Bump. According to Jeffrey Meyers, Hemingway's "unsatisfactory romance with Marjorie inspired two sour Nick Adams stories, 'The End of Something' and 'The Three-Day Blow,'" but they were written "when his love for his first wife was disintegrating" and are "more closely related to the fictional portrayals of the end of his marriage to Hadley ... in 'Cat in the Rain' and 'Out of Season' than to his brief liaison with Marjorie."[22] In satirizing in *Torrents* his current emotional entanglements in Paris with two women, Hemingway returned once again to Petoskey where he had earlier been involved in a similar situation. He had apparently had sexual relations with an older waitress named Pauline Snow, the subject of a 1919 "Crossroads" sketch and the model for Liz Coates of "Up in Michigan," while at the same time he was attracted to the teenaged Marjorie Bump.[23]

"Up in Michigan," a Petoskey story written around 1921–22 when he was newly married, contains one of Hemingway's earliest attempts to conceal the use of personal experience through misdirection, even at the cost of offending family friends. He gave his characters the names of real Petoskey residents, Jim and Liz Dilworth, calling the man Jim Gilmore and the woman Liz Coates, and caused hard feelings at home according to his sister Marcelline.[24] His purpose was to disguise the real source for the story, his own sexual encounter with Pauline Snow.

Hemingway appropriately sets *Torrents* in Petoskey, the place where he himself first experienced the torrents of spring. Hemingway employed a number of devices found to be successful for the stories, such as the use of real people and actual locations. The Indians, the Blackmer Rotary Pump Factory, Braun's Restaurant (i.e., Brown's Beanery), and the scenic descriptions of the Petoskey area are all factual.[25] The amputee Indian war veteran is based on Billy Gilbert, a decorated hero whose marriage was destroyed by the war, described in another of Hemingway's "Crossroads" sketches.[26] He also used the previously developed technique of concealing the real-life situation by disguising it as something else. To obscure the fact that Mandy has Pauline's personality, Hemingway gives her Marjorie Bump's age and appearance, while the Hadley character, Diana, is presented as Liz Coates. Thus Hemingway is, in effect, presenting current autobiography in the guise of past autobiography.

SELF-RIDICULE IN *TORRENTS*

The theme of physical and emotional impotence resulting from the war, which Hemingway had portrayed in his recently completed novel, *The Sun Also Rises*, also becomes a subject for ridicule in *Torrents* through the character of Yogi Johnson. Yogi has been made impotent through his experiences while a soldier in Europe, and his lack of sexual desire is reminiscent of Krebs, the veteran in another 1924 story, "Soldier's Home." Krebs likewise felt no desire for the young girls he saw when he got back home from the war. The source of Yogi's problem, however, is quite unlike that of Jake or Krebs, whose impotence results from their war experiences. In accounting for Yogi's impotence, Hemingway reveals that it was caused by disappointment in love. Hemingway satirizes Yogi's impotence by presenting the love affair as an anecdote derived from a dirty joke: a man discovers that his sexual encounter with a lovely lady has provided "peep-show" enter-tainment for the customers who pay to watch.[27] Yogi, however, never figures out that the beautiful woman who "seduced" him in Paris is a prostitute, and he is embittered because he believes the beautiful woman abandoned him for another man (78–79). Since the Negro women's laughing at the cuckolded Fred Grey is the only incident in Anderson's novel that remotely corresponds to Yogi's Paris story, we must once more look at Turgenev's *Torrents* to determine what might have inspired Hemingway to include this anecdote.

Yogi's relationship with the prostitute recalls Sanin's relationship with Maria Nikolaevna. Like Sanin, Yogi meets a beautiful, wealthy woman who takes him to her "mansion" and, after seducing him, tells him she can never see him again. Although Maria is not a prostitute, she openly has affairs with a series of men whom she dismisses after tiring of them. Like Yogi, Sanin leads a life of apathy as a result of his encounter with Maria. Not until some thirty years later, when he decides to go to America to see his original beloved, Gemma, does he regain a sense of purpose in life. Yogi's manhood is restored through a character reminiscent of a girlfriend from Hemingway's youth, the American Indian girl Trudy (also called Prudie, for Prudence) whom Hemingway credits with initiating him into manhood. Hemingway had only hinted at their sexual relationship in a story written during the same period as *Torrents*, "Ten Indians," a story in which he emphasized Nick's feeling of betrayal by someone he thought cared for him.[28] Hemingway is here projecting into Nick's feelings of betrayal his own guilt about being unfaithful to Hadley. However, when Yogi's manhood is restored by the naked Indian squaw, we are reminded of the later story, "Fathers and Sons," in which Nick's earlier sexual relations with Trudy are described more explicitly, she being the one who, Nick says, "did first what no one has done better." This motif of sexual impotence, which is presented so strongly in *The Sun Also Rises* and then echoed in *The Torrents of Spring* through Yogi, is very likely a sublimated expression of the young Hemingway's own feelings of sexual frustration over his lack of personal freedom and artistic frustration over not having yet achieved the recognition he craved.

Not only did Hemingway project some of his own frustrations into the character of Yogi, but we also find hints of Hemingway in the portrayal of Yogi's friend Scripps. Scripps O'Neil has been described by critics as a parody on writers who cannot write, but he is also a satirically portrayed Hemingway alter ego—he has had two wives and at the end of the story takes up with a third, telling Mandy repeatedly "You are my woman now" (83). Through Scripps, Hemingway is satirizing some of the attitudes about marriage that he had earlier portrayed seriously in such stories as "Cat in the Rain" and "Out of Season."

Later, in *A Moveable Feast*, he would look back nostalgically on this formative period as a time in which he innocently allowed himself to be misled by others, especially Pauline, into betraying his ideals. Others were to blame for any mistaken decisions he had made. We can see from *Torrents*, however, that he was well aware of the consequences likely to result from the actions he planned to take. *Torrents* reveals to us that by means of a devastating parody he was willing to cut off his association with Sherwood Anderson, who had become an artistic embarrassment, no matter what others thought he might owe Anderson; that by creating this parody, he could be ruthless in his business dealings by placing Liveright in a position where he had no choice but to release Hemingway from his contract. And finally, though satirically disguised, his relationship with Hadley was finished, and he was aware that he was going to begin a new relationship with Pauline, a relationship he did not feel entirely comfortable about.

Torrents is as personal as any of Hemingway's other works, perhaps one of the best reasons why Hemingway insisted so strongly to both Liveright and Perkins that *Torrents* was a work worthy of publication.[29] It shows us a Hemingway we would not see again. Just as he abandoned Turgenev as a guide after learning all that master had to teach him, so did he abandon the use of parody after it had served its purposes. The techniques of disguise and misdirection that Hemingway employed in *Torrents* would become a standard literary device in subsequent works, but he would not again resort to the use of an extended satire as a means of relieving personal and professional frustrations.

NOTES

1. John T. Flanagan in "Hemingway's Debt to Sherwood Anderson," *Journal of English and Germanic Philology* 54 (October 1955): 507–20, provides examples that demonstrate what Hemingway had satirized in Anderson's work; Richard B. Hovey in *"The Torrents of Spring*: Prefigurations in the Early Hemingway," *College English* 26 (March 1965): 460–64, provides typical humorous passages from *Torrents* and explains how they function as satire; Delbert E. Wylder in *"The Torrents of Spring,"* *South Dakota Review* 5 (Winter 1967–68): 23–35, analyzes the characters and situations being parodied in *Torrents* through an extensive comparison with Anderson's *Dark Laughter* and *Many Marriages*; Paul P. Somers, Jr., in "The Mark of Sherwood Anderson on Hemingway: A Look at the Texts," *South Atlantic Quarterly* 73 (Autumn 1974): 487–503, provides a stylistic comparison of *Torrents* and *Dark Laughter*, illustrating the parody on Anderson's writing style. Constance Cappel Montgomery's *Hemingway in Michigan* (New York: Fleet, 1966) identifies the biographical sources.

2. The edition of *Torrents of Spring* cited in this study is found in *The Hemingway Reader* (New York: Charles Scribner's Sons, 1953) 25–86; references are cited parenthetically in the text.

3. Carlos Baker, *Ernest Hemingway: A Life Story* (New York: Charles Scribner's Sons, 1969) 155 and notes to section 22, 590. In a letter to Horace Liveright, dated 28 August 1925, Anderson requested a copy of *Dark Laughter* be sent to Hemingway; see *Letters of Sherwood Anderson*, ed. Howard Mumford Jones and Walter B. Rideout (Boston: Little, Brown, 1953) 146.

With a maximum travel time by ship of about 10 days, the copy of *Dark Laughter* should have reached Hemingway before the end of September.

   4. The dates Hemingway borrowed Turgenev's *Torrents of Spring* from Sylvia Beach's bookstore are cited by Noel Fitch in "Ernest Hemingway—c/o Shakespeare and Company," *Fitzgerald/Hemingway Annual 1977*, 175, as 25 October to 16 November 1925, based on Hemingway's lending library cards in the Sylvia Beach Collection at Princeton University Library. Using the same source, Michael S. Reynolds gives the dates as 27 October to 16 November, in *Hemingway's Reading, 1910–1940* (Princeton: Princeton UP, 1981) 194.

   5. Reprinted in *The Fitzgerald/Hemingway Annual 1977*, 112.

   6. See Myler Wilkinson's *Hemingway and Turgenev: The Nature of Literary Influence* (Ann Arbor: UMI Research P, 1986) for an examination of the influence of Turgenev's *Fathers and Sons* and *A Sportsman's Sketches* on Hemingway's style.

   7. Ivan Turgenev, *The Torrents of Spring*, trans. Constance Garnett (1916; rpt. Freeport, N.Y.: Books for Libraries, 1971) 86–87.

   8. Ernest Hemingway, *The Short Stories of Ernest Hemingway* (New York: Charles Scribner's Sons, 1953) 231.

   9. The review, by Herbert J. Seligman, is reprinted in *Critical Essays on Ernest Hemingway's* In Our Time, ed. Michael S. Reynolds (Boston: G. K. Hall, 1983) 15–16.

   10. *A Moveable Feast* (New York: Charles Scribner's Sons, 1964) 28. Prior to the publication of *Torrents*, Hemingway had expressed his distaste for the sentimental writing and borrowed thinking of *Dark Laughter* in a letter to Edwin L. Peterson dated 30 March 1926, summarized by Ray Lewis White in "Hemingway's Private Explanation of *The Torrents of Spring*," *Modern Fiction Studies* 13 (Summer 1967): 262–63.

   11. Ernest Hemingway, *The Hemingway Reader* (New York: Charles Scribner's Sons, 1953) 24.

   12. *Ernest Hemingway: Selected Letters, 1917–1961*, ed. Carlos Baker (New York: Charles Scribner's Sons, 1981) 173, 185.

   13. Sherwood Anderson, *Dark Laughter* (1925; rpt. Cleveland: World, 1942) 74.

   14. See Kenneth S. Lynn, *Hemingway* (New York: Simon and Schuster, 1987) 303–4.

   15. Leonard Schapiro, *Turgenev: His Life and Times* (New York: Random House, 1978) 250.

   16. Lynn, 305.

   17. *A Moveable Feast*, 209.

18. See Jeffrey Meyers, *Hemingway: A Biography* (New York: Harper & Row, 1985) 172–93, for Hemingway's relationship with Hadley and Pauline during 1925 and 1926.

19. Meyers, 152–53.

20. *Letters*, 180.

21. Baker, *Life*, 133; exchange of letters cited in notes, 585.

22. Meyers, 49.

23. Reynolds states that Bill Smith's letters suggest "Pauline Snow was the actual name of a Horton Bay waitress" who was the biographical source for Liz Coates; see *Critical Essays*, 5. Hemingway's sketch of Pauline Snow has been published in "Crossroads—An Anthology," in Peter Griffin's *Along with Youth: Hemingway, the Early Years* (New York: Oxford UP, 1985) 124.

24. Cited by Meyers (147), who suggests that the last names of the characters came from Oak Park residents, Frances Coates and a department store owner named Gilmore.

25. Montgomery, 167–69.

26. See Griffin, 126–27.

27. Daniel R. Barnes, "Traditional Narrative Sources for Hemingway's *The Torrents of Spring*." *Stadies in Short Fiction* 19 (Spring 1982): 148–49.

28. "Ten Indians" was begun in 1925 and finished in May 1926 in Madrid; see Baker, *Life*, 169. The final revision was completed in May 1927 while on honeymoon with Pauline (Baker, 186).

29. In his letter to Liveright, dated 7 December 1925, Hemingway defends the literary merits of *Torrents*; see *Letters*, 172–74. In a letter to Perkins, 30 December 1925, Scott Fitzgerald states that one of Hemingway's conditions for giving *The Sun Also Rises* to Scribner's is that they publish *Torrents* first; see *The Letters of F. Scott Fitzgerald*, ed. Andrew Turnbull (New York: Charles Scribner's Sons 1963) 195–96.

RICHARD C. HARRIS

First Loves: Willa Cather's Niel Herbert and Ivan Turgenev's Vladimir Petrovich

Marian Forrester of *A Lost Lady* is certainly one of Willa Cather's most fascinating characters. As were most of Cather's major characters, she was, to a great extent, based on an actual person, Mrs. Lyra Garber, of Red Cloud, Nebraska. Lyra Garber, Cather said in 1925, was a woman she "loved very much in [her] childhood."[1] Like the story of Annie Pavelka, the prototype for Ántonia Shimerda of *My Ántonia*, the story of Mrs. Garber "teased" Willa Cather for many years, and *A Lost Lady*, published in 1923, was "a beautiful ghost in [her] mind for twenty years before it came together as a possible subject for presentation."[2]

Willa Cather had, in fact, kept informed about Mrs. Garber's life ever since she, Cather, had left Nebraska in 1896. But it was not until this information had been crystallized in one of those catalytic experiences typical of Cather's artistic imagination that Marian Forrester's story could be written. That event occurred in 1921 while Cather was visiting Isabelle (McClung) Hambourg in Toronto, when she received a forwarded copy of a Red Cloud newspaper and read of the death of the former Mrs. Garber, now Lyra Anderson of Spokane, Washington. "The news shocked her," James Woodress says, "and the day being warm, she went to her room to rest. Within an hour the story was all in her mind as if she had read it somewhere.

From *Studies in American Fiction*, vol. 17, no. 1. © 1989 by Northeastern University.

It was another of those inner explosions, such as she had experienced when she had met [Olive] Fremstad or had seen Annie Pavelka and her children."[3]

Woodress' statement is particularly interesting and evidently contains more truth than he realized, for Willa Cather almost certainly *had* read the story somewhere. That story, it appears, was "First Love," Ivan Turgenev's famous depiction of an adolescent boy's disillusionment at the traumatic loss of his idealized love for an older woman. The "inner explosion" that Cather experienced upon reading of Lyra Garber's death seems clearly to have been the result of the coming together (to paraphrase Cather herself) of various elements, most importantly her memories of Mrs. Garber and her familiarity with Turgenev's story.[4]

Cather's admiration for the works of the great Russian writers, especially Ivan Turgenev and Leo Tolstoy, has long been noted by biographers and critics, though studies of their influences on her fiction have only recently been undertaken.[5] In the late nineteenth and early twentieth centuries, the Russian writers, particularly Tolstoy and Turgenev, captured the imagination of the English-speaking world to such an extent that one critic has asserted that the phenomenon can only be termed a "craze."[6] Cather herself, describing this event in a radio broadcast in 1933, declared that these great Russian writers had "flashed out of the north like a new constellation at about the middle of the last century."[7] The period saw the appearance of many critical articles and reviews in major journals, several significant books on the Russians, numerous translations of Russian works, and a long-term debate over the merits of Tolstoy and Turgenev, with Turgenev generally acknowledged to be the better writer of the two.

Willa Cather developed an early interest in Turgenev and referred to him a number of times in the critical articles and reviews she wrote in the 1890s. Elizabeth Moorhead relates that when Cather moved into the McClung household in Pittsburgh in 1905, she and Isabelle McClung "devoured" the works of Turgenev, Tolstoy, Balzac, and Flaubert and that Cather was "deeply impressed by the great Russian realists."[8] Cather's comments throughout her career, in fact, reveal a lifelong admiration for the works of Turgenev. He was, quite simply, one of those few authors she considered "great."

Finally, two letters in particular indicate that Turgenev was very much on Cather's mind in the early 1920s. In a letter to Dorothy Canfield Fisher in 1922, Cather noted the publication of two new editions of Turgenev's works, praising especially the art of his story "The Quiet Backwater."[9] And, writing to a Mr. Miller in 1924, Cather called Tolstoy and Turgenev the two greatest modern writers of fiction.[10]

Cather's familiarity with Turgenev's "First Love" is apparent in numerous similarities between Turgenev's tale and Cather's *A Lost Lady*. Most obviously, both are narratives in which initiation is an important element: in each a naive and idealistic adolescent boy has his illusions about an older woman shattered. Both boys have seen themselves as chivalric heroes, protecting the lives and virtue of these "lovely ladies."[11] Both are forced to recognize the sexuality of women they at once find physically attractive yet expect to transcend any sexuality. "This is love....This is passion," Vladimir Petrovich of Turgenev's story realizes, having observed a passionate secret meeting between the object of his adoration, Princess Zinaida Zasyekin, and his father. His own love, he continues, "with all its excitements and sufferings, struck me as something very small and childish and trivial beside that other, unknown something which I could scarcely grasp and which frightened me like an unfamiliar, beautiful, but menacing face one tries in vain to make out in the gathering darkness."[12] "Beautiful women, whose beauty meant more than it said," Niel Herbert of *A Lost Lady* wonders upon discovering Marian Forrester's adulterous relationship with Frank Ellinger, "was their brilliancy always fed by something coarse and concealed? Was that their secret?"[13] "What did she do with all her exquisiteness," Niel Herbert burned to ask her, "when she was with a man like Ellinger?" (p. 100).

The nature and extent of these boys' disillusionment is nowhere made clearer, and nowhere are the parallels between the two works more obvious, than in the turning points of the stories. In Turgenev's story Vladimir, having been advised by the villainous Count Malevsky to keep watch at the fountain in the garden, discovers a tryst between Zinaida and his father.[14] Describing his reaction to that revelation years later, he says:

> I did not sob; I did not give myself up to despair; I did not ask myself when and how all this had happened; I did not wonder how it was I had not guessed it all before, long ago; I did not even harbour any ill will against my father. What I had learnt was more than I could cope with: this sudden revelation crushed me utterly. All was at an end. All my flowers were torn out by the roots at one fell swoop and they lay about me, strewn all over the place and trampled underfoot (p. 206).

In *A Lost Lady* Niel suffers a similar shocking discovery and provides a strikingly similar description of his reaction. Enjoying a walk on a beautiful summer morning, Niel decides to leave a bouquet of roses on the windowsill of Marian Forrester's bedroom. As he stoops to place the flowers on the sill, he hears first the soft laughter of Mrs. Forrester and then the laughter of Frank Ellinger. Fleeing in pain and anger, Niel finds himself at the foot of the hill:

> In his hand he still carried the prickly bunch of wild roses. He threw them over the wire fence into a mudhole the cattle had trampled under the bank of the creek. He did not know whether he had left the house by the driveway or had come down through the shrubbery. In that instant between stooping to the window-sill and rising, he had lost one of the most beautiful things in his life. Before the dew dried, the morning had been wrecked for him; and all subsequent mornings, he told himself bitterly. This day saw the end of that admiration and loyalty that had been like a bloom on his existence. He could never recapture it. It was gone, like the morning freshness of the flowers (p. 86).

As narrators relating these experiences in retrospect, both Vladimir Petrovich and Niel Herbert realize that their first loves marked the end of youth and innocence. And both, now distanced from the pain, are able to put those revelations in perspective. Neither man wishes he had not experienced that love and even its attendant painful loss. Indeed, recalling his feelings during his attempt to say goodbye to Zinaida, Vladimir asserts, "I would not wish them ever to be repeated; but I would have considered myself unfortunate had I never experienced them at all" (p. 209). Similarly, Niel reflects that he "came to be very glad that he had known her [Mrs. Forrester], and that she had had a hand in breaking him into life" (p. 171). In fact, both men, older now, have come to cherish the memories of their first painful loves. In Turgenev's story, Vladimir tells his friends, "now when evening shadows are beginning to fall on my life, what have I left that is fresher, that is dearer to me than the memories of the storm that came and passed over so swiftly one spring morning?" (p. 217). Near the end of *A Lost Lady* Cather relates, "it was years before Niel could think of [Marian Forrester] without chagrin. But eventually, after she had drifted out of his ken, when he did not know if Daniel Forrester's widow were living or dead, Daniel Forrester's wife returned to him, a bright, impersonal memory" (p. 171).

An examination of the initiation elements in the two works thus reveals striking thematic parallels between Cather's and Turgenev's stories. In addition, the two stories are similarly constructed. Both stories employ frame devices. Both begin with brief prologues set about twenty-five to thirty-five years after the main events of the narrative occurred. In Turgenev's tale, the narrator, asked by a group of friends to tell the story of his first love, remarks that he is "not very good at telling stories" and promises them instead, much like Jim Burden in *My Ántonia*, to "write down all that [he] can remember" and to read it to them (p. 143). While the prologue employs a third-person point of view, the main part of the narrative, "what he [Vladimir] had written down," is told from the first-person point of view. Cather's novel opens with a general description of the Forrester place as it had been thirty to forty years before, told from an authorial "we" point of view. Then in Part I, Section II, the focus shifts to the center of consciousness, Niel.[15] Moreover, in each case the major narrative section is followed by an epilogue in which the narrator meets an old friend from his youth, learns that his first love had married a "kind" or "splendid" well-to-do man and lived happily. In both epilogues the narrator learns of the woman's recent death.

Equally interesting, and perhaps more significant artistically, is Cather's possible use of several of the traits of Turgenev's Zinaida to "flesh out" her depiction of her own heroine. While she claimed that her depiction of Marian Forrester was so successful that people who had known Lyra Garber said "it was very like her,"[16] it may well have been the synthesis of Cather's memories of Lyra Garber and of Turgenev's Zinaida that finally made Marian Forrester such an interesting creation. Cather declared that *A Lost Lady* was not a "character study" but rather "just a portrait like a thin miniature painted on ivory."[17] If *A Lost Lady* is not a character study, Marian Forrester is none the less one of Cather's most fully realized characters.

First, both Marian and Zinaida are seen in terms of the effects they have on various men, especially Niel and Vladimir. Both young men are struck by the attractiveness of the women they admire. Vladimir, considering Zinaida's beauty shortly after his first brief encounter with her, finds her face "even more lovely than on the previous day: everything in it was so delicate, intelligent, and charming" (p. 153). Niel, similarly charmed by Mrs. Forrester, observes that, "something about her took hold of one in a flash; one became acutely conscious of her, of her fragility and grace, of her mouth which could say so much without words; of her eyes, lively, laughing, intimate, nearly always a little mocking" (p. 35). What an older Vladimir realizes, as he at forty recounts the experiences of twenty-five years before, is what lay behind that pleasing and attractive façade. What did lie behind it were the same qualities that Niel Herbert gradually becomes aware of in Mrs. Forrester: a mocking, manipulative, and at times even cruel playfulness; a passionate sexuality; and, finally, a rather desperate interest in dominant men.

The first time that Vladimir sees Zinaida she is playing an imperious, mocking game with several young men; later, she has them draw straws to see who will be allowed to kiss her hand. She compels Vladimir to jump off a fifteen-foot wall to prove his devotion to her and at another point gleefully drives a straight pin into the finger of an admirer eager to prove his love. Turgenev notes carefully the "particularly malicious pleasure" that Zinaida derives from knowing that she has the young men "completely in her power" (p. 172). Her games are more than merely coquettish, and she even admits to Vladimir that she is heartless and knows that she has "tortured" him (p. 208).

Like Princess Zinaida, Marian Forrester also extracts a price for her attention and affection. In *A Lost Lady*, poor Niel, having agreed in chivalric fashion to amuse Constance Ogden, painfully attempts to fulfill his task while Marian and Frank have taken a sleigh ride "to cut cedar boughs for Christmas." Thinking of Niel, Marian "expressed her feelings in a laugh full of mischief":

> "Well, they're off tomorrow. And Connie! You've reduced her to a state of imbecility, really! What an afternoon Niel must be having!"
> She laughed as if the idea of his predicament delighted her.
> "Who's this kid, anyway?" Ellinger asked her to take the reins for a moment while he drew a cigar from his pocket. "He's a trifle stiff. Does he make himself useful?"
> "Oh, he's a nice boy, stranded here like the rest of us. I'm going to train him to be very useful. He's devoted to Mr. Forrester. Handsome, don't you think?" (p. 63).

While Marian Forrester is certainly not so cruel as Zinaida, neither does she seem simply the portrait of a woman whom Cather "loved very much" as a child, a woman who "made [her] happy clear down to [her] toes" when she was younger.[18]

Secondly, both women, the two narrators reflect, were accomplished actresses. Both play their parts well and respond to people and situations in ways consciously calculated to produce desired effects. Vladimir, as he looks back on that summer many years ago, realizes that every one of Zinaida's admirers was necessary to her. "I am a flirt, I'm heartless, I am an actress by nature," the young Vladimir had overheard Zinaida say to another man. He himself, overwhelmed by his love for her, had become her plaything: "... She amused herself with my passion," he says, "she made a fool of me, petted me, and tormented me" (p. 170).

Similarly, Marian Forrester feigns innocence while playing a seductive role she knows full well holds both boys and men in her power. Turgenev's comment about Zinaida, "all the men who visited the house were madly in love with her, and she kept them all on leading strings at her feet" (pp. 170-71), suggests a woman much like Marian Forrester who very consciously impresses, "bewitches," her husband's gentlemen friends as well as the local boys. Niel, like Vladimir, finally comes to realize the extent to which the charm of Mrs. Forrester is the creation of a very accomplished actress. Her vivacity, her charm, her elegance "seemingly so artless," is, he concludes, "really the most finished artifice" (p. 110). Was it all, Niel finally wonders, merely "fine play-acting?" (p. 172).

Finally, the sexuality of Turgenev's Zinaida and Cather's Marian Forrester is much more fundamental than the largely contrived charm they display. Both Vladimir and Niel are shocked, horrified, bewildered to discover their heroines' passionate sexuality, even though each finds his beloved sexually attractive. If the attraction these two boys feel is more than subconscious, it is certainly repressed. Both see, and prefer to see, these women as "lovely ladies," even, as Cather puts it, as "aesthetic ideal[s]" (p. 87).

As if the sexuality of the two women were not difficult enough to accept, the nature of their sexuality and their relationships is even more incomprehensible to their young admirers. Both Zinaida and Marian desire and seem to need to be dominated by the men with whom they have relationships. Zinaida, who has a sadistic side to her, flatly declares to Vladimir, "I want someone who will master me" (p. 173). Marian Forrester, from her rescue by Daniel Forrester to her unfortunate relationship with the despicable Ivy Peters, is always attracted to strong, aggressive, even disdainful men.

Each story is marked by key passages in which a lover (or lovers) displays a sexual contempt or cruelty that the young boys, Vladimir and Niel, simply cannot comprehend. In a very striking scene near the end of "First Love," Vladimir secretly observes one of his father's meetings with Zinaida. As his father talks to Zinaida at her window, Vladimir is shocked to see him suddenly strike her sharply across the bare arm with his riding crop. His father runs into the house, and Zinaida, her arms open to embrace him, runs toward the door. Vladimir remarks, "I simply did not know what to make of it.... I could not possibly make any sense of what I had just seen. But at the same time I felt sure that however long I lived, I could never forget Zinaida's gesture, her look, her smile; and that image of her, this new image which had so suddenly arisen before me, was forever imprinted on my memory" (p. 213).

In Cather's novel, although Niel early on is disturbed by Frank Ellinger's "muscular energy that [has] something of the cruelty of wild animals in it" (p. 46), Marian Forrester is attracted to and is clearly aroused by this same energy. Cather makes this quite clear in the passage in which Frank and Marian take their sleigh ride. As Adolph Blum looks on, Ellinger "crushes" Marian to his breast before lifting her back into the sleigh. When he leaves her to cut "those damned cedar boughs," Cather writes, "Mrs. Forrester sat with her eyes closed, her cheek pillowed on her muff, a faint, soft smile on her lips. The air was still and blue; the Blum boy could almost hear her breathe. When the strokes of the hatchet rang out from the ravine, he could see her eyelids flutter ... soft shivers went through her body" (p. 67). Niel later observes Ivy Peters, who had earlier sadistically blinded the female woodpecker, walk up behind Marian in her kitchen and "unconcernedly," with total disdain for her, put both arms around her, his hands meeting over her breasts. It is with this image in his mind and "with a weary contempt for her in his heart" (p. 169) that Niel leaves Sweet Water.

Niel Herbert, like Vladimir Petrovich, finds his image of this lovely woman forever changed by his last vision of her. Perhaps understandably, neither boy can comprehend and therefore neither can accept the complexities of these women's personalities. Turgenev's most telling description of Zinaida suggests something akin to what Cather calls "the magic of contradictions" (p. 79) so fundamental to the captivating personality of Marian Forrester:

> Her whole being, so beautiful and so full of vitality, was a curiously fascinating mixture of cunning and carelessness, artificiality and simplicity, calmness and vivacity; there was a subtle, delicate charm about everything she did or said, about every movement of hers; in everything a peculiar, sparklingly vivacious force was at work. Her face too was vivacious and always changing: it expressed almost at one and the same time irony, pensiveness, and passionateness. The most various emotions, light and swift like shadows of clouds on a windy, sunny day, chased each other continuously over her lips and eyes (p. 171).

His reading of "First Love" prompted Gustave Flaubert—another of the authors Cather considered "great"—to write to Turgenev in 1863: "... Everyone of them ['old romantics'] should be grateful to you for that little story, which has such insight into their youth. What an exciting creature Zinotchka

[Zinaida] is. One of your virtues is your power of drawing women. They are both idealized and real. They have charm and haloes."[19] How apt a description of *A Lost Lady* and Marian Forrester.

The question, it seems clear, is not whether Willa Cather had in mind Turgenev's "First Love" when she wrote *A Lost Lady* but how her almost certain familiarity with or memory of that work impinged upon her own narrative.[20] At the same time that a comparison of "First Love" and *A Lost Lady* reveals interesting similiarities in the two narratives, it also indicates some very important differences, one involving the different focus in each work, and a second, the historical dimension of Cather's novel.

Turgenev's "First Love" employs a first-person point of view: the focus is clearly on the narrator. Vladimir's relationship with Princess Zinaida is the central event in an initiation story about Vladimir Petrovich. This characteristic may well be accounted for by the fact that, according to Turgenev himself, the incidents of "First Love" were not invented but were given to him entirely by life. The story, he claimed, was the most autobiographical of all of his stories.[21]

The focus in Cather's novel, on the other hand, is on Marian Forrester. Cather stated in 1925 that "the problem was to get her, not like a standardized heroine in fiction, but as she really was, and not to care about anything else except that one character."[22] What is significant, according to Willa Cather, is the portrait of Marian Forrester and the suggestion of the effect she had on those who knew her. Everything else, Cather claimed, is subordinate. While it is difficult to accept Cather's assertion that Niel is in reality "only a point of view,"[23] as an important participant in the events of the narrative and as the center of consciousness in the story, he plays a major role in the novel. Cather's emphasis in *A Lost Lady* is clearly on the lady more than on Niel's loss of innocence and naiveté. Marian Forrester's charm and attractiveness give way to a loss of direction and dignity after the Captain's death, and the novel poignantly traces her decline and increasing desperation. Marian Forrester is, as James Woodress has remarked, "a kind of Emma Bovary of the prairie."[24] She is certainly a more complex personality than Turgenev's coquettish Zinaida and, as Susan Rosowski notes, her awareness of the loss of beauty and energy in the face of time and change makes the reading of *A Lost Lady* "akin to the reading of a Keatsian ode."[25]

Most importantly, Cather's novel contains an historical dimension completely absent in Turgenev's story. The publication of *A Lost Lady* in 1923 marked the end of Cather's "Nebraska" period, which had begun with *O Pioneers!* in 1913. The four novels that precede *A Lost Lady* describe changing ways of life, attitudes, and values on prairie farms and in small towns from about 1870 to about 1920. That description constitutes a fictional record of the decline of what had once been a noble spirit and an admirable set of values.

In *A Lost Lady* the three men (Captain Forrester, Frank Ellinger, and Ivy Peters) with whom Mrs. Forrester has relationships represent stages in the history and gradual decline not only of Marian Forrester but also of the Midwest. In a world increasingly peopled by the likes of Bayliss Wheeler of *One of Ours* and Ivy Peters, Captain Forrester's "sanity"—a term Cather uses to suggest courage, integrity, vision, discipline, and a certain nobility—does not seem to work any more. Toward the end of *A Lost Lady*, Niel Herbert, preparing to leave Sweet Water, reflects that he "had seen the end of an era, the sunset of the pioneer": "This was the very end of the road-making West; the men who had put the plains and mountains under the iron harness were old; some were poor, and even the successful ones were hunting for rest and a brief reprieve from death. It was already gone, that age; nothing could ever bring it back" (p. 169). As Cather declared in an article that appeared in *The Nation* in the same year *A Lost Lady* was published, "in Nebraska, as in so many other States, we must face the fact that the splendid story of the pioneers is finished, and that no new story worthy to take its place has yet begun."[26]

This sense of decline in American goals and values characterizes Willa Cather's fiction in the early 1920s. The short story collection *Youth and the Bright Medusa* (1920) and the novels that appeared during this time—*One of Ours* (1922), *A Lost Lady* (1923), and *The Professor's House* (1925)—all reflect Cather's disenchantment with life in modern America and evidence a certain doubt about and dissatisfaction with her own life. For her, Cather declared, "the world broke in two in 1922 or thereabouts."[27] Given Cather's own disillusionment, Turgenev's story of the loss of innocence and idealism must have seemed particularly pertinent at this time in her life. According to James Woodress, "the dominant theme in [*A Lost Lady*] is the need to reconcile possibility and loss."[28] Both Vladimir Petrovich and Niel Herbert attempt to do just that. Willa Cather's depiction of Niel's memories of his relationship with Marian Forrester would seem to represent one stage in Cather's own attempt to achieve some kind of acceptance of what had passed in America and what had been lost in her own life.

A comparison of Willa Cather's *A Lost Lady* and Ivan Turgenev's "First Love" suggests that Turgenev's story was almost certainly an important influence upon Cather's own. Like the story of Lyra Garber, the story of Vladimir Petrovich had evidently "teased" Willa Cather for a long time. In the introduction to *My Antonia*, another recollection of a fascinating woman, Jim Burden speaks of Antonia and "all that her name recalls."[29] For Willa Cather the name Lyra Garber must have recalled many memories from her childhood, and one of the very best stories of youthful love and innocence, Turgenev's "First Love." An awareness of the apparent influence of Turgenev's story on Cather's *A Lost Lady* not only reveals another important thread in what Bernice Slote called "a secret web of connections and relationships"[30] in Cather's fiction but also provides interesting insight into the working of her intellect and creative imagination.

NOTES

1. Flora Merrill, "A Short Story Course Can Only Delay, It Cannot Kill an Artist, says Willa Cather," *Willa Cather in Person: Interviews, Speeches, and Letters*, ed. L. Brent Bohlke (Lincoln: Univ. of Nebraska Press, 1986), p. 77.

2. Merrill, p. 79.

3. James Woodress, *Willa Cather: Her Life and Art* (New York: Pegasus, 1970), p. 199. See also Woodress, *Willa Cather: A Literary Life* (Lincoln: Univ. of Nebraska Press, 1987), p. 340.

4. Two previous comments on specific parallels between *A Lost Lady* and other works are particularly notable. In *Willa Cather's Imagination* (Lincoln: Univ. of Nebraska Press, 1975), David Stouck notes that several critics have drawn parallels between *A Lost Lady* and Gustave Flaubert's *Madame Bovary*. Stouck contends, however, that the closer parallels are, in fact, to Flaubert's *L'Education sentimentale* (p. 72). Secondly, in "The Importance of *Hamlet* to Cather's *A Lost Lady*," *Markham Review*, 11 (1981), Paul Comeau points out various similarities between the two works and argues that there is a "close relationship between Willa Cather's understanding of *Hamlet* and her response to the decline of the Old West" (p. 1). Interestingly, Turgenev mentions *Hamlet* in "First Love."

5. At the Third National Willa Cather Seminar held in Hastings, Nebraska, in June 1987, David Stouck, in his talk "Willa Cather and the Russians," and I in a paper titled "Willa Cather, Ivan Turgenev, and the Novel of Character," explored this influence. Both essays are included in a volume forthcoming from the University of Nebraska Press.

6. Royal A. Gettman, *Turgenev in England and America* (Westport: Greenwood Press, 1974), p. 110.

7. NBC Radio Address, *Willa Cather in Person: Interviews, Speeches, and Letters*, ed. L. Brent Bohlke (Lincoln: Univ. of Nebraska Press, 1986), p. 170.

8. Elizabeth Moorhead, "The Novelist: Willa Cather," *These Too Were Here: Louise Homer and Willa Cather* (Pittsburgh: Univ. of Pittsburgh Press, 1950), p. 50.

9. Cather to Fisher (January 26, 1922), Dorothy Canfield Fisher Collection, University of Vermont, Burlington.

10. Cather to Miller (October 24, 1924), Hitz File, Newberry Library, Chicago.

11. For a discussion of the medieval and chivalric themes in Cather's novel, see Evelyn Thomas Helmick, "The Broken World: Medievalism in *A Lost Lady*," *Renascence*, 28 (Autumn, 1975), 39-46.

12. Ivan Turgenev, "First Love" in *First Love and Other Tales*, trans. David Magarshack (New York: W. W. Norton, 1968), p. 214. Subsequent references will be parenthetical.

13. Willa Cather, *A Lost Lady* (New York: Alfred A. Knopf, 1923), p. 87. Subsequent references will be parenthetical.

14. Count Malevsky is an interesting analogue to Cather's Ivy Peters. While he does not have Peters' physical ugliness, to Vladimir he represents, as his name suggests, a sinister and contemptuous evil. Vladimir feels an intense aversion to Malevsky and relates that his blood "used to boil every time Malevsky went up to her [Zinaida], swaying cunningly like a fox, leaned elegantly against the back of her chair, and began whispering into her ear with a self-satisfied and ingratiating little smile..." (p. 172). Vladimir cannot understand Zinaida's apparent failure to realize the false and sinister nature of the man, for every word Malevsky uttered "ran like poison through [his] veins" (p. 199). Cather's Ivy Peters is referred to as "Poison Ivy."

15. It may well have been the influence of Turgenev's story that led to the major problem Cather encountered in writing *A Lost Lady*. She told Flora Merrill that the novel was written in five months but that she worked on it "with some fervor," discarding "ever so many drafts." The problem, Cather said, was finding the proper, the right, "medium" by which to present Marian Forrester most vividly. Cather tried carefully to avoid putting her material in "the usual fictive pattern," a pattern that Turgenev had employed in *First Love*. The "medium" that Cather finally chose was that of the Jamesean "reflector," which enabled her to combine the advantages of both the first and third-person points of view. See Merrill, p. 77.

16. Merrill, p. 77.

17. Merrill, p. 77.

18. Merrill, p. 77.

19. Gustave Flaubert, *Letters*, ed. Richard Rumbold (New York: Philosophical Library, 1951), p. 140.

20. One interesting possibility is that Cather's visit with Isabelle (McClung) Hambourg in 1921 prompted reminiscences of their reading Turgenev almost twenty years before. Cather said that her novel was "a beautiful ghost in her mind for twenty years before it came together as a possible subject for presentation."

21. For an account of Turgenev's own first love, see David Magarshack, *Turgenev: A Life* (New York: Grove Press, 1954), pp. 30-32.

22. Merrill, p. 77.

23. Merrill, p. 77.

24. James Woodress, "Willa Cather: American Experience and the European Tradition," *The Art of Willa Cather*, ed. Bernice Slote and Virginia Faulkner (Lincoln: Univ. of Nebraska Press, 1974), p. 59.

25. Susan J. Rosowski, *The Voyage Perilous: Willa Cather's Romanticism* (Lincoln: Univ. of Nebraska Press, 1986), p. 114.

26. Willa Cather, "Nebraska: The End of the First Cycle," *The Nation*, 117 (1923), 238.

27. Willa Cather, "Prefatory Note," *Not Under Forty* (New York: Alfred A. Knopf, 1936), p. v.

28. James Woodress, *Willa Cather: A Literary Life* (Lincoln: Univ. of Nebraska Press, 1987), p. 349.

29. Willa Cather, *My Antonia* (Boston: Houghton Mifflin, 1926), p. [xi].

30. Bernice Slote, "Willa Cather: The Secret Web," *Five Essays on Willa Cather: The Merrimack Symposium*, ed. John J. Murphy (North Andover: Merrimack College, 1974), p. 2.

HAROLD K. SCHEFSKI

"The Parable of the Prodigal Son" and Turgenev's Fathers and Sons

"The Parable of the Prodigal Son" (Luke 15:11–32) has always appealed to the Russian religious mind with its inherent fascination with kenoticism and monasticism.[1] This motif became a permanent fixture in Russian literature when the blank verse tale "Misery-Luckless-Plight" appeared in the mid-seventeenth century. Written anonymously, this work relates the story of a disobedient son who, failing to heed the thoughtful admonitions of his parents, stubbornly asserts his right to have things his own way:

> The Youth was then young and foolish,
> not in his full senses, and imperfect in mind;
> he was ashamed to submit to his father
> and bow before his mother,
> but wanted to live as he listed.[2]

Against his parents' wishes, the son leaves his home and embarks on a life of debauchery. The few decent people whom he encounters on his sinful path instruct him to return home and repent:

> You are a good fellow,
> so go to your home,

From *Literature and Belief*, vol. 10. © 1990 by the Center for the Study of Christian Values in Literature.

to your beloved, respected parents,
to your father and mother dear,
greet your parents, father and mother,
and receive from them the parental blessing![3]

Returning to his parents with the intention to repent, the son soon realizes that the only true escape from his "Misery-Luckless-Plight" is to become a monk and enter a monastery. As he passes through "the holy gates," he leaves Misery (in her personified form) forever behind.

The prodigal son theme assumes a prodigal daughter variant in Alexander Pushkin's famous tale "The Stationmaster" (1833). Here the protagonist's charming teenage daughter Dunya is abducted by a rakish traveler, but then of her own free will decides to stay with her abductor rather than to return to her heartbroken father. Later as a woman of some means (*baryshnya*), Dunya comes back to visit her father's grave (he drank himself to death from grief) and bursts into teats at her loss.

Pushkin leaves no doubt that he is concerned with "the prodigal son parable" in this story when he describes the paintings decorating the Stationmaster's humble abode in the first scene:

> They illustrated the parable of the Prodigal Son. In the first one, a venerable old man, in nightcap and dressing gown, was bidding farewell to a restless youth who was hastily accepting his blessing and a bag of money. The second one depicted the young man's lewd behavior in vivid colors: he was seated at a table, surrounded by false friends and shameless women. Farther on, the ruined youth, in rags and with a three cornered hat on his head, was tending swine and sharing their meal; deep sorrow and repentance were reflected in his features. The last picture showed his return to his father: the warm-hearted old man in the same nightcap and dressing gown, was running forward to meet him; The Prodigal Son was on his knees; in the background the cook was killing the fatted calf and the elder brother was asking the servants about the cause of all the rejoicing.[4]

It is not surprising that from Pushkin the prodigal son parable passes to Ivan Turgenev, who continues many of his mentor's literary traits.[5] What separates Turgenev's *Fathers and Sons* from Pushkin's story and other examples of the prodigal son motif,[6] however, is that he deals with two prodigal sons simultaneously (Arkady Kirsanov and Evgeny Bazarov), and that these sons have not strayed morally but ideologically. They have purposely distanced themselves from their fathers' way of life—a world of romanticism heightened by the worship of such entrenched values of aristocratic life as poetry, music, and Pushkin himself. In place of these spiritual ideals, the sons have committed themselves to progress and natural science as embodied in the idea of transforming nature from a temple of worship to a workshop, where Russia's innumerable social problems can be assailed.

The sons' ideological betrayal of their fathers is called "nihilism" (and not debauchery as in the original prodigal son motif) because they have rejected what the previous generation has accepted on faith and turned to more materialistic values. The fact that Turgenev shows the reader two prodigal sons at once is significant because there is a comparative value to the different ways they return home to their fathers, as David Lowe persuasively argues in his study of the novel: "Children cannot turn their backs on the world of their fathers.... Children ultimately do go 'home' again, and willingly or grudgingly, they are reconciled to the family hearth.[7]" The purpose of this article is to discuss Turgenev's bifurcation of the prodigal son motif by which he brings Arkady contentedly back to his father, while leaving Bazarov an inveterate rebel, whose return to the fold is prompted only by his physical demise.

As the novel opens, Arkady Nikolaevich is returning home to his father Nikolai Kirsanov's estate after a four-year hiatus which he has spent at the University of St. Petersburg. Like the typical father who has been separated from his son for quite some time, Nikolai awaits the appearance of his son's carriage with great anticipation:

> "Well, Peter, not in sight yet?"
> "No sir; definitely not in sight."
> "Not in sight?" repeated his master.
> "Not in sight," responded the man a second time.[8] (1)

Arkady's eventual arrival, however, signals only his bodily return. Unfortunately there are many other disturbing signs indicating that his physical presence is overshadowed by an ideological estrangement. For instance, the narrator points out that the reunion of father and son is much more pleasing to Nikolai than to Arkady: "Nikolai Petrovich seemed far more excited than his son" (4), and then notes the father's disappointment at his son's spiritual alienation: "I did hope, precisely now, to get on close, intimate terms with Arkady, and it turns out I'm left behind, and he has gone forward, and we can't understand one another" (35).

The reason that the son still remains prodigal even after his physical return is that he has fallen under the influence of his college friend Bazarov, an advanced medical student who accompanies him home as a guest. Though Bazarov is Arkady's senior by only three or four years (He is twenty-six while Arkady is twenty-two), it becomes immediately evident that the maturation gap between them is considerably more, and that Arkady is disciple to the mentor Bazarov.

In introducing Bazarov to his father, Arkady not only sings his comrade's praises: "He's a splendid fellow, so simple—you will see" (5), but he also informs Nikolai just how much the man means to him: "Please, dad, be nice to him. I can't tell you how I prize his friendship" (6). Nikolai senses that there exists here something beyond the normal friendship, and in a dialogue with his son he tries to ascertain the chronological development for such an intense case of hero worship:

[Nikolai] "Have you made friends with him lately?"
[Arkady] "Yes, quite lately."
[Nikolai] "Ah, that's how it is I did not see him last winter." (6)

First of all, this conversation establishes the fact that Arkady and Bazarov have known one another for no more than a year. More importantly, however, it provides a subtle motivation for Bazarov's displacement of Nikolai as Arkady's primary role model, since earlier the authorial narrator had made it known that Nikolai had missed the most recent winter's visit to his son after spending with him each of his first three winters at the University: "In 1855 he (Nikolai) brought his son to the university; he spent three winters with him in Petersburg, hardly going out anywhere, and trying to make acquaintance with Arkady's young companions. The last winter he had not been able to go ..." (3). Clearly Arkady missed his father's visit during his last year at the university and filled the void with Bazarov, who ideologically converted the impressionable young man from his family's reformist attitudes to the young generation's radical revolutionary ideas. And so in the novel's beginning, Nikolai bodily receives his son back into the family fold, but in an ideological sense Arkady has gone astray and for the time being remains lost.

Although Nikolai, unlike his brother Pavel, is too kindhearted and soft-spoken to display openly his concern over Bazarov's ideological seduction of his son, he does attempt to reassert in his son's presence the great importance he attributes to the father-son relationship: "I have always had special ideas as regards the relation of father and son.... We must draw close to one another now, and learn to know each other thoroughly, mustn't we?" (7–9). And yet before Nikolai begins to get his son back ideologically, he first contributes further to his alienation by relinquishing his position of authority in the father-son relationship. In short, he allows Arkady to assume control, which in turn gives Bazarov even greater leverage with his pupil, who desperately needs a stable model of authority.

This step in the wrong direction occurs the moment Nikolai timidly informs his son that he is now living with the servant girl Fenichka outside the sanction of marriage. His embarrassment over this "immoral" behavior not only reveals him as weak, but it also virtually reverses his role with his son. Arkady, now sensing his father's vulnerability, begins to treat him like a prodigal son who is trying to reinstate himself after a moral indiscretion: "Arkady's heart was filled with a feeling of condescending tenderness for his kind, soft-hearted father mixed with a sense of a certain secret superiority" (8). This veritable reversal of roles is further enhanced when Nikolai is unable to tell him directly that a son has been born from the illicit union with Fenichka. Once again the son takes on the role of a forgiving father, paying a formal call on Fenichka to show that he is above condemning this relationship and even magnanimously accepts this new rival for his father's inheritance. No wonder Bazarov prevails as Arkady's authority figure in the first part of the novel. Nikolai, consumed by his own "sins," is unable to provide that rock of stability to which his wayward son can return.

Arkady's enchantment with Bazarov's figure reaches its apogee during their first meeting with the attractive widow Odintsova, when he describes his friend to her in these glowing terms: "Did you notice him? ... He has a splendid face, hasn't he? That's a certain Bazarov, my friend" (58). From this point the narrator further develops Arkady's cult of Bazarov's personality, which impresses Odintsova: "Arkady fell to discussing 'his friend.' He spoke of him in such detail, and with such enthusiasm, that Odintsova turned towards him and looked attentively at him" (58).

Ironically, this scene is also responsible for Arkady's realization that Bazarov falls short of that perfection which he has fashioned for him in his own mind. As the two men discuss Odintsova's attributes and Bazarov, noting her impressive set of shoulders, asks his protege whether she is really "ohh la la" (59), Arkady feels wounded by Bazarov's cynical manner in judging her solely as a physical specimen. Their emerging divergent views on love and women are then reinforced in the next scene where Arkady is enchanted by Odintsova's charm, while Bazarov can think only of her magnificent body, which is "perfect for the dissecting-table" (62). After this disagreement, Arkady gradually begins to retreat from his worship of Bazarov and starts to move back toward those romantic values instilled in him by his biological father.

However, the seeds for Arkady's development as a prodigal son are sewn even earlier, when it becomes apparent that he is unwilling to accept Bazarov's concept of nature as a workshop devoid of emotion and spiritual worth. Even in the first few chapters, where Arkady undoubtedly strives to establish an identity separate from Nikolai's, he still finds himself sharing his father's deep-seated admiration of their home estate's natural beauty. For example, while he at first praises the wonderful aroma of the air: "But what air there is here! How delicious it smells! Really I fancy there's nowhere such fragrance in the world as in these regions!" (7), he then catches himself and categorically rejects Nikolai's idea that a special significance can be attached to the place where one is born: "Come, dad, it makes no difference where a man is born. No; it makes absolutely no difference" (7).

Not surprisingly, Arkady's contradictory stance toward nature is also eventually resolved in favor of his father's romanticism. The first evidence of such a change occurs in that polemical attitude which Arkady adopts with regard to Bazarov's radical views. In an uncharacteristically firm response to his mentor's contention that the only important thing is "that two and two make four, and the rest is all nonsense" (33), Arkady asks "And is nature nonsense?" (33). And as if to answer this question along the lines of Arkady's romantic heritage, the narrator depicts him admiring "the bright colored fields in the distance, in the beautiful soft light of the sun, which was no longer high in the sky" (33).

Although Arkady challenges Bazarov's denigration of nature more frequently after this, he still suffers periodically from his own intimate sense of subordination before his friend's imposing figure. Thus he finds it difficult to admit to his beloved Katya that he shares her romantic love for nature: "Katya adored nature, and Arkady loved it, though he did not dare to acknowledge it" (72). Buoyed by his powerful love for Katya and deeply aware of that common inspiration which they derive from nature, Arkady soon begins to overcome his fear of offending Bazarov. After protracted meditation carried out in the midst of inspirational nature—the narrator stresses that "he had hidden himself in the very thickest part of the garden" (143), Arkady takes a stand against Bazarov and resolves to marry Katya. As James Justus perceptively observes in his article "*Fathers and Sons:* The Novel as Idyll," the union of love and nature in this scene is significant because "it constitutes his [Arkady's] final break with what is essentially an alien spirit;

his alliance with Katya ushers in a domestic period of acceptance. It discards revolution, but not reform" (312).[9] And this, of course, is just another way of saying that at this juncture Arkady eschews Bazarov's influence and as a prodigal son initiates his own return to the family hearth.

Besides love and nature, art also undermines Bazarov's influence over Arkady. The elder Kirsanov, as we know, lives by Pushkin's verse, to which he attributes a wisdom of almost biblical force. When Arkady arrives at the station in the first scene, for example, Nikolai almost immediately finds Pushkin apropos, citing two lines from *Eugene Onegin:*

To me how sad thy coming is,
Spring, spring, the time of love. (9)

This declamation, interrupted by Bazarov's mundane request for a match with which to light his pipe, not only shows the elder generation's great reverence for Pushkin, but also alludes—albeit indirectly—to love and nature, those two other romantic values that together with art will eventually spell Bazarov's doom and signal Arkady's repatriation with his fathers.

With this early reference to *Eugene Onegin*, Pushkin becomes a central motif in the work. While the Kirsanovs see the poet as a symbol for all that is aesthetically moving in life, Bazarov equates him with art without a purpose, and therefore worthy of being rendered obsolete. Finding Nikolai reading Pushkin at his leisure, Bazarov encourages Arkady to confront his father with this useless pursuit of romanticism: "The day before yesterday I saw him reading Pushkin.... Explain to him, please, that that's entirely useless. He's not a boy, you know; it's time to throw up that rubbish. And what an idea to be a romantic these days! Give him something sensible to read" (35). In this instance Arkady complies with his friend's request, giving his father a copy of Ludwig Buchner's *Stoff und Kraft*, but later in the work as his break with Bazarov becomes more imminent, he censures him for misrepresenting Pushkin, the ideal of his fathers: "He (Pushkin) never said anything of the sort ... Pushkin was never a military man! Why, what stories you invent! I declare, it's outright calumny" (104).

Arkady's return to his father's appreciation of art is suggested by more than merely his defense of Pushkin; he also gradually liberates his intense feeling for music, which had long been suppressed by his strict adherence to Bazarov's philosophy. In his conversation with Odintsova, Arkady clearly prefers "launching into a discourse upon the significance of national melodies" (62) rather than talking about those subjects—medicine, homeopathy, and botany—which are of interest to Bazarov. Moreover, one of Arkady's first silent polemics with his mentor is associated with his father's love for music. As Bazarov bursts into sarcastic laughter upon hearing Nikolai playing Shubert's "Expectation" on the violoncello, Arkady, by contrast, "does not even smile ... much as he revered his mentor" (34).

Bazarov's relentless criticism of the Kirsanov family delivers the final blow that sends Arkady back into his elders' camp. When Bazarov labels Pavel Petrovich "an idiot" (105), Arkady responds with the phrase "this is intolerable!" (105), and aggressively defends himself against his friend's accusation that family comes before ideology in his scheme of things: "It was a simple sense of justice spoke in me and not family feeling at all.... But since that's a sense you don't understand, since you haven't that sensation, you can't judge it" (105). At that point the narrator intercedes, informing the reader that the friendship between Bazarov and Arkady which dominated the first half of the novel is about to become a thing of the past: "But no friendship can long survive such collisions" (106).

What is important about Arkady's role as a prodigal son is that it demonstrates that he is not the static uninteresting figure that N. Strakhov has suggested: "What could be weaker or more significant than Bazarov's friend Arkady. He apparently submits to every passing influence; he is the most ordinary of mortals" (220).[10] On the contrary, he evolves from a naive boy, hypnotized by the radical philosophy of Bazarov, to a prodigal son who once again gravitates toward the reformist ways of his father Nikolai. As shown here, the romantic values of love, nature, and art comprise the catalyst for the change, although Arkady is inclined toward them from the start. When all these traits converge in the person of Katya, with whom Arkady sees the chance to begin a family after the example of his father, Arkady realizes that his evolution is complete and explains this to his beloved: "I certainly have changed a great deal, and you know that better than anyone else—you to whom I really owe this change.... I am not now the conceited boy I was when I came here ... I've not reached twenty-three for nothing; as before, I want to be useful, I want to devote all my powers to the truth; but I no longer look for my ideals where I did; they present themselves to me ... much closer at hand" (144).

Arkady's role as a prodigal son is not only meaningful in isolation; it also is designed to be compared with Bazarov's similar role. While Arkady comes home willingly, Bazarov returns to his parents grudgingly and only as a last resort following the failure of his philosophy. His first flight to his parents occurs when he realizes that his love for Odintsova would negate his own denial of human sentiments and could also lead to her possible rejection of him—a thought totally unacceptable to his boundless vanity. His second retreat results from the disappointing loss of his disciple Arkady to the very romanticism which he berates.

In both instances Bazarov's mother and father greet him with an overt display of emotion that is reminiscent of Nikolai Kirsanov's unrestrained joy upon welcoming Arkady in the opening scene. Like the elder Kirsanov, Evgeny's parents belong to the old generation of romantics and prize the values of love, nature, and art. Arina Vlasyevna is so enamored of her son that she cannot take her eyes (or hands) off him, as her unbridled response to his visit so aptly shows: "Ah ... for what ages, my dear one, my darling Enyusha ... and not unclasping her hands she drew her wrinkled face, wet with tears and working with tenderness, a little away from Bazarov, and gazed at him with blissful and comic-looking eyes, and again fell on his neck" (90).

His father Vassily Ivanovich, on the other hand, knowing that such an emotional scene is unpleasant for their son and runs counter to his philosophy, tries to excuse it in a condescending manner: "You understand a woman's weakness, and well, a mother's heart ..." (90), but it is soon revealed that he himself has suppressed a similar emotional response: "But his lips and eyebrows, too, were twitching, and his beard was quivering.... He was obviously trying to control himself and appear almost indifferent" (90).

Unlike Arkady, who has come home for good and gradually begins to fit in, Bazarov is restless at home and ready to leave after only a couple of days. His poor mother, who intuitively senses that he never belongs to them for long, is afraid to ask him about the length of his stay: "'What if he says for two days?,' she thought and her heart sank" (96). As Bazarov prepares to depart, he shows no pity for this sensitive woman: "I hear her sighing the other side of the wall, and when I go to her, there is nothing to say to her" (109). He is similarly callous in informing his father of his intentions: "When he was just saying good-night to him in the study, he observed, with a feigned yawn—'Oh ... I was almost forgetting to tell you.... Send to Fedot's for our horses tomorrow'" (109).

The only consolation the parents can take from such news is that their prodigal son promises to return to them on his way back to St. Petersburg: "We shall soon see each other again, father, really" (110). After Bazarov's departure his mother can justify the painful nature of their relationship with their son only through highly emotive language: "There's no help for it, Vasya! A son is a piece cut off. He's like the falcon that flies home and flies away at his pleasure; while you and I are like mushrooms in the hollow of a tree, we sit side by side, and don't move from our place. Only I remain unchanged for you, forever, as you for me" (111).

Although Bazarov's second visit to his parents is scheduled to last for six weeks, it is doubtful he would have stayed so long if he had not become deathly ill after cutting himself on a contaminated instrument as he performed an autopsy on a typhus victim. In many ways his ensuing death was less of a tragedy for his parents than at first one might imagine. After all, only in death were they able to keep this rebellious and restless soul in their midst. Only buried in the country graveyard was this prodigal son returned to them for good: "However passionate, sinning, and rebellious the heart hidden in the tomb, the flowers growing over it peep serenely at us with their innocent eyes; they tell us not of eternal peace alone, of that great peace of 'indifferent' nature; they tell us, too, of eternal reconciliation and of life without end" (166).

As we have seen here, Turgenev's *Fathers and Sons* is a novel about two prodigal sons, one of whom is returned to his family in life while the other is reconciled only in death. The use of this important biblical archetype suggests that the writer's ties with Christianity deserve to be reexamined. Classified by Dostoevsky as an atheist and by others (including himself) as an agnostic,[11] Turgenev has long been regarded as possessing at best a tenuous connection with religion. Yet there is every indication in his works and letters that he never entirely rejected Christianity but rather found himself perpetually suspended between belief and disbelief.

NOTES

1. According to G. P. Fedotov, *The Russian Religious Mind* (New York: Harper, 1946), the three major components of Russian kenoticism are poverty, humility, and love, while Russian monasticism stresses the values of poverty, humility, and obedience. All these traits are central to "The Parable of the Prodigal Son," which relates the story of a rebellious son who forsakes his family and squanders his money on vice. Impoverished and remorseful, he returns humbly to a loving father, who is overjoyed to see that the sins of pride and disobedience have been overcome by the virtues of humility and obedience.

2. Serge Zenkovsky, ed., *Medieval Russia's Epics, Chronicles, and Tales* (E. P. Dutton, 1964) 412.

3. Zenkovsky 420.

4. Paul Debreczeny, *Alexander Pushkin, Complete Prose Fiction* (Stanford: Stanford UP, 1983) 95.

5. Kathryn Feuer, "Fathers and Sons: Fathers and Children," *The*

Russian Novel from Pushkin to Pasternak, ed. John Garrard (New Haven: Yale UP, 1983), most astutely summarizes the close relationship between Pushkin and Turgenev as follows: "For most writers there are other writers whose lines, paragraphs, works exist as part of their consciousness, touchstones which may only occasionally be specified but whose presence is constant. For Turgenev, Pushkin was such a writer." One of the best examples of such literary inheritance is the character configuration of powerful women and ineffectual men which Turgenev, following the Pushkin archetype of Tatyana and Eugene in *Eugene Omegin*, patterned into his trademark.

6. It is interesting to note that the Prodigal Son motif continues to thrive even during the Soviet regime, as Prokoviev's ballet of that name (1928–29) attests. Moreover, Rembrandt's painting *The Return of the Prodigal Son* (1668–69), which is permanently displayed at the Hermitage Museum in Leningrad, attracts the attention of countless visitors. One interpretation is that it relates to the artist's tragic personal life (e.g., he witnessed the death of two wives and nearly all his children along with suffering bankruptcy and other kinds of degradation) and symbolized his own wish to be returned to God the Father.

7. David Lowe, *Turgenev's* Fathers and Sons (Ann Arbor: Ardis, 1983) 16.

8. All passages cited from Turgenev's novel are taken from the English version *Fathers and Sons*, ed. and trans., Ralph E. Matlaw (New York: Norton, 1966). Page numbers are provided in parenthesis following the citation.

9. James Justus, "Fathers and Sons: The Novel as Idyll," *Western Humanities Review* XV (1961): 259–65. Reprinted in Ivan Turgenev, *Fathers and Sons*, ed. and trans., Ralph E. Matlaw (New York: Norton, 1966) 307–14.

10. N. Strakhov, *Kriticheskie stat'i* (Kiev, 1908) 1–39. Reprinted in Ivan Turgenev, *Fathers and Sons*, ed. and trans., Ralph E. Matlaw (New York: Norton, 1966) 219–30.

11. For example, Leonard Schapiro, *Turgenev, His Life and Times* (New York: Random, 1978) 214, writes about Turgenev's agnosticism as follows: "Turgenev was not a determined atheist; there is ample evidence which shows that he was an agnostic who would have been happy to embrace the consolations of religion, but was, except perhaps on some rare occasions, unable to do so"; and Edgar Lehrman, *Turgenev's Letters* (New York: Knopf, 1961) xi, presents still another interpretation for Turgenev's lack of religion, suggesting literature as a possible substitution: "Sometimes Turgenev's attitude toward literature makes us wonder whether, for him, literature was not a surrogate for religion—something in which he could believe

unhesitatingly, unreservedly, and enthusiastically, something that somehow would make man in general and Turgenev in particular a little happier."

PATRICK WADDINGTON

No Smoke Without Fire:
the Genesis of Turgenev's Dym

It is customary to consider *Dym* ('Smoke') the weakest of Turgenev's novels, yet everything points to his having wished it to be the strongest. Certainly few books in the nineteenth century can have aroused such national controversy. A storm of protest followed its first appearance in *Russkii vestnik* for March 1867, with but a few lonely voices raised in its defence. Turgenev was accused of absenteeism, of being out of touch, of a lack of knowledge of contemporary Russia and Russian life. The novel was a slander on his native land and its people. 'As far as I can see', he told A. I. Herzen, 'it has stirred up against me in Russia religious people, high society, Slavophiles and patriots.... Everyone is swearing at me—both reds and whites, from above, below and the side, especially from the side.'[1]

Criticism at the time was levelled chiefly at the person and sayings of Potugin. To Herzen, who claimed to be bored by him and thought his prattling should have been cut by half, Turgenev retorted: '*I* find that he doesn't say enough, and am strengthened in that opinion by the universal fury unleashed upon me by this character.'[2] More recent critics have objected to Potugin for a different reason: they find his role in the actual plot less significant than the political and philosophical message of the work should imply. As always in the six books he referred to as *romany* (novels),[3] Turgenev sought to combine in *Dym* a tale of personal love, ambition and hope, with a

From *From Pushkin to Palisandriia: Essays on the Russian Novel in Honor of Richard Freeborn.* © 1990 by the School of Slavonic and East European Studies, University of London.

study of contemporary Russian society, but whereas in the others both elements seem adequately centred on the principal male character, in the case of *Dym* they are largely separated. For all the obvious differences between *Rudin* (1856), *Dvorianskoe gnezdo* ('A Nest of the Gentry', 1859), *Nakanune* ('On the Eve', 1860), *Ottsy i deti* ('Fathers and Children', 1862) and *Nov'* ('Virgin Soil', 1877), a single hero is centrifugal in each—Rudin, Lavretskii, Insarov, Bazarov, Nezhdanov. There are other male characters of varying importance, some sharing in the love theme, some in the social, some in both, but only of *Dym* is it possible to argue that there are two heroes, not bound significantly together by the plot: Litvinov and Potugin. The alleged effect is thus that there are two books rather than one.[4]

It is important to understand that Turgenev deliberately brought this problem upon himself. As always with his novels, *Dym* was conceived both in love and in politics, but it had a specially complex genesis in his thinking and experience. The purpose of this chapter is to consider its earliest origins in relation to the finished work.

Although some aspects of the future plot of *Dym* had been in Turgenev's mind for years, its principal lines developed out of *Ottsy i deti*. It is an opinion universally held and scarcely refutable that the highest tide in Turgenev's literary career was marked by the composition and publication of *Ottsy i deti*. To alter the metaphor, he believed that with it he could at last sail into the haven of old age.[5] At the same time, with Bazarov, he was opening a gateway to the future, away from the paternalism of pre-Emancipation Russia and out on to the long road of reform and change.[6] The novel thus offered hope, however fragile. It was both an end and a beginning, as befitted the transitional nature of the epoch.

Ottsy i deti came out in *Russkii vestnik* in the first days of March (Old Style) 1862.[7] At this time Turgenev, in Paris, was already writing the sad and world-weary sketch *Dovol'no* ('Enough'), subtitled *Otryvok iz zapisok umershego khudozhnika* ('An Extract from the Notes of a Dead Artist'). Things were not going well, either with his work or in his relations with Pauline Viardot: as is echoed in Section V of *Dovol'no*, these seemed practically cut off. But he then took up another sketch, *Prizraki* ('Phantoms'), left in abeyance for some months, and told F. M. Dostoevskii (for whose magazine it was intended) that progress on it would be rapid.[8] Not long afterwards, he wrote to inform his publisher M. N. Katkov, editor of *Russkii vestnik*, that he hoped to have ready for the autumn a new work, not so long as *Ottsy i deti* but 'meditated with love' (*zadumannyi s liubov'iu*). This statement of 26 April 1862 has been taken to be the earliest reference to *Dym*.[9] If indeed it was, the first character list for the future novel could also date from mid-April rather than—as has generally been supposed—from the end of this year or the beginning of the next.[10] Furthermore, mentions of a 'big new story' (*povest'*) in letters of June and July cannot refer to anything else that he was doing at the time, given the proposed length and publishing arrangements; but although he now rashly promised the work for the end of 1862 it is obvious that he was doing little more than think about it.[11] Indeed, he had good reason to wait: he needed to digest the myriad reactions to *Ottsy i deti*. *Dym* would then become very different and much weightier than he had at first intended.

Home at Spasskoe in June, Turgenev tried to put on a brave face in the gale of hostile comment on *Ottsy i deti*. He told Pauline Viardot that it even pleased him, as a reflection of the novel's deliberate controversiality.[12] But this is not how he described things to most other people. Ever since reports had started coming in, from April on, he had known that *Ottsy i deti* was angering, upsetting or bewildering many whose opinion he esteemed, as well as many he had wanted to disturb. As he repeated some years later in his essay on the novel ('Po povodu "Ottsov i detei"'), what troubled him most was that his worst enemies tended to adore it.[13] Moreover, it was not only in Russia that Turgenev had problems. The two leading centres of Russian so-called democratic influence abroad—London and Heidelberg—were coming out against his work. He himself visited both this year and each was to play a significant role in *Dym*.

Turgenev had spent a week in London in mid-May, talking over Russia's future with Herzen and his aide, the poet and pamphleteer N. P. Ogarev, as well as with the notorious anarchist M. A. Bakunin who had recently escaped from exile in Siberia. The arguments between these long-standing colleagues had become increasingly bitter and uncivil. All loved and believed in their country and still hoped that good would come from the recent Emancipation; but whereas the London trio proposed various brands of social and political revolution, based on the will of the people for change, Turgenev foresaw a continuation of lethargy, stagnation, and resistance to European enlightenment. While in England he presumably went to the International Exhibition at Brompton and perhaps also to the Crystal Palace at Sydenham, gaining from the one or both the impression that Russian civilization scarcely counted for the nations of the earth, for in Chapter 14 of *Dym* he would put into Potugin's mouth in this respect some of his strongest and, it seems, most intensely personal observations.[14] Although Potugin's pro-Western views were here deliberately pushed to the extreme and do not represent Turgenev's own position with complete accuracy, they doubtless draw directly upon the arguments that their author found himself forced to make in answer to the nascent Russian agrarian socialism which he discovered in Herzen. After he had gone back to Paris, Herzen pursued him, as it were, with a series of eight letters called *Kontsy i nachala* ('Ends and Beginnings'), published in *Kolokol* from July 1862 to February 1863 and secretly addressed to Turgenev. In these, Herzen reproached his former good friend for wishing to retire to a quiet life, resting on the autumnal laurels of Western culture, just when the East was reawakening. In page after page of heavy, obscure and boring prose, he ironically urged Turgenev to portray the sad and aimless Don Quixotes of revolution before they finally died out and were replaced by stronger men. Battling to emerge from a plethora of tangential remarks was the idea that Europe was finished and that Russia would make a new beginning for humanity.[15]

Turgenev came across the first two letters not long after he had settled in Baden-Baden on 21 August for an exploratory sojourn in the train of the Viardots, who were considering whether to remove there. He determined to reply in the pages of *Kolokol*, asking Herzen only to maintain the secrecy of their exchange, but although he started one such response he soon came to realise that everyone would recognise his authorship, and indeed a high Russian official travelling in Germany warned him that to publish in Herzen's paper could only further incriminate him in the eyes of Imperial justice, which was actually now investigating his connections with the London exiles. Turgenev thus abandoned his original plan in favour of continued private correspondence with his philosophical antagonist.[16] There were, however, other reasons for the change of tack. One was the sudden sense of wellbeing that he experienced in the charming environment of Baden-Baden; a second, strangely enough, was the discovery that in neighbouring Heidelberg dwelt still fiercer opponents of his literary endeavours than Herzen and Ogarev themselves. In September and October he made two sorties in the direction of these 'wild young Russians', so different from the 'top flight and therefore lowest kind' of his compatriots by whom he found himself surrounded in large numbers in the baths resort itself.[17]

Heidelberg at that time was the intellectual haven of progressive Russian students, its prestige resting principally on the natural and experimental sciences with teachers like Bunsen, Kirchhoff, Helmholtz and Wundt. Lacking direct personal knowledge of this and assuming it to be largely fashion, Turgenev had somewhat casually and cruelly attacked those young and not-so-young Russians in Heidelberg who, according to what one reads in Chapters 13 and 28 of *Ottsy i deti*, often tagged along for the experience and could not tell oxygen from nitrogen. In 1862 Heidelberg was in fact filling up with some of the best Russian minds, as well as with some of the most radical. The closure of their own universities after the fires and disorders which followed the Emancipation Decree during the previous year led still more students to Germany than previously. But this really only made more obvious something which Turgenev certainly already knew, namely that a centre capable of attracting men like S. P. Botkin, I. M. Sechenov, D. I. Mendeleev and A. P. Borodin was not deserving of his satire alone.[18]

This at least was the view taken by a group of indignant young men and women in Heidelberg who read *Ottsy i deti* in the spring. Infuriated by the implication that they were all ignorant and lazy good-for-nothings, they had one of their number known to the author, the soldier, poet and student K. K. Sluchevskii (1837–1904), write to Turgenev with a list of counts on which they chiefly accused him. These amounted to the belief that he had vilified the 'children' and extolled the 'fathers', to the detriment of political advancement in Russia. Turgenev urbanely yet vigorously contested such a view in a reply from Paris on 26 April, but determined to face the challenge in person when he had the opportunity.[19] This came sooner perhaps than he expected, in the autumn of the same year, and although Sluchevskii was absent from Heidelberg on at least one of his trips there, he was able to talk to several other supporters of Herzen and Ogarev, founders of the local Russian reading-room, including V. I. Bakst (1835–74), V. F. Luginin (1834–1911) and presumably the brothers de Roberti. Whether he addressed a large gathering of students there, as one historian has claimed, cannot at present be affirmed, but he did penetrate very quickly into the spirit of their arguments and perceived, indeed, that the continuing leadership of the London émigrés had become something of a *pis aller*.[20] None of this prevented him, however, from persisting in the opinion that Heidelberg for the Russians was a hive of scandal, mediocrity and waste. The so-called 'Heidelberg arabesques' in *Dym* show clearly what he thought of all their scurrying but purposeless activity. As he told one interviewer in 1867, after the novel had appeared, its political tendency was largely inspired by his disappointment with the younger generation of Russians, especially students abroad, who had lost all idealism or sense of beauty. They were positivists, utilitarians, realists, or what you would; but they seemed primarily intent on putting out the 'sacred fire of humanity'.[21] Turgenev's own purpose was to keep that fire burning through Potugin.

And so the political, social and philosophical origins of *Dym* are clear: Turgenev wished to vent his spleen upon both the disciples and the masters, all those supposedly forward-looking Russians whom he now considered to be fossils, history's dead-ends. In particular, he wanted to make public the reasons for his disgust with Herzen, Ogarev and Bakunin.[22] But the novel's personal and moral origins are harder to determine, being more diffuse. This was an especially dark period in Turgenev's career, which it would take a whole book to elucidate. It was as if he had lost everything that had been meaningful in life: youth, energy, success, inspiration and love. For a time, Baden-Baden may have seemed a new start; and even back in Paris a significant event occurred when Pauline Viardot, on a visit to his apartment in the rue de Rivoli on 6 November, drew a seal of Solomon in his current manuscript book as an apparent pledge of her affection.[23] Not long after this, he took up again the old sketch *Poezdka v Poles'e* ('An Outing to the Forest Belt', 1857) and tried to continue a 'third day' for it which he had earlier interrupted. But he quickly abandoned the attempt, leaving nothing but the complaint: 'Oh, the sweet feelings, the soft sounds, the goodness, and the stilling of a troubled soul, the melting joy of love's first emotions—where are you, where?[24] And on 3 January 1863, referring to the lack of progress on *Dym*, he told one correspondent that although things were turning in his head he could get none of them down on paper, and another—his publisher Katkov—that he had composed not a single line for three months: his mood was black, and he could not say when he might break out of it.[25]

By the end of January Turgenev had again begun to work a little, probably on *Prizraki*, but things were still going sluggishly when he learnt officially from the Imperial Embassy in Paris that he must return soon to Russia to face certain charges relating to his contacts with the editors of *Kolokol*. Stunned and shaken, he drafted letters to the Tsar and generally gave himself up to thoughts about his own and Russia's future.[26] With the personal and political now intensely combined, further impetus was given to put down on paper his intentions for the future novel *Dym*. Perhaps it was now that he drew up the first list of characters (the one already known to scholars); but, as has been argued, that doubtless took place nine months earlier. More certain is the fact that a second character list and a plot summary held in a private collection and dated 'Paris, 1863' were elaborated this spring before Turgenev's departure for Baden-Baden at the beginning of May. Already by the end of February he was starting to gain courage and buck up, and on 1 March he promised his close friend and counsellor P. V. Annenkov that he would show his radical denigrators on the editorial staff of *Sovremennik* how wrong they were to think him dead and buried.[27] About this period he was also receiving strong inducement to start writing seriously again by the praise of Russian friends in Paris for his former work and by the unexpected adulation of Gustave Flaubert, whom he had just met.[28]

Although he kept telling correspondents that he had been idle all winter, his stated resolve to work hard in Baden-Baden was equally insistent.[29] As most of April was taken up with business of various kinds including his official and highly careful response to a list of questions sent him by the investigating committee of the Russian Senate, March appears to be the most likely month to which the preparatory materials for *Dym* can be reasonably assigned.[30] They must have taken him at least a week to set down on paper, but beyond that one can only speculate; a paucity of published letters for the month of March makes it impossible to specify his activity with any great accuracy. The fact that he had already completed the new documents before leaving for Baden-Baden is shown by his subsequent reference to work on the novel and by the circumstance that he only spent a very few more days in Paris, and on business, later in this same year.[31]

It is time now to consider quite what Turgenev had in mind when calling his new novel *Dym*. That this title was important to him is shown by the fact that it stands already at the head of the first list of characters.[32] It is true that the second character list and the plot summary refer only to 'the new story'. It is also true that Turgenev much later thought of entitling the novel 'Dve zhizni' ('Two Lives'), perhaps as an indication of the two possible outcomes for Litvinov (or of the contrast between Russia's rulers and protesters, or of Litvinov and Potugin in relation to Irina),[33] and after the novel had appeared he had doubts again and wondered if the French translation should be called not *Fumée* but 'Incertitude', 'Entre le passé et l'avenir', 'Sans rivage' or 'Dans le brouillard'.[34] Yet all these alternatives still connote vagueness or ephemerality and the last reverts practically to *Dym*. Prosper Mérimée, in urging that the title *Fumée* be retained, argued that it would properly arouse the reader's curiosity.[35] Another way of saying this is that it has poetic ambiguity and charm.

To examine all the certain, probable, possible and doubtful implications of the word *dym*—or *fumée*, or *smoke*—in relation to Turgenev's novel would take a thesis. In view of Litvinov's celebrated meditations in the train from Baden-Baden to Heidelberg (see Chapter 26 of *Dym*), it is unlikely that any *positive* meaning should be sought. Some have found relevance in A. S. Griboedov's saying, turned against Turgenev in an epigram by F. I. Tiutchev, 'The very smoke of the fatherland is sweet and pleasant to us.'[36] This actually has a very long history. Griboedov was quoting, in trivially altered form, a line from the end of G. R. Derzhavin's poem *Arfa* ('The Harp') which had become a dictum. Derzhavin in turn was adapting an idea which descends from the *Odyssey* and Lucian via Joachim du Bellay to its neatest formulation in John Ray's 'English proverb' of 1670: 'The smoke of a man's own house is better than the fire of another's.' But although Turgenev may secretly have felt all this—who completely hates even native infamy?—it has no place in the novel and is more appropriate as an expression of the views of Herzen, Ogarev and other exiles and, of course, of Dostoevskii.

Another usage which appears to be only peripheral to *Dym* is the Judaeo-Christian concept of smoke as a portent, a sign of judgement and destruction: smoke consumes the wicked, God drives away His (or Her) enemies as smoke before the wind.[37] On the other hand, the cognate view that our life is consumed like smoke, whether by judgement, by fate, or by our own free acts, is very fitting with respect to Litvinov's own experience up to his final break with Irina. Smoke as a symbol of the darkness or night that awaits us all is certainly relevant, and indeed Turgenev extended this to cover those who are already enveloped in smoke, or fog, like the London exiles and their counterparts in his fictional recreation.[38] Much of Russia, in his view, did not know where it was, could not see itself for the smog of its own making. For some time he had been struck by the 'gaseousness' (*gazoobraznost'*) of his country, not yet in a planetary state.[39] The various little references to smoke and fog, worked into the novel so carefully by the author, reveal that neither the actual rulers nor those who wished to overturn them could see or be seen with clarity. In Chapters 4 and 6 Litvinov's head is made to turn and ache from the cigar smoke of the Gubarev circle; in Chapter 10 he has to suffer from the better-quality smoke of the generals. Meanwhile, he knows already in Chapter 17 that his only means of escape— a railway journey back to Russia—will be smoky, and as he leaves Baden-Baden at the end of Chapter 25 Irina herself appears to dissolve in a kind of fog with which he afterwards associates her. There follow his reflections on the smoke and steam in Chapter 26, his train speeds away through mist and low cloud: the endless puffs of smoke keep changing shape yet always remain the same. Back in Russia at the very end of the novel, Litvinov's new-found happiness with the white-robed Tat'iana is contrasted with the censer-like smoke of the expiring aristocracy.[40]

One other significant mention of smoke is found, in Chapter 23, where Litvinov uses the expression *dym i prakh* ('smoke and ashes') to describe the ruin of his hopes and aspirations.[41] The fact that at this time he thinks his love for Irina will recompense him for his lost past only makes his statement the more poignant. We come here to the truest meaning of smoke: the transitoriness of human life and endeavour. Russian, like English and French and many other languages, speaks of things disappearing like smoke—which is illusion, false hope and trust, vainglory and vanity. From Virgil's smoke fading into thin air to Milton's 'smoke and stir' and Shakespeare's 'helpless smoke of words', poets down the centuries have sought to show through such images the seeming pointlessness of all we think and say and do.[42] Turgenev himself was in the habit of speaking in this way in his correspondence with friends. In 1859, for example, we find him saying that all his fine plans have been dissipated like smoke;[43] and at the beginning of 1861 he writes: 'These three months have gone like smoke from a funnel: grey puffs running on and on, each as if different from the other yet monotonously the same.'[44] This last formulation is so similar to Litvinov's in the train that Turgenev must already have been rehearsing that; indeed, everything points to his whole being and experience in these years leading up to and culminating in such a striking meditation:

> 'Smoke, smoke', he repeated several times; and everything suddenly seemed to him as smoke, everything, his own life, Russian life—everything human and especially everything Russian. All is smoke and steam, he thought; all seems to be continually changing, everywhere there are new forms, scene chases after scene, and in reality everything is always the same, just the same; all is hurrying somewhere, rushes along—and all disappears without trace, attaining nothing; another wind blows, and everything is thrown in the opposite direction, there again to start its unwearied, disquieting and unnecessary game. He recalled much that had been accomplished before his eyes with sound and fury in the last few years.... Smoke, he whispered, smoke. He remembered the heated quarrels, talk and cries at Gubarev's, and with other people high- and low-ranked, young and old.... Smoke, he repeated, smoke and steam. He remembered at last the famous picnic, remembered other judgements and speeches of other people of state—and even all that Potugin had preached.... Smoke, smoke and nothing more. And his own aspirations, and feelings, and ventures, and dreams? He merely threw up his hand.[45]

This extraordinarily evocative passage, like something from Ecclesiastes, is made to cover the whole of Litvinov's (and his generation's) experience—personal, moral, social and political. It includes not only everything that Potugin had railed against, but also his railings themselves. Vanity, all is vanity, says the preacher—who is now Turgenev himself. In seeking to determine the source of such pessimism in *Dym*, many commentators have pointed to the influence of Schopenhauer.[46] Certainly

Schopenhauer excited Turgenev around 1862, at the time when the novel was conceived and when other disconsolate writings, notably *Dovol'no* and *Prizraki*, were in prospect. The correct interpretation of Schopenhauer was one subject of Turgenev's bitter dispute with Herzen, and it has been argued that he discussed the German philosopher's impact on him with Prosper Mérimée.[47] But one has also the re-emerging, originally much earlier influence on Turgenev of Pascal, too celebrated for comment,[48] seen now specifically in Section XIII of *Dovol'no*; and the French thinker even has somewhere that our soul is only wind and smoke. Going back further still in Turgenev's life, there is, besides, the whole Romantic background against which he himself was brought up and which in one sense had never died. Hippolyte Taine, in his *Voyage aux eaux des Pyrénées* (1855), had declared not long since that human life was a pure accident due to a variation in heat, and would last but a minute in eternity. Though realistically couched, this remains in the tradition of Chateaubriand who in *René* (originally of 1802) wrote that: 'The family of man lives but a day; god's breath scatters it like smoke.'

For whatever reason, then, Turgenev had become obsessed with the symbol of smoke in his renewed awareness of human transience and fragility. At the end of *Gamlet i Don-Kikhot* ('Hamlet and Don Quixote', 1860), that fine study of the polarity of types making up the human race, he quoted from Schiller's *Siegesfest* in the translation by V. A. Zhukovskii: 'All that is great on earth is dissipated like smoke.' Here he still contested this, claiming that good works remain and that love is omnipotent. At the end of *Ottsy i deti* his conclusion was more or less the same. But in *Dovol'no* the stance would change. Art is more durable than politics, yet even our greatest works are images from the dust; all is ultimately delusion and life is monotonously repetitive. In *Prizraki*, meanwhile, he was showing a similar disgust at the history and present state of humankind, matched by terror before the destructive force of nature. Tableau dissolved into tableau, age into age, and the whole proceeded from mist and reverted into nothingness. Both in this last piece, which he completed in Baden-Baden in the summer of 1863, and in the other, which dragged on for two more years, Turgenev was careful not to use the actual word 'smoke'; but in each the mood and outcome overwhelmingly echo this image. And he stayed with it right up to the publication of *Dym* in 1867, despite that novel's happy final twist.

It must, however, be emphasised that Turgenev never lost for long his faith in the power of love. That faith, indeed, caused the peripeteia in *Dym* and enabled him to go through with the novel in the first place. The five-year gap between its conception and completion was filled increasingly with a new-found emotional stability in Baden-Baden, a greater closeness to Pauline Viardot and a reborn joy in their relationship. After some time of relative idleness, he was inspired by her to start in earnest on *Dym* and did so on 18 November 1865.[49] On the front of the large notebook that he had bought for this purpose he stuck a label marked 's.i.P.', followed by what seems to be a small cross. When at long last he had finished the manuscript, on 29 January 1867, he made some of his strongest-ever recorded confessions of love for Pauline and explained that he must always have her approval, her imprimatur, that everything must be 's.i.P.'.[50] André Mazon proposed that this secret formula should be read as 'sub invocatione Paulinae'. Another possibility is 'sub imperio Paulinae'.[51] Either way, it certainly means that *Dym*, in its final form, was intimately and absolutely connected with Turgenev's love for Pauline Viardot, just as it was resolutely set against all that seemed trivial, hypocritical or corrupt in the life of contemporary Russia. Fire now shone through the smoke.

The best indication of how Turgenev put together all these factors in the characters of *Dym* is seen in a conversation that he had some years later with the Norwegian–American teacher and writer Hjalmar Hjorth Boyesen (1848–95). Boyesen was particularly intrigued by Irina, whom he found convincing and even admirable despite her immorality, and Turgenev responded that she was in fact drawn from life. But he quickly went on to describe how life, once observed, was transformed into a different, fictional reality.

> I hardly know how to explain to you how characters develop in my mind. Every line I have written has been inspired by something which has happened to me or come within my observation. Not that I copy actual scenes and lives of actual persons— no; but they teach me a lesson and furnish me with the rough material for building. So also with a character. I seldom find it suitable to my purpose to copy directly a person of my own acquaintance, because it is but rarely that one finds a pure type. I then ask myself what nature intended with this or that person; what this or that trait of character would be if developed to its last psychological consequences. I do not take a single feature or a single peculiarity and make a man or a woman of it; on the contrary, I endeavour not to give undue prominence to any one trait; even if ever so characteristic, I try to show my men and women *en face* as well as *de profil*, and in fact in every attitude which has at the same time natural and artistic value. I cannot

pride myself on strength of imagination; I have not the faculty of building in the air.[52]

While there can be no certainty that every word of this was Turgenev's, rather than Boyesen's, the whole rings most authentically true. And what is very interesting is that, in this interview of 1873, Turgenev went on immediately to talk about Bazarov. The revolutionary *Ottsy i deti* and *Dym* were still inseparable in his mind, the more so since both novels had 'failed'. But he had by then largely overcome the sense of failure, and remained confident of the justice of his purpose in each. Many others by now were as aware as he of the smoke that arose from his compatriots. Near the end of Chapter 26 of *Dym* he had reaffirmed the uselessness, in his opinion, of the cream of young Russian life that had gone to study in Heidelberg. No one had led him to change his mind, in the five years since he had first thought of writing on this theme. A year later still, in the spring of 1868, he warmly thanked his English friend W. R. S. Ralston for a piece on *Dym* in the *Spectator*.[53] In this, as it were on Turgenev's behalf, Ralston had vehemently defended the author against accusations of cynicism or contempt. 'But what renders him angry and impatient', he continued, 'is the senseless self-glorification in which certain Slavonic enthusiasts indulge, the useless building of visionary fabrics in which they waste their time.' This then was the smoke that Turgenev wished to eradicate from Russia; and it was to men like a revivified Litvinov that he would look 'for the kindling of that sacred fire which is some day to consume the rank and noisome element of Russian life'. While Turgenev did not live to achieve this, and might not have liked the conflagration when it came, he had already struck some sparks among the smoke and was convinced he had been absolutely right.

NOTES

1. Letters of 17 May and 4 June (both New Style) 1867, in I. S. Turgenev, *Polnoe sobranie sochinenii i pisem v dvadtsati vos'mi tomakh* (Moscow and Leningrad, 1960–68): *Pis'ma*, Vol. VI (1963), pp. 247 and 260. This collection, which comprises 13 volumes of Letters (Pis'ma) and 15 of Works (Sochineniia) is being replaced by a second, revised and augmented edition in 30 volumes (Moscow, 1978–, comprising *Sochineniia*, 12 vols; *Pis'ma*, 18 vols), but only the works series is complete. It is thus necessary to use the first edition of *Pis'ma*, with occasional corrections and additions from those volumes of the second edition that have already appeared. In the case of

Sochineniia the second edition can be used, but it unfortunately omits the manuscript and other textual variants which are such a useful feature of the earlier one. In the present notes, following the practice observed by the Soviet editors on the covers of each, volumes of *Sochineniia* and *Pis'ma* in the first edition are identified by Roman numerals, those in the second by Arabic ones. It is not the purpose of this article to investigate in detail the contemporary reception of *Dym*: a good summary of it will be found in *Sochineniia*, Vol. 7, pp. 531–44.

2. *Pis'ma*, Vol. VI, pp. 252, 550.

3. This appellation received definitive force only *ex post facto*, in Turgenev's preface to Vol. III in the 1880 edition of his collected works; see *Sochineniia*, Vol. 9, p. 390. Earlier, and especially in his manuscripts, he had more commonly called the works *povesti* (long stories or tales).

4. There is of course nothing new in this analysis. Richard Freeborn himself is one of several who have argued it persuasively: see his *Turgenev: the Novelist's Novelist* (Oxford, 1960), pp. 142–4. Among those who have attempted to refute such a view and plead for the unity of *Dym* is James B. Woodward, who believes that the central character is neither Litvinov nor Potugin but Irina: see his article 'Turgenev's "New Manner": a Reassessment of His Novel *Dym*', *Canadian Slavonic Papers*, XXVI, no. 1 (1984), 65–80.

5. See *Pis'ma*, Vol. IV, p. 108 (and also pp. 125, 136). For a discussion of this, see Patrick Waddington, *Turgenev and England* (London, Macmillan, 1980), p. 114.

6. *Pis'ma*, Vol. IV, p. 381.

7. M. K. Kleman, *Letopis' zhizni i tvorchestva 1. S. Turgeneva* (Moscow and Leningrad, 1934), p. 131.

8. *Pis'ma*, Vol. IV, pp. 348, 359.

9. Ibid., pp. 379, 639; see also p. 376, where there is a perhaps related reference of two days earlier.

10. André Mazon, *Manuscrits parisiens d'Ivan Tourguénev. Notices et extraits* (Paris, Honoré Champion, 1930), pp. 23, 62; *Sochineniia*, Vol. IX, pp. 396–7, Vol. 7, pp. 510–11. Careful study of the original manuscript at the Bibliothèque Nationale in Paris (Slave 88, ff. 87 recto and 86 verso) has persuaded me that the argument in favour of December 1862–January 1863, though appealing, is by no means overwhelming.

11. *Pis'ma*, Vol. V, pp. 9, 31, 496, 505.

12. Ivan Tourguénev, *Nouvelle correspondance inédite*, edited by Alexandre Zviguilsky, 2 vols (Paris, Librairie des Cinq Continents, 1971–72), Vol. I, p. 101.

13. *Sochineniia*, vol. 11, p. 87; *Pis'ma*, vol. V, pp. 22–3, 41.

14. For a fuller discussion of this, as also of his visit to London in general, see my *Turgenev and England*, pp. 130–32, 297–8. On the similarities and differences between Turgenev's views and Potugin's, see *I. S. Turgenev v vospominaniiakh sovremennikov*, edited by S. M. Petrov and V. G. Fridliand, 2 vols (Moscow, 1969), Vol. II, p. 101 (reminiscence of V. V. Stasov).

15. See the 1863 collected version of the letters in A. I. Gertsen [Herzen], *Sobranie sochinenii v tridtsati tomakh* (Moscow, 1954–65), Vol. XVI, pp. 129–98; see also *Pis'ma*, Vol. V, pp. 394–5.

16. *Pis'ma*, Vol. V, pp. 38–40, 51–6, 64–8, 73–5, 508, 516.

17. Ibid., pp. 41, 44, 46–7, 56, 58.

18. See on this the article by S. G. Svatikov, 'I. S. Turgenev i russkaia molodezh' v Geidel'berge (1861–1862)', *Novaia zhizn'*, XII (1912), 148–85.

19. *Pis'ma*, Vol. IV, pp. 379–82, 640.

20. Ibid., Vol.V, pp. 47, 50, 56, 74, etc.; Svatikov, pp. 162, 175–6.

21. P. P. Suvorov, *Zapiski o proshlom* (Moscow, 1889), Vol. I, p. 100. On Turgenev's long-standing prejudice against Heidelberg, see *Pis'ma*, Vol. IV, p. 147. On the 'Heidelberg arabesques' in *Dym*, see, for example, I. A. Vinnikova, 'Turgenev i Pisemskii', *Turgenevskii sbornik*, V (Leningrad, 1969), pp. 261–5; A. B. Muratov, '"Geidel'bergskiearabeski" v "Dyme"', *Literaturnoe nasledstvo*, LXXVI (1967), 71–105; and the same author's *I. S. Turgenev posle 'Ottsov i detei' (60-e gody)* (Leningrad, 1972), pp. 124–44.

22. For a fuller discussion of this, see Henri Granjard, *Ivan Tourguénev et les courants politiques et sociaux de son temps*, 2nd ed. (Paris, Institut d'Etudes Slaves, 1966), pp. 353–4. For a different analysis of Turgenev's dispute with Herzen, more sympathetic to Herzen, see Leonard Schapiro, *Turgenev: His Life and Times* (Oxford: Oxford University Press, 1978), pp. 195–203, 210–13, and also Freeborn, pp. 135–8.

23. Mazon, p. 61.

24. *Sochineniia*, Vol. VII, p. 301; Mazon, p. 62.

25. *Pis'ma*, Vol. V, pp. 80–81.

26. Ibid., pp. 82, 87, 89, 382–4, 387–9, 537–8, 543, 691; Mazon, p. 62.

27. *Pis'ma*, Vol. V, p. 103.

28. Ibid., pp. 105–6, 556–7.

29. Ibid., pp. 111–12, 116.

30. Ibid., pp. 107, 391–401, 694–97.

31. Ibid., p. 173. The second character list and the plot summary here referred to will be found fully discussed in my article 'Turgenev's Notebooks for *Dym*', *New Zealand Slavonic Journal*, 1989–90, pp. 41–6.

32. See the reproductions of this in Mazon, p. 23, and *Literaturnoe nasledstvo*, LXXVI (1967), 93.

33. See the reproduced title-page of the manuscript (not begun until 18 November 1865) in *Sochineniia*, Vol. IX, p. 145; it shows hesitation between 'Dve zhizni' and 'Dym'. See also Mazon, p. 69, but note that what is said there is somewhat modified by the fact that 'Dve zhizni' stands alone at the head of the novel proper in the manuscript at the Bibliothèque Nationale (Slave 84, f. 2).

34. *Pis'ma*, Vol. VI, pp. 283–4, and see ibid., p. 233.

35. Prosper Mérimée, *Correspondance générale*, edited by Maurice Parturier, second series, 11 vols (Toulouse, Edouard Privat, 1953–64), Vol. VII (1953), p. 550.

36. *Gore ot uma* ('Woe from Wit'), line 386. See the discussion of this in A. I. Batiuto, *Turgenev-romanist* (Leningrad, 1972), pp. 359–60. On the various connotations of *dym* see also Peter Thiergen, 'Turgenevs *Dym*: Titel und Thema', in *Studien zu Literatur und Kultur in Osteuropa. Bonner Beiträge zum 9. Internationalen Slawistenkongress in Kiew*, edited by Hans-Bernd Harder and Hans Rothe (Cologne and Vienna, Böhlau, 1983), pp. 277–311.

37. Psalms 37:20; 68:2; 102:3; Acts 2:19.

38. See *Pis'ma*, Vol. V, pp. 52, 68.

39. Ibid., Vol. IV, p. 238.

40. *Sochineniia*, Vol. 7, pp. 267, 279, 296, 347, 396–9, 401, 407.

41. Ibid., p. 384.

42. *Aeneid*, V, 740; *Comus*, 5; *The Rape of Lucrece*, 1027.

43. *Pis'ma*, Vol. 4, p. 69 (not in the first edition).

44. *Pis'ma*, Vol. IV, p. 190.

45. *Sochineniia*, Vol. 7, pp. 397–8.

46. See, for example, Sigrid McLaughlin, *Schopenhauer in Rus'sland. Zur Literarischen Rezeption bei Turgenev* (Wiesbaden, Otto Harrassowitz, 1984).

47. *Pis'ma*, Vol. V, pp. 65, 74, 530–31; *Sochineniia*, Vol. IX, p. 379; Prosper Mérimée, *Oeuvres complètes. Etudes de littérature russe*, edited by Henri Mongault (Paris, 1932), Vol. II, pp. 549–50; Granjard, pp. 325–6.

48. See, for example, *Pis'ma*, Vol. V, pp. 245–6; A. I. Batiuto, 'Turgenev i Paskal', *Russkaia literatura*, 1964, no. 1, pp. 153–62.

49. *Quelques lettres d'Ivan Tourguénev à Pauline Viardot*, edited by Henri Granjard (Paris and The Hague, Mouton, 1974), pp. 133–4; Mazon, pp. 68–9.

50. *Nouvelle correspondance inédite*, Vol. I, p. 140; Henri Granjard and Alexandre Zviguilsky (eds), *Lettres inédites de Tourguénev à Pauline Viardot et à sa famille* (Lausanne, L'Age d'Homme, 1972), pp. 126–7; *New Zealand Slavonic Journal*, 1983, p. 229; *Pis'ma*, Vol. VI, p. 139, 141, 142.

51. See Mazon, pp. 61–2, 68. The label on Turgenev's manuscript book is somewhat coffin-like in shape, adding perhaps to an earlier (but surely wrong) surmise that 's.i.P.' should be construed as 'sit in pace'. As is shown also by similar labels on other notebooks at the Bibliothèque Nationale (Slave 84, 85, 86), the 'P.' is definitely a capital. Some other interpretations, such as 'sub iudice Paulina' or 'sic iuvit Paulinam', seem less likely as Turgenev, in these situations, would probably have used a 'j'.

52. H. H. Boyesen, 'A visit to Tourguéneff', *Galaxy*, XVII (1874), p. 462.

53. *Pis'ma*, Vol. VII, p. 202; (unsigned), 'Smoke', *Spectator*, 28 March 1868, pp. 379–81.

IRENE MASING-DELIC

Philosophy, Myth, and Art in Turgenev's Notes of a Hunter

In "Hamlet from Shchigry District," one of the sketches in Ivan Turgenev's *Notes of a Hunter* (1852), the narrator's unknown interlocutor refuses to give his name, merely calling himself a provincial Hamlet. The reason is that he bitterly resents what he calls his lack of originality. He keenly feels the irony of being deemed original by his naive rural neighbors whereas he himself is convinced that he lacks uniqueness. Representing an as yet novel type in the Russian provinces, he was nevertheless "born a copy of someone else"[1] and spent his life imitating various models, mainly culled from Western literature. Incapable of the creative acts of rearing a son and heir, or educating a disciple, he instead reproduces himself by cloning. Twin brothers of his are beginning to appear even in remote rural districts, he states, and apparently he is right. Among the guests in the manor house which offers the setting for the sketch, its author catches a glimpse of a "young man of about twenty years of age, myopic, with fair hair and draped in black from head to foot." He is painfully shy and self-conscious, but he "smiles caustically."[2] In another twenty years' time he will probably be telling a life story which in all essential aspects duplicates the one the reader is about to learn from the current Hamlet. Perhaps he already senses this outcome, since his caustic smile betrays that, like all Hamlets, he too is fatally self-centered.

From *The Russian Review*, vol. 50, no. 4. © 1991 by The Ohio State University Press.

Self-consciousness makes the Hamlets "unoriginal" (to use their own terminology) and the more they cultivate an artificial eccentricity, such as draping themselves in black, the more they emphasize that they are copying someone else, for example, Shakespeare's hero. Needless to say, their imitation is but a caricature, since Shakespeare's Western prince, being the first Hamlet, was original and tragic whereas his Russian rural copies are actors in a farce, a notoriously imitative genre.

However, the senior Hamlet of the present story has gathered enough life experience to be done with caustic irony aimed at others. Self-conscious posing has, in his case, yielded to a redeeming self-critical assessment of his personality type. Thus Hamlet from Shchigry attempts putting the psychological-social phenomenon he represents in a cultural context. Not ignoring his genetic inheritance, that is, regretting that his parents were dull people, incapable of bestowing original features on their offspring, he explores mainly cultural factors in his investigation of Russian Hamletism.

It emerges from his story that these factors include an over-protected childhood. Although occasionally subjected to corporal punishment, Hamlet was an overly sheltered proto-Oblomov who grew up under "the cover of a feather-bed."[3] Accustomed to the womb of a self-contained microworld, he began to fear exposure to reality. However, it was during his university years that a fatal spiritual atrophy set in that precluded forever his becoming an "original" (genuine, vital) personality capable of shaping his life in accordance with his own vision. At fault was German Idealist philosophy in its Muscovite setting, the philosophical debating societies of the 1830s and 1840s (the *kruzhki*). Hamlet is absolutely certain that it was precisely this apparently innocuous and friendly Muscovite philosophical debating society which "spelled the end to any development of originality."[4] What then, in Hamlet's view, was so dangerous about philosophizing with Idealist Muscovite student friends?

Apparently it was the high-powered glorification of the *Absolute* which created an impenetrable screen between a philosopher and reality. It put the individual, as it were, in a bell jar of brittle oversensitivity, or a hall of mocking mirrors. Seized by fear of the "base phenomena" of life, the philosopher learned to subsist on surrogates, on "words, words, words" *about* friendship, love and wisdom, as opposed to the genuine article. The overpowering presence of the *Absolute* spiritually castrates a man, replacing his creative potency with laming self-consciousness. A philosophical circle is a depraved monastic order, a caste of eunuchs, who, according to Hamlet, in spite of their sterility, lack purity. Thus the Muscovite philosopher is not only incapable of creativity but he also feels compelled to rationalize away the creative activities of others leaving his "dirty fingerprints" all over their souls.[5] He also destroys his own noble impulses by overindulgence in self-analysis. Studying himself in the hall of mocking mirrors, the philosopher discovers that, measured by the standards of the *Absolute*, he is as imperfect as his fellowmen, if not more.

In fact, injured vanity obliges him to exaggerate his shortcomings and to distort his image, in order to attract, if not admiration, then at least attention. Thus he becomes a clown instead of a man, a mouse that, at the slightest threat to his delicate sensibilities, scurries into his hole.[6] Playing the part, Hamlet wears a clownish nightcap and still practices his childhood habit of diving into his featherbeds at the slightest alarm.[7] Hamlets are poseurs or *lomaki* whose lives have an ironic quality. Their claims to have a panacea for all ills of reality because of their close knowledge of the Ideal are at best a joke. On the contrary, they destroy those faint vestiges of Truth, Goodness, and Beauty that actually do exist in the midst of imperfect life by their constant *Kritik*. Hamlet's marriage to a woman named *Sofya* demonstrates the ironic quality of a Russian *wisdom* lover's unoriginality with particular force. Like the philosophy he is trapped by, this marriage had a German prologue.

As a student in Berlin, Hamlet had the prospect of entry into German academic and private life by marrying into a professorial family. He eventually rejected this opportunity perhaps for the same reasons that made the *Underground Man* sneer at German idealist philosophers. According to the Underground Man, these philosophers have an astounding capacity to "dwell among the stars" in verbose discourses, while living in the dreariest philistine surroundings possible. In any case, Hamlet flees from his German professor, as well as his two daughters Minkhen and Linkhen, opting for Russian life instead. The latter is represented by an impoverished general's widow, a tyrannical steppe estate landowner who has two ailing but eligible daughters Vera and Sofya (Faith and Wisdom). But the encounter with Russian reality proves as much a failure as the German, specifically in his marriage to Sofya.

It is characteristic of Hamlet's courtship that he fell in love with his bride when he had his back turned on her, perchance following Hegelian injunctions to ignore mere *Wirklichkeit*. Sitting on a terrace facing a rose garden and gazing into the sunset, he listened to Sofya—well hidden in the inner recesses of the house—playing a certain Beethoven piano motif over and over again. On the strength of this, Hamlet persuaded himself that he loved her. Confronting her as a wife, he pondered flight, even suicide. It could be argued that the reason why Hamlet's and Sofya's love "got stuck" on a certain motif, in spite of numerous efforts to play the piece to the end, should be sought in Sofya. She clearly did not qualify as the earthly incarnation of Divine Wisdom when examined more closely.

Not only was Sofya bald and tubercular, but also spiritually warped.[8] She reminded Hamlet of a canary he once owned. First a playful cat frightened the bird beyond recovery, then a rat bit off its beak and finally it died, never having chirped happily for a single day of its short existence. Bald Sofya is a "plucked canary" also.[9] A provincial, timid, and old-maidenish young woman, she harbored a minute but never-healing wound in the depths of her soul, where some metaphysical "cat" or "rat" once bit her. Incapable of "chirping" her song, she made pathetic attempts at reproducing the few notes of the Beethoven phrase she had learned. It could be argued that such a woman cannot be loved.

A Russian idealist nurtured in Muscovite philosophical circles would argue thus, since, unlike the German, he is unable to tolerate too wide a gap between the real and the Ideal. Therefore he assiduously applies his *Kritik* of mere reality to all imperfect manifestations of the Ideal, of which there are many in his native land. Russian spiritual-cultural life, if it were to be incarnated in a woman, could well turn out bald, silly, and moribund, a pathetic and ludicrous realization of her transcendental model *Sophiia*. Hamlet states that he would like to "take lessons from her, Russian life that is," but, unfortunately, "the little dove [*golubushka*] is silent."[10] The Russian idealist trained to perceive abstract perfection is offended by this lack of opinion and aspirations among the Russian people, who, as Pushkin already stated in his stage directions for *Boris Godunov*, invariably "keep silent."[11] Rejecting his own culture, he does not feel comfortable in any other, however. Herein lies the tragedy of Russian Hamlets.

Furthermore, they are aesthetes. Extolling both the Good *and* the Beautiful, they favor the latter. Unfortunately, Sofya embodied only the good. In the ethical sphere she could not be faulted, as Hamlet emphasizes, but aesthetically she was flawed.[12] Thus he had to face the sunset, when he persuaded himself that he loved her. He needed the protection of mood (*nastroenie*) and the lofty Ideal somewhere beyond the sunset to imitate the feeling of love. Presumably the German professorial home was lacking in poetic atmosphere, and the coffee brewed by the sisters, although excellent, was no substitute for *nastroenie*. In the dilapidated "gentry nest" of the two Russian sisters Vera and Sofya there was poetry, however, albeit of the elegiac mode. In addition, it offered some faith and wisdom, not because the two sisters incarnated these ideals, but because they offered Hamlet the opportunity to demonstrate a little faith and gain some wisdom. Had he done what he should have done—to pity and love the real, even though it was not ideal, or even to bring it just one step closer to the Ideal—he would have been a better philosopher and human being.

It could in fact be argued that Hamlet, by the time he meets the narrator, has come to realize that "the excessive rationalism of Western culture had destroyed the 'integrity' of [his] self, and led to a profound inner split in [his] personality that could only be healed by faith."[13] Perhaps he is beginning to realize that faith in Russia's innate wisdom, in spite of her humble appearance, could have given him the originality he covets.[14] In his humble wife, he should perhaps have seen an incarnation of that Russia which, according to the Slavophiles, was now a "stepchild of historical Providence,"[15] but destined to become an original, even unique nation and carrier of Divine Wisdom. For that matter, had not Western Romantic Idealist philosophy taught them that a national culture incarnates itself in *das ewig Weibliche*?

Instead of gazing into the sunset, Hamlet should have had a good look at his mousy Cinderella and perceived her future redeemed hypostasis, not to mention her pathetic but possibly quite lovable actual form. Blinded by self-pity, Hamlet was bitterly disappointed in his bald Sofya, forgetting that he himself was little more than a clown and "mouse." In other words, his poetic mood could not be sustained and philosophy proved to be an insufficient shield against reality. Poor Sofya had to repeat Ophelia's fate and die insulted by her prince, falling very short of her Hamlet's vision of the Ideal. Under the insult of his critical glances, or, worse, of his avoiding eyes, her festering wound could not heal. The rat which bit off her "beak" was thus perhaps Hamlet from Shchigry himself. After all, the sentimental provincial maiden presumably believed she had married a philosopher, not a clown whose opinions need not be taken seriously.[16] Sickly Russian culture, harboring its festering inferiority complex, may well die also, withering under the overly critical glances of its moping *intelligenty*, who do nothing to initiate a creative transformation.

The paradox of the philosopher becoming increasingly trapped by delusions in the overly critical quest for Truth is reversed in that of the mythmaker, who in fabricating an "ennobling lie" (Pushkin), establishes contact with real life, at least emotionally. Indifferent to abstract logic, arid philosophical categories, and other depersonalizing thought patterns, he has that originality for which Hamlet strives in "the sweat of his brow" without ever achieving it.[17] This reversal is demonstrated in the sketch "The District Doctor."

Here the author-narrator again is the recipient of a confession, this time from a provincial *intelligent* who perchance was destined for something better than his actual lot. This "Hamlet"[18] learned to live with his unappealing looks and lowly status, however, making a compromise settlement with reality by marrying one of those solidly real (read stout) merchants' daughters whom Hamlet from Shchigry despises.[19] Before his marriage, however, the district doctor was loved by a beautiful woman from a noble but impoverished family, who enshrouded him in a romantic myth, in spite of his lack of appeal. This female mythmaker, who was determined to see in him what he was not, presented him with the most tormenting, as well as rewarding, moments of his life.

Summoned to the sick-bed of Aleksandra Andreevna, the un-remarkable country doctor became the hero of a myth, fabricated by her. As he himself realized—not without injury to his self-esteem—she created this myth of hers out of feverish fantasies and her yearning for love in the face of death, rather than from a sober assessment of his personality. Normally this fastidious young woman would never have paid any attention to him. Once she asked for his name and disappointed to learn that it was the inelegant "Trifon," she responded contemptuously in whispered French. It could be argued that in her dying state, Aleksandra Andreevna, no less than Hamlet from Shchigry, loved only under the impulse of certain mood. But there is a difference. Hamlets submit passively to outer stimuli at a congenial moment. Mythmakers act creatively in spite of the resistance of the "raw material." Aleksandra Andreevna, far from surrendering to a fragile mood, feverishly created a persuasive myth that turned a timid district doctor, in spite of himself, into a knight in shining armor. Here an effort was made to create a myth out of flawed reality and live it, as opposed to the fearful withdrawal from imperfect life into unsustainable moods.

The difference between the two is further emphasized by the fact that Aleksandra Andreevna was able to create her beautiful myth in spite of her lover's unaesthetic, "Trifonesque" aspect because she discerned his ethical validity. Even when the author meets him, the doctor is still a man who perceives service to others as his prime duty, in spite of his newly acquired "bourgeois" status. It is the perception of his sense of honor that enables Aleksandra Andreevna to aesthetically enhance his image, whereas Hamlet, painfully aware of Sofya's flawless character, was incapable of not noticing her baldness. The mythmaker pays homage to ethics within the Good-True-Beautiful triad of *Prekrasnoe*.

It is true, however, that Aleksandra Andreevna's creative originality stems from the extraordinary situation of her illness, that fatal circumstances turn her into a mythmaker, and that she is an original person capable of forgetting her conventional self and letting her true self come to the fore. Had it not been for her "lofty malady" (Pasternak), she would have remained an entirely proper young lady. She is thus not the genuine foil to Hamlet who represents the well known social phenomenon and cultural type of the superfluous man. The *intelligentsiia* philosophers in Turgenev's *Notes* find their contrast, not in the "mythmakers by chance" but in the *narod*, whose *mifotvorchestvo* is rooted in collective creativity rather than personal tragedy.[20] The sectarian utopian Kasyan from Krasivaya Mech', the peasant visionary Lukerya, the boys in "Bezhin Meadow," the "pantheist" Kalinych and others do not regale the author-narrator with confessions but with tales and attitudes that are anchored in religious imagery, popular history and prehistory, in the "racial unconscious" of Jungian discourse, and the texts of nature itself, as opposed to the individual ego. They are woven into the contexts of prophecy, superstition, fairytales, folklore, and nature myths and thus possess a wider validity, more objectivity and organic unity than the splintered consciousness of individual confessions. Although the folk mythmakers, like the philosophers, are outsiders, often ridiculed by their social peers (Kasyan is deemed a "holy fool" with the emphasis more on "fool" than "holy"), they are not peripheral characters. In their own perception at least, they are firmly anchored in belief systems and myths of the *narod*.

Certainly they possess that which Hamlet lacks, namely, the ability to be themselves as they forget themselves. Their lives are therefore full of enticing visions of bliss—a fairytale paradise somewhere in the South, an afterlife where Christ the Bridegroom exalts his poor bride Lukerya; alternatively they are haunted by portents, since death is always announcing itself, although it invariably takes its victims by surprise. This mythic attitude toward existence would thus seem to offer a positive contrast to Hamlet's individualistic self-laceration parading as philosophy, offering in cultural-ideological terms the Slavophile religious alternative to Westernizing negativism.[21]

The world of Turgenev's *Notes* is, however, not easily divisible along clear-cut Slavophile/Westernizing lines. If classification is to be applied to the author of *Notes* at all, he answers the description of Westernizer and "Friend of Philosophy" rather than the Slavophile "Hunter for Russia's Hidden Spiritual Treasures." On the other hand, the Westernizer Turgenev did produce Slavophile texts also (such as the novel *A Nest of Gentle Folk*). Should he perhaps be seen as closer to the Slavophiles than is commonly assumed? Or are the two ideological positions ultimately so inextricably intertwined in Turgenev's world that classifications should not be attempted?

It has been argued that the "conjunctive narratives" of the *Notes* rests on "the precarious coexistence of opposites" linked by *and*, such as "Khor' *and* Kalinych" and "Forest *and* Steppe."[22] This precarious balance of opposites includes the Slavophile/Westernizer issue, too often seen in terms of absolute opposites.[23] This issue is further debated below, but let it be noted here that the creative, "mythic" attitude toward life, represented in the *Notes* by members of the *narod* and resident landowner types, is not devoid of its specific problems. Myth does not remedy the unresolved problems of philosophy.

Idealists, insulted by a reality which does not correspond to their vision of the Ideal, pour venom over mere *phenomena*; the mythmakers distort reality to suit their vision or else ignore it, since their vision of the Ideal is so real to them. If they were to be classified philosophically, they would certainly not qualify as empiricists, deeming factual evidence irrelevant as they do. Thus Aleksandra Andreevna's making a hero out of her district doctor creates a beautiful myth, though "objectively" it is "a parody of Prince Charming as he sloshes through the foul 'enchanted forest' of a Russian countryside to reach his 'Sleeping Beauty' for whom he can do nothing except bestow one last kiss of death."[24] The sectarian Kasyan expounds on his promised land, complete with golden apples and enchanting song,[25] in a setting that is an ecological hell with its parched earth and wanton "murder" of trees felled for the sake of greed. It is true that Kasyan is not oblivious to what is happening around him—indeed, he condemns greed as a deadly sin, and fearlessly speaks out against the hunter who "exposes blood to the light of day," repeating Cain's mortal sin for his own amusement.[26] Yet his reaction to evil is somehow impersonal, as if it did not really concern him. He has no intention of struggling against it, as his sect is that of the "runners" (*beguny*), whose flight (*begstvo*) from the waste land of reality seeks the greener pastures of the imagination and myth (a popular equivalent of the *Absolute*).

Naturally Kasyan, who not only is a serf but also a dwarf, is both socially and physically unable to change reality in even the smallest measure. It is interesting, however, that he has no impulse to leave the ugly locality where he now dwells for Krasivaia Mech, his idyllic home. This "fair place" has already fulfilled its aesthetic function of stimulating his mythmaking and has therefore become redundant. Now the Land of Golden Apples is dearer to Kasyan than both the deforested wasteland where he dwells and the fair Russian landscape of his past. Reality is ultimately uninteresting to the utopian mythmaker and he abandons it (whereas the philosopher hates it, but is riveted to it, since he enjoys denouncing and defaming it). Kasyan, the *begun*, represents a native tradition of abandoning the unacceptable,[27] but he also forsakes the more positive aspects of reality.[28] He wanders for the sake of wandering, remaining forever a "stranger" in the world of reality (a "nonresident" in R. Gustafson's gnostic terminology).[29]

Kasyan's sectarian attitude is socially significant since it rejects Russian reality as a whole and even reality in general. The mythmakers refuse to deal with the problems of everyday life, devoting themselves to a futile search of mythic paradises instead. Unlike the resentful philosophers, they feel no need to ridicule flawed reality, have no wish to tear people or institutions to shreds, and harbor no inclinations to self-laceration, since they simply do not think themselves or reality important enough to fret about. Thus the mythmakers are original, creative, and imaginative, but also fatally passive and noninvolved with earthly reality. Without feeling fatally alienated or desperately unhappy in this world as the philosophers do, the mythmakers simply dwell in "another" place. Evil is likewise mythical to them and therefore they do not seek to fight it in social institutions but, again, in myth—in the two-horned Anti-Christ of czars Aleksei and his son Peter the Great.[30] The task of overcoming this Beast is best left to the "Savior on His white steed,"[31] however, while His flock waits for the Last Judgment and the deliverance from "Babylon." Thus myth, however inspiring and original, like philosophy causes a man to turn his back on reality and in the end it does not matter whether the turned back demonstrates disgust caused by too close a scrutiny, or the indifference of apocalypticmythic expectations.

The picture that emerges in *Notes* is that Russia is inhabited by a fatalistic race of myth-makers, largely drawn from the *narod* and imaginative women, and by an *intelligentsiia* of paralyzed philosophers, neither of which is capable of dealing with the country's real problems.[32] These are left in the care of a third category of Russia's inhabitants, its "dead souls" who, never questioning anything, live in "the best of all possible worlds," or that realm of complacency and stagnation where both critique and creativity, philosophy and myth, are equally unacceptable. Perhaps the first category is the most active of the three. It does after all keep the myths of the national heritage alive and guards the buried treasures of the national spirit, whereas the second largely nurtures its own anxieties. The third category, as has been stated, displays no activity whatsoever except for lackeyism, conformity, and mismanagement (see the first "Gogolian" part of "Hamlet from Shchigry" with its satirical description of the landowners). Thus an original people, creating, developing, and guarding its myths, is seen as abandoned not only by absentee landlords but also by an absentee intelligentsia of Hamletian philosophers who turned the search-light of their foreign-honed erudition inward, instead of illuminating dark Russian reality, of helping to raise the *Kitezh-grad* of a submerged popular-national culture to the surface, making positive myths real. A question—not posed but implied—in *Notes* is: how can this raising of *Kitezh-grad* be accomplished, when those trained to diagnose and cure national ills indulge in futile self-laceration and, the "patient" (Mother Russia), furthermore, is content with "her" comforting fever fantasies, some of which are very beautiful.

One answer to the above questions is given in the very first sketch of *Notes*, the programmatic "Khor and Kalinych." In it, the author launches a theory of the Russian national character and Russia's destiny that forms part of the long prehistory of Dostoevsky's famous Pushkin speech of 1880. Here Dostoevsky proclaims Russia to be the most culturally receptive of all nations in the world, wherefore its historical destiny is to become a conciliator and synthesizer of peoples and cultures. Although this "prophetic" vision of Dostoevsky's was greeted with frenzied enthusiasm in 1880,[33] it was not a sudden revelation to Dostoevsky alone, but the culmination of a gradually developing myth.[34] Thus "Belinskij anticipated the myth"[35] and Gogol formulated its fundamental tenets in his *Dead Souls*, sharing with Belinsky "a firm belief in the 'national spirit'" and, like him, paying particular attention to the inner form of language as an expression of this spirit.[36] Turgenev's *Notes of a Hunter* also contributed to the myth of Russia as the universal nation, offering a synthesis where both Belinsky's admiration of Peter the Great and Gogol's vision of Russia as a speeding *troika* are given their due.

In regard to Russian universality, the author of *Notes*, in a direct address to his readers, asserts that "Peter the Great was predominantly Russian," not in spite, but because of his Western reform activities.[37] Clearly dissenting from the Slavophile and sectarian evaluation of Peter, the author states that his Westernism was his Russianness and his Russianness, his Westernism. The hallmark of the genuine Russian is precisely creative receptivity to all good ideas regardless of their source, as opposed to slavish imitativeness, or lack of originality. Hamlet from Shchigry was unable to salvage his personality after his encounter with German culture, but his fate is not inevitable. The genuine Russian character is sufficiently self-confident that no amount of cultural borrowing can obliterate it. Peter the Great certainly did not lose an ounce of his originality after his encounter with Western culture, and it was his bold translation of ideas into action that made him a Russian Westerner and a Western Russian, a universal man, mythmaker and philosopher rolled into one. Perhaps genius and intense receptivity are one and the same, since receptivity need not be imitative, as philosophers should note.

Had Hamlet from Shchigry—on his own modest scale—been more receptive to all facets of German culture rather than fearfully guarding himself against it, he may well have turned out an innovator in the realm of philosophy and not a parrot. But, apart from Minkhen and Linkhen and book knowledge, he ignored German life. Nor did he learn anything from traveling in other European countries and he returned to Russia without any practicable ideas. No wonder the poor plants entrusted in his care—anemic Vera and bald Sofya—withered and died. To state it once more, it was not overexposure but underexposure to the cultural riches of Europe that made Hamlet unoriginal. Culture is after all much more than abstract philosophy. Lara in Pasternak's *Doctor Zhivago* states that philosophy is not the staple of life and should be enjoyed in small doses, like horseradish. Hamlet from Shchigry would have profited from her insight. Indeed, being a Hamlet does not automatically spell disaster if a "philosophical" disposition is counterbalanced by practical activity.

Khor, a peasant Hamlet of sorts, does not commit the mistake of his intelligentsia *confrère*. Critical of pedantic Germans, he also well knows that they have "something to teach others" and he is willing to learn.[38] Prone to "philosophical" bouts of self-pity[39] and deeply distrustful of his fellowmen, Khor is also indefatigably active, which, together with his cultural receptivity, saves him from the sterility of Hamletism. Khor is a splendid organizer, shrewd economist, and diligent worker—a man who has learned from the practical men of the West, a realm where not only abstract philosophy but also practical commerce and other useful activities flourish. In Khor, the Hamlet-like analysis and critical attention to detail do not degenerate into self-laceration, but are applied for practical tasks. Nor does Khor scorn the native heritage. Part of his Russian, hence universal nature is his capacity for friendship with the diametrically opposed personality Kalinych, the pantheist mythmaker. Thus the Russian Khor, receptive to everything good from West and East, is capable of positive accomplishments in spite of a certain egocentricity. A misogynist like Hamlet from Shchigry, he does not psychologically ruin his (shrewish) wife. He is in fact a Peter the Great in his own small world and, on his own modest level, an incarnation of the Russian genius that blends creativity and receptivity, the mind and heart. Khor is one of the forerunners of the Dostoevskian *vsechelovek*, certainly a peasant anticipation of Stolz[40] and Turgenev's own Solomin in *Virgin Soil*. Thus he offers a promise for the future and it is not fortuitous that he has numerous children. One of his sons, the handsome, talented, and literate

Fedya, a strapping *bogatyr*, holds out the prospect that the Russian people will choose the path of harmonious synthesis where poetic originality is not wasted in futile dreams, nor where the critique of native ways is transformed into a slavish imitation of foreign models. Russians will one day strike the right balance between philosophical analysis and inspiring mythmaking, Turgenev assures us.

The quest for the *Prekrasnoe* and the Russian, yet universal, man may be the nation's guarantee of originality (the "Russian idea"), as some members of the intelligentsia perceive. This group does not solely consist of jaded philosophers, but also of uniquely creative men of letters. Writers, as *Notes* demonstrates, are "hunters" for the hidden treasures of the Russian people who do not lose sight of those offered by an advanced Europe. Writers, including the author of *Notes*, are the Peters of their times who embrace all of humanity. They are indeed the inheritors of Pushkin, who was portrayed as the universal Russian genius and incarnation of panhumanity by Gogol and Dostoevsky. Like him, they understand, see, and show everything, at the same time indicating what ought to be done.

To further exemplify, the narrator of the sketch "Death" sympathetically portrays a young German steward who is aghast at the wastage of timber cutting he witnesses on a Russian estate. The narrator finds it ironic that a foreigner should have more pity for Russian natural resources than the Russians themselves. At the same time he perceives that the young German is rather pedantic and his taste in literature not of the best (he reads Johanna Schopenhauer's novels). Thus he balances his evaluation of foreigners, just like Khor. Although a minor detail in the sketch, it demonstrates that the Hunter of *Notes* is not blindly enamored with foreign culture but a critical judge of its trivial aspects.

Perhaps the author is best called a Russian who knows that his country must learn from the West in preserving its natural and human resources, but still fervently hopes that his people will make a significant contribution to world culture. Since the Russians have the mythopoeic talent, or faith, to meet death itself with calm dignity (as the sketch shows), there is no reason to assume that their courage will fail them in creating a unique future for themselves. But the people need guidance and this is what the creative intelligentsia can give it. As an "all-seeing eye," the writer can ensure that his nation follows a road of national originality based on cultural synthesis. Art, notably verbal art, can combine philosophy with myth, ideas with imagery, (initial) analysis with (ultimate) synthesis, merging content with form.[41] It can "think in images," as Belinsky, following the German philosophical tradition, avers. Thus art will help Russia realize its destiny as the "universal nation" opening up ever new vistas of cultural synthesis to an "astonished world" (Gogol).

The literature of Pushkin, Gogol, and Turgenev himself offer productive myths that lead not away from, but toward reality. Gogol's vision of the Russian land as a *troika*, for example, is linked to historical time, whereas Kasyan's apocalyptic myth belongs to a "dream time" outside history. Firmly anchored in history, yet embracing the *goût de l'infini*, Gogol's vision can stimulate positive action, as opposed to sectarian *begstvo*. It could be argued that the author of *Notes* uses Gogol's *Dead Souls* as a subtext offering the challenge of filling Russian sheer potential—in the novel symbolized by the endless steppe—with valid content in historical time.

Gogol is distinctly present in *Notes*, both as a satirist (in the first half of the Hamlet sketch) and as a visionary.[42] As a visionary he is evoked in the final lyrical sketch, "Forest and Steppe." Its placement not only forms a suitable coda in its glorification of the beauties of the Russian land, but also an ideological summary and conclusion, harmoniously synthesizing both its main "images" and "thoughts." Having in the first sketch stated the archetypal Russian quality of constant self-renewal through creative adaptation to and absorption of new ideas regardless of their origin, the author in the last sketch conjures up a vision of Russia as a carriage[43] traversing "the limitless, unsurveyable steppe"[44] and a future fraught with endless potential.[45] It is true that the narrator is not in a Gogolian *troika* but in a *telega* and that he takes along his *samovar*, not indifferent to cozy comfort.[46] But although Turgenev's epilogue to *Notes*, by some called *Living Souls*, offers a more modest variant to the ecstatic coda of *Dead Souls* (1842), there is, nevertheless, the same endless perspective and promise of endless achievement. The fact that Turgenev's prosaic sketches move more slowly than Gogol's *poèma* perhaps ensures a more successful outcome, since Russian popular wisdom holds that "one gets farther if one travels slower." Less poetic than Gogol's, Turgenev's "steeds" (*koni*) are not devoid of mythic enchantment either, as they too carry their rider "farther and farther" into the land of the future where the unique Russian destiny is to be realized.[47]

Turgenev's vision of the future Russian "omniman" (Hingley) is also more modest than the grandiose vision of Dostoevsky's 1880 Pushkin speech.[48] The author's underlying concept of the artist is not that of mythmaker and prophet but that of moderator between the worlds of myth and philosophy on one hand and reality on the other. Turgenev's narrator is a self-effacing[49] yet richly endowed observer who, employing the "poetics of mimicry," serves his nation by letting it speak for itself.[50] Art brings together philosophical analysis and mythic synthesis, offering the common ground for aristocratic artists of the word and singers from the people ("The Singers"). It has room for philosophers and mythmakers from all social strata and all peoples. As the synthesizer par excellence, the Russian artist finds his uniquely individual voice as he becomes increasingly more receptive to other voices, just as his land finds "her" unique destiny by synthesizing her Western and Eastern cultural legacies. A true *Sophiia* at last, Russia merges philosophical thought with the mythic imagination in transformational creativity, just as the "father of her history," Peter the Great, himself taught and demonstrated.

NOTES

1. I. S. Turgenev, *Polnoe sobranie sochinenii i pisem, v tridtsati tomakh* (Moscow: Nauka, 1979), 3:259.

2. Ibid., 250.

3. Ibid., 262. Oblomov too is a Hamletian character, in his fastidiousness, fatness (Hamlet being fat according to some editions) and vacillation between "being and non-being," or, in his case, "living" and "vegetating." The relation between the Russian Hamlet Oblomov and his Horatio, the half German Stolz, is symbolic of the Russia-Europe constellation, a theme important in *Notes* also. Turgenev planned to include sketches on the "Russian German" in *Notes*, but these remained unfinished.

4. Turgenev, *Polnoe sobranie sochinenii* 3:262.

5. Ibid.

6. Turgenev's Hamlet, as G. Bialy has shown, is at times virtually indistinguishable from Dostoevsky's "Underground Man." See Bialy, *Turgenev i russkii realizm* (Moscow and Leningrad: Sovetskii pisatel', 1962).

7. This ridiculous figure may also be seen as a man victimized by Russian reality, of a 'man made socially superfluous, as opposed to a man *feeling* superfluous. The most appropriate is perhaps the mixed reaction of ridicule and pity, of Gogolian "laughter through tears."

8. Turgenev, *Potnot sobranie tochinenu* 3:257.

9. One is led to doubt that Hamlet ever owned a canary but invents the bird symbolism in order to express Sofya's character. His captivating style in narrating his life story leads one to believe that he is a potential writer, and perhaps more original than he gives himself credit for.

10. Turgenev, *Polnoe sobranie sochinenii* 3:260.

11. Gogol also in his famous *troika* vision begs Russia to reveal "her" destiny, but "she gives no answers." Turgenev later transposes this notion

into the image of Russia as the sphinx which poses riddles but never resolves them.

12. Turgenev, *Polnoe sobranie sochinenii* 3:266, 268.

13. Joseph Frank, *Through the Russian Prism* (Princeton: Princeton University Press, 1990), 64.

14. The theme that faith is the sole rewarding approach to Russia is common in Slavophile literature. Tyutchev would in 1866 state «Умом Россию не понять. . .в Россию можно только верить».

15. Frank, *Through the Russian Prism*, 63.

16. Following Silbajoris, who in the two Chertopkhanov stories perceives a parody on the Bela story (in Lermontov's *A Hero of Our Times*), one could in the Hamlet sketch see a parody on *Evgeny Onegin*. Unlike Tatyana, poor Sofya presumably never discovers that her hero imitates literary models.

17. Turgenev, *Polnoe sobranie sochinenii* 3:259.

18. It could be argued that the doctor is not a genuine Hamlet. Recent Turgenev criticism aims at transcending its standard typology of "Hamlet and Don Quixote" (inspired by Turgenev's famous article from 1869). Thus J. Woodward feels that these clichés do more harm than good, since every Turgenevan character, regardless of the time of his creation, is forced to conform to these two prototypes.

19. It may be recalled that Shakespeare's Hamlet was contemptuous of the "too solid flesh."

20. That popular myth is seen as a collective phenomenon is confirmed by the fact that the boys in "Bezhin Meadow" know the same myth of an ideal land in the South which is recorded in "Kasyan from Krasivaya Mech'." Iu. Lebedev emphasizes that in "The Singers" the main theme is not individual talent but the "giftedness of the masses." See Lebedev, *"Zapiski okhotnika" I. S. Turgeneva* (Moscow: Prosveshchenie, 1977), 50. Perhaps "celebration of a secular *sobornost'* in shared aesthetic experience" is a more accurate formulation, but "collectivity" is indisputably a constituent aspect of myth and other facets of popular culture in *Notes*.

21. Dale Peterson points to a paradoxical contrast in types in *Notes*; the physically mobile Hamlet is spiritually paralyzed, whereas the physically paralyzed Lukerya is spiritually free. See Peterson, "Hamlets and Hesychasts: Paralysis and Illumination in Turgenev" (Paper delivered at the Twentieth National Convention of the AAASS, Honolulu, Hawaii, 1988).

22. Dale Peterson, "The Origin and End of Turgenev's *Sportsman's Notebook*: The Poetics and Politics of a Precarious Balance," *Russian Literature* 16 (1984): 355–56.

23. Victor Ripp discerns a coexistence of Slavophile and Westernizing motifs in *Notes*, since "the Slavophiles' basic assumptions" and "Westernizing ones" are shared. See Ripp, *Turgenev's Russia from* Notes of a Hunter *to* Fathers and Sons (Ithaca: Cornell University Press, 1980), 50, 51.

24. Rimvydas Silbajoris, "Images and Structures in Turgenev's *Sportsman's Notebook*," *Slavic and East European Journal* 28, no. 2 (1984): 188.

25. Kasyan's vision has a great deal in common with Lermontov's dream in the famous poem «Выхожу один я на дорогу», where an eternally green oak tree and the never-ceasing "sweet voice" of a fairytale bird (the siren bird Sirin perhaps) form the mythologemes of the poet's dream.

26. Turgenev, *Polnoe sobranie sochinenii* 3:116.

27. N. Brodskii, *I. S. Turgenev i russkie sektanty* (Moscow, 1922), 4, 13, 18.

28. Nicolas Berdyaev in his *The Russian Idea* (1947) states that the "urge to wander" is a "very characteristic Russian phenomenon." It means that the wanderer "has no abiding earthly city, but is directed toward the City-to-Come." Wanderers are well known among the *narod* but also the creative intelligentsia, notably its radical wing, are very much "wanderers" as well, rarely "at ease with anything finite," finding even pleasant aspects of earthly reality wanting. See David Bethea, *The Shape of Apocalypse in Modern Russian Fiction* (Princeton: Princeton University Press, 1989), 27, 28. It would seem that Turgenev, in his representation of Russian sectarians, anticipates what Bethea calls "a subgenre of the modern Russian novel," namely, "apocalyptic fiction" (p. 33).

29. See Richard Gustafson, *Leo Tolstoy: Resident and Stranger* (Princeton: Princeton University Press, 1986).

30. Brodskii, *Turgenev i russkie sektanty*, 3.

31. Ibid., 18.

32. See Peterson, "Hamlets and Hesychasts."

33. For details of the "pentecostal mood" with which the speech was received see Marcus C. Levitt, *Russian Literary Politics and the Pushkin Celebration of 1880* (Ithaca: Cornell University Press, 1989).

34. Russian intellectual history borrowed this presumed "Russian idea" from German romanticism, which proclaimed the *Germans* to be the most universal nation in the world.

35. Victor Terras, *Belinskij and Russian Literary Criticism* (Madison: University of Wisconsin Press, 1974), 96.

36. See *Dead Souls*, ch. 5; Terras, *Belinskij*, 29; Gogol's "Pushkin speech," and his 1932 article on Gogol.

37. Turgenev, *Polnoe sobranie sochinenii* 3:16.

38. Ibid.

39. Ibid., 18.

40. See footnote 3.

41. On Turgenevan notions of analysis versus synthesis see my "Bazarov pered sfinksom: Forma i dissektsiia v romane Turgeneva *Ottsy i deti*," *Revue des Études Slaves* 57, no. 3 (1985). In regard to the content-form relation, Turgenev was fond of merging myth and folklore (from all nations) with highly stylized *Kunstformen*, as in his late supernatural "Song of Triumphant Love." This pastiche of an Italian renaissance novella is based on a Grimm fairy tale, ("The Glass Coffin").

42. See footnote 11.

43. Turgenev, *Polnoe sobranie sochinenii* 3:355.

44. Ibid., 359.

45. As Bethea points out, by the first half of the nineteenth century, the steppe, "with its sprawling expanse and seemingly endless horizon line, became a metaphor for the openness and infinite possibility of Russian historical time." See Bethea, *Shape of Apocalypse*, 68. Pushkin's "proud steed" (in *The Bronze Horseman*) and Gogol's "fiery steeds" in his words had opened the path into "other dimensions."

46. Turgenev, *Polnoe sobranie sochinenii* 3:354.

47. Ibid., 355, 359.

48. Turgenev's Pushkin speech delivered on the same occasion as Dostoevsky's likewise dispensed with prophecy and therefore went relatively unnoticed.

49. A. Chicherin noted the narrator's ability *"stushevyvat'sia,"* as well as his enormous "receptivity." Quoted from Lebedev, *"Zapiski okhotnika"*, 16.

50. Like Pasternak's persona, the self-effacing narrator of *Notes* is a "sponge," absorbing the endless richness and variety of external reality into himself, subsequently "squeezing out" the transformed mélange in the form of art. See also the preceding footnote. Thus it is by not "foregrounding" oneself but by merging with one's surroundings to the point of mimicry that one may achieve genuine originality, as all Hamlets should note. The modest, yet highly original Hamlet of *Doctor Zhivago's* eponymous poem of course knows this well.

GLYN TURTON

Turgenev in the Critical Outlook of Henry James

> Turgenev is in a peculiar degree what I may call the novelist's novelist—an artistic influence extraordinarily valuable and ineradicably established.
>
> (*FON*, 228)[1]

The affection, affinity and reverence felt by Henry James for Turgenev, and the personal contacts through which these developed, represent one of the best attested and documented relationships between writers of different nationalities. The copious references to Turgenev in James's writings have formed the basis of studies of both their personal connection and the artistic influence of Turgenev's fiction on that of James.

Of these accounts, three deserve particular mention. The first volume of Leon Edel's *The Life of Henry James* (1977) provides a comprehensive record of their relations from the time of James's arrival in Paris in 1875 until Turgenev's death in 1883. Edel gives an evaluative summary of the apparent reasons for James's attraction towards the older Russian writer, emphasising the common factor of their exile in Paris, and the 'powerful ferment in the "provinces"' (Edel 1977, I: 436) of which, he suggests, they were both products. Though essentially biographical, Edel's account of the relationship of Turgenev with James offers, *en passant*, a highly condensed assessment of

From *Turgenev and the Context of English Literature* 1850-1900. © 1992 by Routledge.

the similarities of their respective themes and methods. Daniel Lerner's 1941 article, 'The Influence of Turgenev on Henry James', published in the *Slavonic and East European Review*, emphasises Turgenev's 'cosmopolitan, humanist aestheticism' as the main ground of affinity on which the personal relationship was founded. Patrick Waddington's study, *Turgenev and England* (1980), provides an exhaustive documentary record of those of James's contacts with Turgenev which appertain to England, shedding much light on the precise links between James and figures such as W. R. S. Ralston, Turgenev's English translator and publicist.

Because the facts are already so well documented, the present study does not attempt a comprehensive account of Turgenev's personal links with Henry James. Instead it is proposed to select only those biographical and documentary points of reference that will serve the main purpose of this and the following chapter, which is to make a fresh comparative assessment of their work. By viewing James and Turgenev in a single critical and historical perspective, I hope to explore not only questions of positive influence and affinity, but also areas of difference, which, I believe, are both governed by, and shed light on, the radically differing cultural situations of the two.

Such an assessment needs to focus upon the two areas of James's fiction and his criticism, particularly those three or four extended critiques of Turgenev that James wrote over a twenty-five-year period and which are the main testimony of his unswerving admiration for Turgenev as a human and artistic influence, 'extraordinarily valuable and ineradicably established'.

As a preliminary to that assessment, it is necessary to identify the important transatlantic literary context in which James's lifelong attachment to Turgenev developed in the early 1870s and to link it to that surge of interest in Turgenev among a small but influential circle of New England critics and writers whose main members were T. S. Perry, William Dean Howells, Hjalmar Boyesen and James himself.

The very earliest source of Henry James's enthusiasm for Turgenev lies, as Daniel Lerner has pointed out (1941: 29–30), in the admiration of his father and elder brother for the Russian writer. Lerner speculates that James's earliest reading of Turgenev may well have preceded his fifteenth birthday, cites the numerous laudatory references to him in the letters of William and Henry James Senior, and observes that 'Turgenev established himself firmly, as well as early, as a favorite in the James household' (1941: 29). When James embarked on his literary career in the 1870s, the 'favorite' immediately became a model, at times almost a totem, ardently recommended by the elder, and willingly accepted by the younger Henry James. In his autobiographical *Notes of a Son and Brother*, writing of the year 1872,

James warmly and nostalgically recalls his father's sympathy for his, Henry Junior's, 'fondest preoccupations', which were 'now quite frankly recognised as the arduous attempt to learn somehow or other to write' and quotes the following extract from a letter from his father at the time:

> I send you *The Nation*, though there seems nothing in it of your own, and I think I never fail to recognise you. A notice of Gustave Droz's Babolain (By T. S. P., I suppose) there is; which book I read the other day. This fumbling in the cadaver of the old world, however, only disgusts me when so unrelieved as in this case by any contrast or souffle of inspiration such as you get in Tourgueneff.
>
> (James 1956b: 408)

James readily agreed with his father's high valuation of Turgenev; the following year he completed his first critical appraisal of the Russian, sending it to his father for comment, and in 1874, during his visit to Europe, he wrote home proudly announcing his intention of visiting Turgenev at Baden (James 1974b, I: 458).[2] Plainly, for James, Turgenev was already the hero as man of letters, albeit in a somewhat un-Carlylean mould, and his pilgrimage to Europe in the middle 1870s had the Russian writer as its specific object of veneration.

But it is clear that James's admiration for Turgenev typifies the enthusiasm of a wider circle of New England literati, for by the early 1870s the prominent New England reviews under the direction of T. S. Perry and W. D. Howells had adopted his work as a criterion of excellence. He was commended as a model for what one might call the ideal of pictorial realism with a moral face, which Perry and Howells saw as the desirable basis for the practice of American writers and the taste of American readers. Turgenev's work was perceived as a golden mean that avoided both the vapidities of many English novels of plot and incident and the excessively cerebral approach of French fiction. It is during the early 1870s that the New England periodicals can be observed trying to establish a code of principles and practice for the novel, resting on the assumption that the genre has both moral and aesthetic functions. In so doing the American editors clearly hoped to safeguard the dignity and high seriousness of a literary form peculiarly susceptible to debasement by popular taste and careless practice. Turgenev's novels, realist in essence, pictorial and dramatic in method and moral in outlook, came to be used as a benchmark by which Perry and Howells in particular judged fiction, and they accorded him generous treatment and hyperbolic praise in their reviews. As Royal Gettmann has observed, 'The *Atlantic Monthly*...was studded with commendations of Turgenev, and the *Nation* brought him forward at every opportunity' (Gettmann 1974: 43).

It is evident that James's passion for the spirit and method of Turgenev's fiction must be seen in the context of the general enthusiasm of this small but influential group of American critics and writers. They were his friends, associates and correspondents, and with them he conducted a debate on the nature of the art of fiction, lasting—certainly in the case of his relationship with Howells—for many years. In its turn this general enthusiasm for Turgenev as an example of a realist, capable and worthy of being imitated, must be seen as typifying a new spirit of intellectual inquiry, a quest for new intellectual and artistic frontiers, prevailing among the circles that centred on W. D. Howells and the *Atlantic Monthly* during the early years of his editorship. The desire to establish and affirm the principle and methods of realism in fiction is one important aspect of a wider effort to define a moral, intellectual and cultural framework within which American thought and letters might thrive. Edwin Cady, editing Howells's criticism, has written of this period in terms of a post-Civil War New England impulse of renaissance:

> A decided newness in thought and sensibility, varying somewhat between generations and from person to person, of course, became epidemic in Howells's Cambridge circles and in his generation. To put the situation paradigmatically, everything intellectual history means by 'Darwinism' drove these minds towards the stance of agnosticism. As agnostics they turned away from supernaturalism, whether Hebraic or Platonic, towards forms of humanism. The resultant metaphysical and emotional tensions they resolved as pragmatism in philosophy and realism in art. As Henry Adams rejected the Unitarian optimism of the hereditary 'Boston solution', Howells, in company with William and Henry James, rejected the romantic idealism of his father and entered upon the newness.... From the heart of Cambridge as far as the eye of the age could see, in every intellectually respectable direction the newness flourished.
>
> (Howells 1973: 24–5)

Cady's assessment of this spirit of new departure in intellectual and artistic circles gives us the key to Turgenev's popularity with Howells, James and other New England advocates of realism, for in replacing the romantic idealism of an earlier New England generation, the younger men were sufficiently imbued with a sense of high seriousness not to want to throw out the baby of morality with the bathwater of idealism. Turgenev, possessed of a moral sense and a truthful eye, yet in no way transcendental in his vision, was a perfect example of a morally reponsible and emotionally responsive realist. He had, moreover, the distinct advantage of belonging to neither of the two Western European cultures from which Howells, at least, was keen to distance the new American realism.

It was in this climate of receptivity to Turgenev in particular, and to discriminating realism generally, that James's own enthusiasm for Turgenev was fostered before he left for Europe in the mid-1870s. The Russian academic, M. M. Kovalevsky, who visited both England and America during the last decade of Turgenev's life, noted that the Russian writer had 'even managed to create something of a little school among American novelists' (Petrov and Fridlyand 1969, II: 142).[3] In part, of course, the formation of Turgenev's American 'school' is attributable to the sensitive pride of an emerging culture, ready to look to anywhere but Western Europe for its models. Nevertheless, the New England critics did enunciate precise aesthetic grounds for their high estimation of Turgenev. These grounds, and the idiom in which they were expressed, were to characterise the aesthetic which Henry James himself developed in the course of his career as a critic and novelist. Thus, the analogy of pictorial art pervades the criticism of T. S. Perry in particular, while in both Perry and Howells such terms as 'the art of fiction', 'the air of reality' and 'the power of choice' recur.

In the opinion of Perry and Howells, the 'art' of Turgenev's fiction is manifested in three main characteristics of his work—the centrality of dramatically presented character, the absence of the apparatus of plot and melodramatic incident, and the unobtrusive and seemingly dispassionate narrative stance. Royal Gettmann has fully demonstrated the importance which the 'Turgenev enthusiasts' attached to these qualities of their master's work (Gettmann 1974: chapter 2), and I do not intend to duplicate the many quotations from the *Atlantic* and the *Nation*, which he uses as illustrations. To grasp the exemplary force which Turgenev's novels possessed for James's New England contemporaries, it is necessary only to quote a remark by Howells, written in the article 'My Favorite Novelist' in 1897 after his passion for Turgenev had been superseded by an even stronger admiration for Tolstoy:

> The business of the novelist is to put certain characters before
> you and keep them before you, with as little of the author

apparent as possible. In a play the people have no obvious interference from the author at all. Of course he creates them, but there is no comment; there can be none. The characters do it all. The novelist who carries the play method furthest is Tourgenief and for a long time I preferred him to any other.

(Howells 1973: 270)

Among American novelists it is James whom Howells considers the finest exponent of the 'play method' which he praises so highly in Turgenev. In his article 'Henry James, Jnr' for the *Century Magazine* of November 1882, he warmly commends James for his 'artistic impartiality' ('one of the qualities most valuable in the eyes of those who care how things are done') (Howells 1973: 66) and for the precedence given to character and situation over 'the moving accident' and 'all manner of dire catastrophes'. For Howells, James is the leader of a new school of American novelists, committed to the Turgenevan brand of sensitively discriminating realism, dramatic in method without being sensational in effects. It was particularly important for Howells to liberate the concept of fiction from both the 'deviant' tendencies of the present and the massive burden of the past—from the monumental, but inimitable examples of Dickens and George Eliot, as much as from the excesses of contemporary naturalism. If fiction could be claimed to be an 'art' with identifiable techniques, it followed that it could be learnt without undue reference (or deference) to the massively individual genius of Dickens, the intellectually exhaustive manner of George Eliot, or, for that matter, the idiosyncrasies of any notable writer of the previous generation. More than that, it could be practised just as well in the rarer cultural atmosphere of the United States as in Europe.

When he moved to Europe, James took with him both the concept of the 'art' of fiction and the idea of Turgenev as its exemplar. Throughout his life he was to regard Turgenev's work as the absolute epitome of his own aesthetic. But the Jamesian notion of the art of fiction carries with it, for all its commitment to 'the air of reality', an assumption of the ontological independence of imaginative literature. It is this assumption which reflects a fundamental difference in the cultural situations—and, therefore, in the artistic outlooks—of James and Turgenev. Moreover, it is a difference of which I believe James to have been quite unaware in his appraisals of Turgenev's writing. James believed that the artist enjoys an absolute freedom to reconstitute the facts of reality in a formal order that transcends life itself. By contrast, Turgenev possessed a strong sense of the historical determinants of culture. Insistent though he was up on the artist's right to claim impartiality amidst the heat of political controversy, Turgenev none the less recognised that 'there are epochs when literature cannot *merely* be artistic, there are interests higher than poetry' (Letter to Botkin, 29 June 1855, *Letters*, II, 282). I propose to focus upon this difference in outlook in order to add a contrastive dimension to the frequently undertaken comparative studies of James and Turgenev, and, additionally, to shed light on the difference between a politicised and a non-politicised culture.

The emphasis in James's aesthetic upon form, upon the autonomy of the novelist's imagination, upon the growth of a novel out of a picture of character, inwardly conceived—these may be construed, despite James's ostensible realism, as a form of crypto-romanticism. The difference between 'reality' and 'the air of reality' is three words and a wealth of arguably problematical meaning. The term 'the air of reality' may be read as no more than a corrective to, and a refinement of, naïve notions of mimesis, but it conceals a critical shift away from that sense of art's subordinate and relative relationship to life, in which the realist movement had its origins. Of course, the phrase is intentionally ambivalent and might be seen, quite simply, as an assertion of the axiom that art is not life. But in James's aesthetic, I believe the concept of the air of reality is handled with a licence which moves the absolute centre of value towards art itself and away from the life it mirrors.

There is much evidence to suggest that James lived intensely, but vicariously, through and by art. 'It is art', he wrote, 'that makes life, makes interest, makes importance for our consideration and application of these things, and I know of no substitute whatever for the force and beauty of its process' (James 1970, II: 490). The notion that 'art makes life' leads to a certain epistemological ambiguity when it is combined, as it is in James's aesthetic, with ostensibly realist intentions. Arthur Mizener has written interestingly of what he terms 'the troubled uncertainty about objective reality' apparent in James's work (quoted in Gorley Putt 1968: 15). What Mizener speaks of is that elision between the act of observation and the phenomena observed which occurs in James's conception of the artistic process.

The following lines spoken by the narrator in *The Author of Beltraffio* (p. 8) illustrate the point:

> 'That was the way many things struck me at that time, in England—as reproductions of something that existed primarily in art or literature. It was not the picture, the poem, the fictive page that seemed to me a copy; these things were the originals, and the life of happy and distinguished people was fashioned in their image'.[4]

It is the sheer density of James's sense of things, what F. Gorley Putt (1968: 51) calls 'his vast, bland sensitivity to impressions' that renders problematical his use of terms such as 'the air of reality', for, in its very formulation, the phrase subtly evades the question of whether the artistically achieved 'air' relates subordinately or transcendentally to 'reality'.

We are here at the very heart of James's conception of his own fiction, and that of those writers of whom he approved. It is clear that in enunciating such criteria of the art of fiction as its right and power to select, to discriminate, to present without discursively explaining, James was in part undertaking an arguably legitimate defence of art against the relentless advance of scientific rationalism and its literary 'fifth column', naturalism. But James's insistence upon marrying artistic rights of imaginative subjectivity to the objectivist claims of realism becomes especially contestable when the artist's chosen *donnée* is historical or social forces. It is in such cases that doubt may be cast on James's requirement that the reader should take on trust his own assumption that causality is realiably, truthfully subsumed in fictional effects. To appropriate the facts of reality to serve as the furniture of the House of Fiction is one thing; to change them into adornments for the Palace of Art is quite another.

What illustrates this fundamental question of the method and manner of James's treatment of reality is the repeated use, throughout his criticism, of the analogy of pictorial art—to the point, almost, where one is inclined to think of him as believing that all art aspires to the condition of painting. James's insistence upon preserving the integrity of form, upon allowing the 'portrait' to stand by itself without discursive elaboration or moral commentary, is really an appeal not to tear open the canvas upon which the 'portrait' is 'painted', since both effect and cause are compressed, assimilated to the single pictorial dimension, the one surface on which they are portrayed.

It is in the light of his insistence on the art of fiction as the 'painting' of portraits that we should view James's objections to Tolstoy and his reservations about George Eliot. Ostensibly those reservations concern the absence of shaped form in such novels as *Middlemarch* and *War and Peace*, but in essence his objections are to any attempt to probe the achieved image, to create an art of three-dimensional relief in which effect is extended back to cause, a fiction more analogous to plastic than pictorial art and sharing its procedures with the human and social sciences. James's critical challenge to the form of *Middlemarch*—'If we write novels so, how shall we write History?' (*FON*, 89)—precisely encapsulates his uncompromisingly aesthetic conception of fiction. Nothing so suggestively illustrates the different approaches to character as portraiture taken by James and George Eliot as the continual, ironical play in *Middlemarch* upon the discrepancy between painted images and the reality of flesh, blood and emotion. Indeed, it might be argued that *Middlemarch*, deprecated by James for its lack of 'form', is as much a sustained illustration of the essential disparities between portraits done in oils and those executed in language as James's work is an appeal for the correspondences between the two.

This recurrent treatment of the novel by analogy with painting is the single most prominent identifying feature of James's critical writings and, notably, of that most influential of his pieces, 'The Art of Fiction' (AOF), in which he wrote 'the analogy between the art of the painter and the art of the novelist is, so far as I am able to see, complete' (pp. 50–1). In James's aesthetic it is not just content (idea) and form that are assimilated to each other, but also, by the processes of art, cause and effect ('A psychological reason is to my imagination an object adorably pictorial' (AOF, 64)). Such a process of assimilation may appear incontrovertible when confined to the psychological and emotional plane of meaning—James's finest dramatisations of moral conflict such as *Washington Square* and *Portrait of a Lady* bear out the author's view. But when the frame of reference of a novel is widened to take in historical and social forces, the question of whether and how 'the aspect of things' embodies their cause and origin becomes problematical. It is then that account must be taken of art as a determined as well as a determining activity.

The point I wish to make is that despite their very real similarities of method and process, Turgenev, by virtue of a difference in temperament, vision and, above all, cultural situation, had a keener sense than James of the manifestation of impersonal forces in personal lives and a stronger awareness that, although it might suffer outrageous injustice in the process, fiction had to be tried at the bar of history, as well as that of art.

Correspondingly, there is to be found in Turgenev a proportionately greater concession made to the determining power of historical reality over a writer's work than, I believe, James could ever have conceded. Throughout the nineteenth century Russia underwent a protracted political crisis, from which the personal destiny of its people could not be detached or abstracted imaginatively, any more then it could be freed literally. In writing about that 'rapidly changing physiognomy of Russians of the educated class' ('Foreword to the Novels', 1880; *PSS*, XII, 303), Turgenev was inevitably involved in creating 'pictures' of characters which were, at the same time, 'readings' of history, pictures picked out in relief from the ground of history. James's procedure was to seize upon a situation which was morally interesting and, even in a novel such as *The Princess Casamassima*, the theme of which is ostensibly political, to adjust and accommodate the sociopolitical focus to the personal drama inherent in that situation. James's response to the challenge of determinism is to transmute social and historical phenomena into moral drama in its emotional and psychological aspects. Turgenev, albeit with varying degrees of artistic success, chose to meet history on its own ground, but to counterbalance it with that profound, pessimistic sense of mortality which James found the only negative feature of his master's art.

I propose to illustrate this point in two ways. First, I shall compare what may be taken as the critical and artistic testimonies of Turgenev and James—the latter's 'The Art of Fiction' of 1884 and the former's foreword to the collected edition of his novels of 1880. To the best of my knowledge, such a comparison has not been undertaken before and I believe it sheds light on what is often assumed to be the complete affinity between James and Turgenev. Second, I shall examine James's critical writings on Turgenev, writings which, while accurately perceptive of many aspects of the latter's artistic method, nevertheless show James to be distinctly blind to other important tests of the Russian's artistic success—tests by which Turgenev was, and indeed expected to be, judged. At first glance, placed side by side, Turgenev's foreword and James's essay appear to share, as their central concern, a preoccupation with what Morris Roberts called 'the integrity of the artist's vision' (1929: 59). Both testimonies assert the unquestionable and inalienable right of the author to freedom from constraint and direction by agencies other than his own imagination. The apparent similarities go further; both Turgenev and James affirm the image, as apprehended by the artist, as the irreducible building block of fiction, and, by that token, proof of the inviolable nature of the artistic imagination.

But beneath this resemblance lies a fundamental difference of emphasis which amounts to a difference in conception and meaning. Running through Turgenev's foreword is an awareness of the extrinsic significance of the art of fiction, an acknowledgement—however 'free' the artist may be—of the way in which historical reality impinges upon imaginative writing. In James's essay, I find no such concession to the power of historical circumstance; for him the value of art is entirely intrinsic and his reaction to the question of what differentiates and what connects art and history is not to concede their interpenetration, but, by characteristic 'sleight' of style, to locate fiction within a hall of mirrors in which, no matter where you turn, alternative analogies, rather than direct, unmediated connections, provide the meaning of the art of fiction. Thus fiction is held by James to be at once analogous to painting and to history and, by implication, greater than either: 'It seems to me to give him [the novelist] a great character, the fact that he has at once so much in common with the philosopher and the painter; this double analogy is a magnificent heritage' (AOF, 22).

To insist upon this double analogy is to create an essentially reflexive proposition in which art appears as both subject and predicate. It is a proposition that can only hold if we admit the prior assumption upon which James's aesthetic is founded, that what the imagination seizes upon must be true (AOF, 51), and that the novelist competes with 'his brother the painter in rendering *the look of things, the look that conveys their meaning*' (AOF, 57; my italics).

James, writing in a culture in which the question of the relationship, much less the subservience, of art to historical and political life, had not assumed the acute and pervasive form that it has traditionally and historically had in Russia, perceived no ideological challenge to the view that 'the look' of a thing 'conveys its meaning'. By contrast, Turgenev was frequently arraigned, particularly by the younger generation of Russian radicals, for allegedly presenting in his novels a 'look' which did not convey the meaning of history, for failing to offer what they regarded as a faithful picture of the progressive forces subterraneously at work in Tsarist society. The hostile reception by young Russian radicalism of *On the Eve, Fathers and Sons* and *Virgin Soil* represented a challenge to the integrity of the artist's vision in politico-historical, rather than artistic, terms. In defending himself against charges of inaccuracy and betrayal, Turgenev, it is clear, felt obliged to insist, just as strongly as James does, on the primacy and prerogatives of the artist's imagination, but—and it is a crucial difference—to concede, far more than James is prepared to, the determining power of circumambient reality. In James's writings so much emphasis is placed upon the processes of receiving, collecting and selecting the impressions upon which the imagination feeds that the sense of the autonomous active power of the cause and origins of these impressions is frequently lost. Turgenev, challenged by hostile critics with the view that there is both a higher reality and a higher necessity than imaginative art, was compelled to argue his case in terms of a causation external to the artistic process.

Two sections in particular of Turgenev's 1880 foreword are of relevance to the point in question. In his opening remarks, making a vigorous response to those critics who have accused him of deviating from the direction he had first taken as a novelist more than twenty years earlier, he states that, on the contrary, he might be more justifiably accused of excessive consistency. He continues:

The author of *Rudin*, written in 1855, and the author of *Virgin Soil*, written in 1876, are one and the same man. In all that time I have striven, as far as strength and ability have permitted, conscientiously and dispassionately to depict and embody in appropriate human types what Shakespeare calls 'the body and pressure of time', and that rapidly changing face of Russians of the educated class, who have formed the predominant subject of my observations.

('Foreword to the Novels', 303)

Turgenev's use of the quotation from *Hamlet*, and his insistence upon the novel as chronicle, seem to me to represent a recognition of the power of actuality that is far less equivocal than James's perception and interpretation of the way in which the 'the novel is history'.

But it is in his conclusion that Turgenev in one sense most nearly approaches, and yet in another crucially differentiates himself from, James's position in 'The Art of Fiction'. After completing a self-justificatory commentary upon the conception and often hostile reception of each of his six major works and launching a counterattack upon the tendentiousness of recent criticism, Turgenev delivers a robust defence of artistic freedom:

Every writer, who has talent—which is, of course, a pre-requisite—every writer, I maintain, tries above all to reproduce, in a living and faithful form, those impressions which he has culled from his own life and that of others: every reader has the right to judge to what extent he has succeeded in this and where he has gone wrong: but who has the right to tell him which impressions are suitable for literature and which are not? If he is thoughtful, then he is right, and if he has not talent, no amount of 'objectivity' will help him....

Everyone is familiar with the saying: *the poet thinks in images*; the saying is indisputably true. But on what grounds do you, the poet's judge and critic, allow him to reproduce images of nature, of national life, of life in the raw (yet another of those wretched terms), while shouting 'stop!' if he should dare to touch upon something obscure, something psychologically complicated, even morbid—especially if that something is not a personal, individual fact but is instead thrown up by that self-same public and national life?...

Believe me, real talent never serves extraneous ends, it is its own satisfaction: it draws its content from the life that surrounds it; it is the concentrated reflection of that life; but it is just as incapable of producing a panegyric as it is a lampoon…. In the last analysis such things are beneath it. Only those who are incapable of doing anything better can submit themselves to a given theme or adhere to a programme.

('Foreword to the Novels', 309—10)

Turgenev's defence of artistic freedom appears to touch that of James in 'The Art of Fiction' at numerous points. Turgenev's insistence that 'every artist … tries to reproduce … those impressions which he has culled from his own life and that of others', that the artist may not be dictated to, appears close to James's statement that

a novel is, in its broadest sense, a personal, a direct impression of life: that, to begin with, constitutes its value, which is greater or less according to the intensity of the impression. But there will be no intensity at all, and therefore no value, unless there is freedom to feel and to say. The tracing of a line to be followed, of a tone to be taken, of a form to be filled out is a limitation of that freedom.

(AOF, 54)

Similarly, James's contention that 'we must grant the artist … his donnée, our criticism is applied only to what he makes of it' appears equivalent to Turgenev's 'every reader has the right to judge to what extent he has succeeded', while his quotation of the maxim 'every poet thinks in images' reminds one of the emphasis in 'The Art of Fiction' (and throughout James's criticism) on the literary imagination as inwardly visual.

But the essential difference between 'The Art of Fiction' and Turgenev's foreword is that the former is a defence of aesthetic freedom against artistic constraints, while the latter is a defence of artistic and imaginative freedom against ideological constraints. To James questions of art 'are questions (in the widest sense) of execution' (AOF, 65) and the artist, in striving to capture the 'air of reality', produces 'the illusion of life'; by an exquisite process, he '*competes with life*' (AOF, 57; my italics). For all that James insists on 'solidity of specification' as the 'supreme virtue of the novel', there is at work pervasively in 'The Art of Fiction' an underlying subjective aestheticism that foreshadows the preciosity of his last phase of writing, a stealthy if subtle translation, by processes of questionable logic, of the objective into the subjective, an assimilation of life to art: 'If experience consists of impressions, it may be said that impressions *are* experience just as they are the very air we breathe' (AOF, 57).

In James's aesthetic, the 'body and pressure of time', the 'surrounding life' of which art is the concentrated reflection, these solid points of reference, the fundamental determinants of fiction, upon acceptance of which Turgenev's artistic testimony is based, are vaporised into 'the very air we breathe', the 'airborne particles', the 'very atmosphere of the mind'. The difference is essentially between a conception of fictional art as synthesis, on the one hand, and as assimilation on the other, between art as absolute in value and transfigurative in effect, and art, as Turgenev came to see it, as conditional upon the historical moment and ultimately relative to time and death.

For although Turgenev may never have entirely lost the traces of romantic idealism and, in particular, Hegelianism which clung to him from that youthful 'headlong plunge' into 'the German sea' (*PSS*, XIV, 9), in the course of time the Hegelian idea of art as representing a higher reality than nature was superseded by the sense that permeates his mature work of the blind indifference of the cosmos to man and his works. The deeply pessimistic (and unquestionably autobiographical) fragment 'Enough!' of 1864 takes art to be subject to decay, like all other human artefacts. The disillusioned artist-narrator speaks of how he can endure the thought that beauty and art are relative rather than absolute, but he is driven to despair by the thought that art, like everything else human, is perishable:

> But it is not the relative nature of art that bothers me; it is its transience—its decay, its ruin—that disheartens me and makes me lose faith. Of course, at any given moment, you may say that it is stronger than nature because in nature there is no symphony by Beethoven, no painting by Rouisal, no poem of Goethe's—and it is only dull-minded pedants or dishonest fools who would claim art to be imitation of nature; but in the end nature is irresistible. She has no need to hurry, for sooner or later she will prevail. Unconsciously and unswervingly obedient to her own laws, she does not recognise art, just as she does not recognise freedom or goodness.... How can we poor humans, we poor artists, come to terms with this mute, blind force, which does not even celebrate its own victories, but goes relentlessly onward, consuming everything. How can we withstand the rude shock of these

endlessly and indefatigably oncoming waves, how in the end can
we believe in the significance, the value of those perishable
images which we, in darkness and on the very edge of the
precipice, fashion for a moment from the dust.

('Enough', *PSS*, IX, 119—20)

There is simply no equivalent in James to the unmitigated pessimism
of this view of art, no corresponding sense of the ultimate futility of all the
works of man, including the highest. For Henry James, art was a distillation
from, rather than of, life. For Turgenev, as we have seen, the reverse was true,
and thus art must ultimately perish from the same cause as life itself,
dissolved in 'the endlessly and indefatigably oncoming waves' of time.

When we turn to a consideration of James's writings on Turgenev, what
we find is a remarkable consistency and loyalty lasting over forty years—
consistency not merely in the level of enthusiasm, but in the qualities which
James continued to appreciate. Much of what James saw and praised in
Turgenev is there for the praising. Much of what James felt himself to have
in common with Turgenev was indeed common to the two. But, at certain
points and over certain aspects in his critical writings on Turgenev, James
errs, omits or stumbles in his judgement; at certain times he unwittingly
exposes differences in artistic outlook between himself and Turgenev. I
would submit that it is, in a sense, the evidence of limitations in his
understanding of the Russian novelist that constitutes the most interesting
aspect of James's lifelong devotion.

James's principal writings on Turgenev consist of the following pieces:
a long article entitled 'Ivan Turgeniew' for the *North American Review* of
April 1874, ostensibly a review of German translations of 'The Torrents of
Spring' and 'A King Lear of the Steppe', but in fact a survey and appreciation
of Turgenev's work as a whole; 'Ivan Turgenef's New Novel', a review of
Virgin Soil in its French form for the *Nation*, 26 April 1877; 'Ivan Turgenieff',
James's reminiscences about Turgenev written immediately after his death
and published first in the *Atlantic Monthly* of 1884 and subsequently in *Partial
Portraits (PP)*; a contribution to the *Library of the World's Best Literature* (New
York) of 1897 (reprinted in *FON*). Additionally, two pieces which allude to
Turgenev incidentally are of relevance—the preface to Scribner's Sons'
edition of *Portrait of a Lady* (1908) (reprinted in *The Art of the Novel* (*AON*; it
is to this edition that page references are given)); and James's 1877 piece,
'Daniel Deronda: a Conversation' (reprinted in *PP*).

We may enumerate those main features of Turgenev's art to which
James recurrently draws attention throughout his writings on the Russian

novelist. The most salient of these are: Turgenev's emphasis upon character portrayal and moral situation, rather than upon story or plot; his 'ironical' detachment; the quality of 'poetic' realism by which his work is distinguished and, as a corollary, its avoidance of the excesses of naturalism; his conciseness; the consistently impressive moral character of his heroines; his sensitive treatment of the theme of failure in his male characters; and, to James, the one blemish on his master's otherwise spotless record, his pessimism.

Of these aspects of Turgenev's work the one most often high-lighted by James is that of character and its 'morally interesting' potentialities as the germ of Turgenev's art. It is this that, among James's positive and accurate insights into Turgenev, deserves the closest attention, not simply because it is the cornerstone of his own art of fiction, but also because of Turgenev's invaluable usefulness to James at the height of his campaign in the middle 1880s to break down and break with the Anglo-Saxon habituation to novels of plot and intrigue, and gain acceptance for a more mature fiction judged by moral and psychological density and depth, rather than on more superficial criteria.

In his *North American Review* article (hereafter referred to as *NAR*), James goes out of his way to distinguish Turgenev's virtues from those of the British fiction with which his American readers might be expected to be more familiar, insisting that Turgenev has qualities which more than compensate for the absence of exuberant inventiveness and plot interest of Scott, Dickens or George Eliot (*NAR*, 330). 'His figures', James tells his readers, 'are all portraits' (*NAR*, 331).

This feature of Turgenev's work is adverted to with redoubled enthusiasm by James in his memorial tribute of 1884, the date being of especial significance if we consider that it is the year in which 'The Art of Fiction' appears, incorporating James's efforts to disabuse readers and writers of the false distinction between incident and character. So while in 'The Art of Fiction' James is asking rhetorically 'What is character but the determination of incident? What is incident but the illustration of character?' (AOF, 58), he is, in the same year, to be found illustrating that axiom by reference to Turgenev's practice:

> The germ of a story with him was never an affair of plot—that was the last thing he thought of; it was the representation of certain persons. The first form in which a tale appeared to him was as the figure of an individual, or a combination of individuals, whom he wished to see in action, being sure that such people must do something very special and interesting.
>
> (*PP*, 314)

This observation James develops into a chastisement of Anglo-Saxon critics for their failure even to begin to grasp the need for a debate on the meaning and relative importance of plot and character in fiction:

> We have not yet in England and America arrived at the point of treating such questions with passion, for we have not yet arrived at the point of feeling them intensely, or indeed, for that matter of understanding them very well. It is not open to us as yet to discuss whether a novel had better be an excision from life or a structure built up of picture cards, for we have not yet made up our minds as to whether life in general may be described. There is evidence of a good deal of shyness on this point—a tendency rather to put up fences than to jump over them. Among us, therefore, even a certain ridicule attaches to the consideration of such alternatives. But individuals may feel their way, and perhaps even pass unchallenged, if they remark that for them the manner in which Turgenieff worked will always seem the most fruitful.
>
> (*PP*, 315–16)

Although James felt able to speak of the plot–character issue as a neglected one in Anglo-American literary life, his words may be construed more as a gentle taunt than a statement of fact. Kenneth Graham, in his study *English Criticism of the Novel, 1865–1900*, has drawn attention to the fact that the controversy over whether plot or character formed the basis of fiction did indeed figure in the columns of English periodicals at precisely the time of 'The Art of Fiction' and the obsequy to Turgenev, and that critics and reviewers tended to approach the questions more in a spirit of chauvinistic resentment at the impertinence of the 'American school' and their attempts to discredit plot than in one of real intellectual debate (Graham 1965: 107–10). Graham maintains that 'as part of the reaction against analysis in the eighties, came a resurgence of interest in "plot" and "incident"' and that 'reviewers everywhere seized on any evidence of plot contrivance of "strong situations" in a novel to hold it up as an example of heroic resistance to the foreign invasion.' His case is well substantiated by quotations culled from the *Quarterly Review*, the *Saturday Review* and *National Review*. Consequently, James's *Partial Portraits* article may be seen as more than a mere obituary, or even a critical appreciation of Turgenev; it may also be seen as a counterblow in his own campaign for acceptance of the novel of character and the pictorial method of presentation. It is, moreover, a blow struck by invoking the example of Turgenev's work at just the moment at which English appreciation of him was finally shifting from politico-historical to literary grounds.

James continued to pay tribute to Turgenev's method of composition, and to invoke it in support of his own method, until close to the end of his life. When, however, we consider James's final tribute to the fundamental place of character portrayal in Turgenev's art—the 1908 preface to *Portrait of a Lady*—we sense that a subtle shift in James's conception of character as organising principle has developed since the time of *Partial Portraits*. No longer is the choice one between primacy of plot and primacy of character, formulated in the robust terms of a choice between life and the unlifelike ('an excision from life or a structure built up of picture cards'); rather the blossoming of an entire novel from the seminal image of a character, or group of characters, is taken as simultaneously signifying, proving and endorsing the authority of the subjective imagination. By now, character, as the author apprehends it, 'is unattached, the image en disponibilité', a 'stray figure', and the novelist makes of it what he will rather by the laws of art than the laws of life. The entire emphasis of the preface to *The Portrait of a Lady* is on 'the kind and degree of the artist's prime sensibility, which is the soil out of which his subject springs' (*AON*, 45). It is as if, by having shown that 'the House of Fiction has … not one window, but a million' (*AON*, 46) and that the individual imagination of the artist is paramount ('Tell me what the artist is, and I will tell you of what he has been conscious'), James has performed a vanishing trick upon that 'spreading field, that human scene' on to which the windows of the House of Fiction are meant to give; or, at least, he has made vanish the question of what that spreading field objectively is.

Yet if we look at the remarks by Turgenev, recalled verbatim by James in the preface, remarks intended to justify and legitimise his own subjective mode of imaginative creation, we find, alongside an account of his pictorial or visionary conception of his subject, a strong acknowledgement of the life, the reality that provides the germ of all fiction:

> As for the origin of one's wind-blown germs themselves, who shall say, as you ask, where *they* come from? We have to go too far back, too far behind, to say. Isn't it all we can say that they come from every quarter of heaven, that they are *there* at almost any turn of the road? They accumulate, and we are always picking them over, selecting among them. They are the breath of life—by which I mean that life, in its own way, breathes them upon us.

They are so, in a manner prescribed and imposed—floated into our minds by the current of life.

(*AON*, 50)

The subtle but real difference of emphasis in the preface between Turgenev's words (as James recalls them) and James's own—between, on the one hand, a sense of the conceptual freedom of the imagination which none the less strongly and plainly acknowledges life as its source and, on the other, a sense of imaginative licence so strong that life itself is annexed to the 'artist's prime sensibility', 'the soil out of which his subject springs'—seems to me to be just that same difference of emphasis that distinguishes 'The Art of Fiction' from Turgenev's 1880 'Foreword'. Perhaps the key to this distinction lies in James's comments on Turgenev's nature in *Partial Portraits* and the article for the *Library of the World's Best Literature*. In the former James wrote 'his [Turgenev's] was not, I should say, predominantly, or even in a high degree, the artistic nature, though it was deeply, if I may make the distinction, poetic' (*PP*, 300), while in the article for the *Library* he wrote, 'he is of a spirit so human that we almost wonder at his control of his matter' (*FON*, 231). Coming from so supremely artistic a nature as James's, these comments on Turgenev convey clearly a sense of the distinctively different character of their two talents, a difference which, if James is to be believed, manifested itself in Turgenev's lukewarmness towards James's works:

> He cared, more than anything else, for the air of reality, and my reality was not to the purpose. I do not think my stories struck him as quite meat for men. The manner was more apparent than the matter; they were too *tarabiscoté*, as I once heard him say of the style of a book—had on the surface, too many little flowers and knots of ribbon.
>
> (*PP*, 298–9)

Of course, I am far from suggesting a radical misreading of Turgenev on James's part. On the contrary, many of the qualities of Turgenev's fiction to which James draws attention are indeed essential characteristics of his work. In an age still labouring under the burden of the three-decker novel, James was right to make Turgenev's economy a salutary example ('His great external mark is probably his concision' (*FON*, 228), 'He is remarkable for concision' (*NAR*, 332). He was right, too, to point to Turgenev's trick of anatomising character without killing the novel's vital form ('M. Turgeniew, with his incisive psychology ... might often be a vain demonstrator if he were

not so constantly careful to be a dramatist (*NAR*, 335)). Above all, he is right
to stress Turgenev's ability to invest his realism with a 'poetic' sense of pathos
('The element of poetry in him is constant and yet reality stares through it
without the loss of a wrinkle' (*FON*, 262)), and to insist upon his broad
impartiality and understanding ('a view of the great spectacle of human life
more general, more impartial, more unreservedly intelligent, than that of any
novelist we know' (*NAR*, 330)).

Nevertheless, there are aspects of Turgenev's work over which James
seems to me to err on the side of generosity. First, he is inclined to overrate,
to the point of serious misjudgement, the artistic success of Turgenev's
portraits of young women for, like Turgenev, James tended to favour
idealised images of youth, beauty and moral constancy in the female sex.
Second, as I have already suggested above, James judged 'portraits' by self-
validating standards of dramatic effectiveness, without due regard for the
accuracy of social or historical reference. Where Turgenev's novels claim
such reference, James takes their accuracy on trust. James devotes
considerable space in his writings on Turgenev to praise for the noble-
natured maidens of the latter's work whose function it is to expose, by their
strength of will, the tragic weaknesses of his male characters. In his *NAR*
article of 1874, James is most fulsome in his praise for this aspect of
Turgenev's fiction: 'It would be difficult to point, in the blooming fields of
fiction, to a group of young girls more radiant with maidenly charm than M.
Turgeniew's Helene, his Liza, his Katia, his Tatiana and his Gemma' (*NAR*,
329).

Clearly feeling Turgenev's virtuous women to be the aspect of his work
that will commend itself most to British and American readers, James is
ready to draw parallels with the maidenly ideals of both his native and his
adopted countries. He writes, 'these fair Muscovites have a spontaneity, an
independence, quite akin to the English ideal of maidenly loveliness' (*NAR*,
336–7), and later in the same article:

> American readers of Turgeniew have been struck with certain
> points of resemblance between American and Russian life. The
> resemblance is generally superficial; but it does not seem to us
> altogether fanciful to say that Russian young girls, as represented
> by Liza, Tatiana, Maria Alexandrovna, have to our sense a touch
> of the faintly acrid perfume of the New England temperament—
> a hint of Puritan angularity.
>
> (*NAR*, 340)

This high valuation of Turgenev's heroines James repeats in his 1897 article, stating that it is the 'question of will' which most exercised the Russian novelist, and, while his heroes exhibit the want of that faculty, his heroines more than make up for their weakness:

> But if the men, for the most part, let it go, it takes refuge in the other sex; many of the representatives of which, in his pages, are supremely strong—in wonderful addition, in various cases, to being otherwise admirable. This is true of such a number—the younger women, the girls, the 'heroines' in especial—that they form in themselves, on the ground of moral beauty, of the finest distinction of soul, one of the most striking groups the modern novel has given us. They are heroines to the letter, and of a heroism obscure and undecorated: it is almost they alone who have the energy to determine and to act.
>
> (*FON*, 232)

Morris Roberts, in his study *Henry James's Criticism*, instances James's predilection for Turgenev's heroines as evidence of that taste for moral refinement, amounting almost to puritan priggishness, which led James to an exaggerated dislike of the greater sexual and moral candour of the French novel in its Flaubertian and post-Flaubertian form:

> It is difficult to escape the impression that James's morality is sometimes only a genteel distaste for the uglier facts of life, and that his 'richness' of inspiration might upon occasion be more exactly described as purity of inspiration, as a kind of conventual fragrance which is the opposite of 'richness'.
>
> (Roberts 1929: 45–6)

Roberts, in passing, contrasts James's intense enthusiasm for Turgenev's women characters with the dislike of them on the part of Chekhov, otherwise an appreciative admirer of Turgenev's work. Chekhov's opinion, given in a letter to Suvorin of 24 February 1893, is indeed worth citing in full, for it explodes precisely that illusion under which James laboured—that Turgenev's heroines were not only the quintessence of real moral goodness, but also the quintessence of Russian womanhood:

> Except for the old woman in *Fathers and Children*—that is Bazarov's mother—and the mothers as a rule, especially the

society ladies, who are, however, all alike (Liza's mother, Elena's mother), and Lavretsky's mother, who had been a serf, and the humble peasant women, all Turgeniev's girls and women are insufferable in their artificiality, and—forgive my saying it— falsity. Liza and Elena are not Russian girls, but some sort of Pythian prophetesses, full of extravagant pretensions. Irina in *Smoke*, Madame Odintsov in *Fathers and Children*, all the lionesses, in fact, fiery, alluring, insatiable creatures forever craving for something are all nonsensical. When one thinks of Tolstoy's *Anna Karenina*, all these young ladies of Turgeniev's, with their seductive shoulders, fade away into nothing. The negative types of women where Turgeniev is slightly caricaturing (Kukshina) or jesting (the description of balls) are wonderfully drawn, and so successful, that, as the saying is, you can't pick a hole in it.

(Chekhov 1966: 242–3)

There is no doubt that Chekhov's is the more accurate judgement, that James is the victim of the idealising tendencies of his own imagination, and that, as Roberts suggests, an element of either prudishness or fear finds its way into his preferences. That his last suggestion is true seems borne out by the ambivalence and reservations on James's part when he speaks of one of Turgenev's women characters who is truly convincing in her demonic powers of seductiveness, Madame Polozova in 'The Torrents of Spring'. Of her James writes:

Madame Polosow, though her exploits are related in a short sixty-five pages, is unfolded in the large dramatic manner. We seem to be in her presence, to listen to her provoking bewildering talk, to feel the danger of her audacious conscious frankness. *Her quite peculiar cruelty and depravity make a large demand on our credulity; she is perhaps a trifle too picturesquely vicious.* But she is strangely, vividly natural, and our imagination goes with her in the same charmed mood as with M. Turgeniew's other evil-doers.

(*NAR*, 348; my italics)

It is difficult to know what James means by the apparent contradictions of a 'large demand on our credulity' and 'strangely, vividly natural', just as it is hard to concur with his reservations about the seduction of Sanin away from the virginal Gemma by Madame Polozova ('Not without an effort, too, do we accept the possibility of Sanin's immediate infidelity to the object of the pure silk passion with which his heart even yet overflows' (*NAR*, 348)). These are the words of a 'romancer' (to coin James's own term), rather than a realist. Even if we admit the motive of concern for the sensibilities of his New England readers, we are still left with the impression that, in the matter of women and sexual relations, it remains questionable how much the James of 1874—like his heroine, Maisie—really knew.

At the same time James's judgement of Turgenev's heroines may, to a significant degree, be attributed to the thorough going aestheticism of his outlook, his belief that 'as the picture is reality, so the novel is history'. This conviction—that the aspect of things, as that aspect is manifested in the author's imagination, yields their truth—informs the whole of James's writing on Turgenev. So, trusting implicitly to Turgenev's imaginative eye, James is capable of erring critically at those points where the former errs imaginatively. Where Turgenev falters or fails in his imaginative apprehension of historical reality, James, with an apparently superficial acquaintance with Russian politics and society, is doubly prone to misjudgement. As a matter of principle, he takes the fictional picture as reality, and, in any case, knows little of the reality on which the picture is based. Two examples of James's writing on Turgenev—the review of *Virgin Soil* of 1877 and the critique of *Daniel Deronda*—illustrate the point.

James's review of *Virgin Soil*, published in the *Nation* in April 1877, contains a number of interesting features, not the least of which is a striking discrepancy in its judgement of the novel from that made in private to T.S. Perry in the same month. On 18 April 1877, James wrote to Perry:

> I send you herewith the cheap (and nasty) reprint of *Terres Vierges* which John Turgenieff lately sent me—having kept it only to review it. The nice edition is not yet out. The book will disappoint you, as it did me; it has fine things, but I think it the weakest of his long stories (quite) and it has been such a failure in Russia, I hear, that it has not been reprinted from the Review in which it appeared. Poor T is much cut down. He wrote me the other day: 'La fortune n'aime pas les vieillards' and the miserable prospect of war (which is all that is talked of here) won't cheer him up. I should not find myself able conscientiously to recommend any American publisher to undertake *Terres Vierges*. It would have no success.
>
> (James 1974b; II: 108)

By contrast, the review (to which James refers in his letter) is generous in its praise of the novel, containing no adverse criticism at all. The charitable explanation of this discrepancy (and, probably, the correct one) is that James wished to spare Turgenev's already sorely bruised feelings. In his private opinion, expressed to Perry, James is stating no more than Turgenev himself was ready to acknowledge—that the novel was indeed a failure and that it was so largely because Turgenev was physically and mentally out of touch with his native country and its current mood.[5] It scarcely seems possible that James's laudatory review was a disingenuous act committed for the purpose of continuing to cultivate his famous friend.

James's review of *Virgin Soil* is of interest also because of its acknowledgement of the problems of translation from so obscure a language as Russian and the question of erroneous or contaminated texts. To his credit, James, the stylist *par excellence*, consistently recognised the importance of accurate and sensitive translation and remained highly conscious of the problem up to the time of the Garnett translations of the 1890s:

> the impatience of his admirers was increased by the fact that—
> Russian scholars being few—the book would be for some time
> before the world and yet be inaccessible. *Nov'* [*Virgin Soil*]
> appeared in Russian during the first weeks of the present year;
> but it has been translated into French with commendable
> promptitude—with what degree of accuracy we are unable to say,
> though we may suppose that as the translation was made under
> the eyes of the author it is fairly satisfactory.
>
> (James 1957: 190)

Exactly twenty years later, when parts, but not all, of the Garnett translations were available, James expresses himself strongly and acutely on the question of Turgenev's great achievement, his style, and combines his remarks with what we may take to be an implicit plea for translations that approach, as closely as possible, 'his personal tone, his individual accent' (*FON*, 229).

But, notwithstanding that an element of well-meaning insincerity may inform the review, when it comes to the matter rather than the manner of *Virgin Soil*, we observe that it is to the 'morally interesting' aspect of a situation, its 'moral and psychological side', not to the accuracy and appositeness of its social and political reference, that James attends. However much James may be feigning admiration for *Virgin Soil*, we may be clear that the terms in which he discusses it typify his general tendency in the theory and practice of fiction to judge 'pictures' as if they had no 'frame'. When Donald Mackenzie Wallace, writing in 1905, added several chapters on the revolutionary movement to his famous work, *Russia* (which James reviewed in the same year as *Virgin Soil*), he reflected that by 1877 'propaganda and agitation among the masses were being abandoned for the system of terrorism' (Mackenzie Wallace 1905, II: 337).

As Richard Freeborn and others have pointed out, what is wrong with *Virgin Soil*, apart from its weak and schematic conception, is that it is simply not relevant to the state of the revolutionary movement in 1877, by which date long-delayed trials were bringing to an end the first idealistic and agitational phase of 'going to the people' and were ushering in the phase of terrorism which characterised the last three years of Alexander II's reign. *Virgin Soil*, set in 1868–70 and toyed with by Turgenev for at least seven years, was out of touch and out of date before it was published. It lacks precisely that solidity of specification which James prescribed as the *sine qua non* of realistic fiction. James, however, appears to take the picture offered on trust, and the comfort he takes in the innocuous (because incompetent) nature of the young *narodniki* seems ironical when one considers that it is expressed on the eve of a period of terrorist violence and government reaction:

> The outside world knows in a vague way of the existence of secret societies in Russia, and of the belief entertained by some people that their revolutionary agitation forms a sufficient embarrassment at home to keep the Government of the Czar from extending his conquests abroad. Of one of these secret societies M. Turgenef has given a picture, though it must be said that the particular association he describes hardly appears to be of a nature seriously to alarm the powers of order.
>
> (James 1957: 191)

In one sense, James's ignorance of Russia is simply that of most Westerners. Objective information on Russia was lacking, while the Russo-Turkish war and the anti-Russian sentiments it aroused disposed even the educated towards an uncritical acceptance of sources, fictional or otherwise.[6] Nevertheless, James's acceptance of the fidelity of *Virgin Soil* to the historical situation it treats is strongly reinforced by his personal tendency to view fictional material almost exclusively in terms of its potential for studies in character and dramatic situation. James conceives of the theme of *Virgin Soil* solely as 'the opposition of different natures convoked together by a common ideal' (James 1957: 191). Judging its subject purely on its potential as a 'morally interesting situation', James fails to recognise the way in which an ideological dimension, superimposed upon 'character', mars the work both as a study of characters under moral stress and as a study of a political movement. As Richard Freeborn points out in his study of Turgenev, 'the distinction which he makes between the aims of the populists and their persons was artificial, especially for a writer like Turgenev who had been used to accepting both the man and his ideas' (Freeborn 1960: 169). When James maintains that in *Virgin Soil* Turgenev achieves 'the union of the deepest reality of substance ... with the most imaginative, most poetic touches' (James 1957: 196), he is simply placing trust in his own maxim that 'as the picture is reality, so the novel is history'.

A similar judgement on Turgenev from '*Daniel Deronda*: a Conversation' affords further evidence that for James 'reality of substance' is subsumed in the artistically achieved image. In the 'conversation', Turgenev's *On the Eve* and its principal characters, Insarov and Elena Nikolaevna, are invoked by Pulcheria as superior artistic achievements to *Deronda*:

> PULCHERIA. Pulcheria likes very much a novel which she read three or four years ago, but which she has not forgotten. It was by Ivan Turgenieff, and it was called *On the Eve*. Theodora has read it. I know because she admires Turgenieff and Constantius has read it, I suppose because he has read everything.
>
> CONSTANTIUS. If I had not reason but that for my reading it would be small. But Turgenieff is my man.
>
> PULCHERIA. You were just now praising George Eliot's general ideas. The tale of which I speak contains in the portrait of the hero very much such a general idea as you find in the portrait of Deronda. Don't you remember the young Bulgarian student, Insaroff, who gives himself the mission of rescuing his country from its subjection to the Turks? Poor man, if he had foreseen the horrible summer of 1876! His character is the picture of a race-passion, of patriotic hopes and dreams. But what a difference in the vividness of the two figures. Insaroff is a man; he stands up on his feet; we see him, hear him, touch him. And it has taken the author but a couple of hundred pages—not eight volumes—to do it.
>
> THEODORA. I don't remember Insaroff at all, but I perfectly remember the heroine, Helena. She is certainly most remarkable,

but, remarkable as she is, I should never dream of calling her as wonderful as Gwendolen.

CONSTANTIUS. Turgenieff is a magician, which I don't think I should call George Eliot. One is a poet, the other is a philosopher. One cares for the aspect of things and the other cares for the reason of things. George Eliot, in embarking with Deronda, took aboard, as it were, a far heavier cargo than Turgenieff with his Insaroff. She proposed consciously to strike more notes.

PULCHERIA. Oh, consciously, yes!

(*PP*, 77–8)

As in the case of *Virgin Soil*, James's judgement here is partially defective. Insarov is not a vividly conceived 'picture of a race-passion', but a cipher, a wooden and unconvincingly 'heroic' creation, lacking credibility, like many of the characters in *Virgin Soil*, because he is made to bear the superimposed weight of an ideological destiny. By contrast the 'non-ideological' characters in *On the Eve*, Shubin and Bersenev, though secondary, have an inner reality that Insarov quite lacks. In the case of Insarov 'the aspect of things' is insufficiently grounded in 'the reason of things'.[7]

What these lapses of critical judgement illustrate is that James, generally speaking, had no real conception of the problems of correlating the moral drama of particular human predicaments with the wider movements of social history. A full sense of these problems—and a successful resolution of them—came to him only when, in the middle 1880s, his emotional involvement in the historical destiny of America became critical. The novel that came out of this crisis, *The Bostonians*, while owing far less thematically to Turgenev than other novels by James, seems to me the most Turgenevan, for its source is the same anxious engagement with the fate of the writer's native country that exercised Turgenev throughout his career. Superficially, *The Princess of Casamassima* owes most to Turgenev, but, as I hope to show, it dramatises personal destinies without dramatising the issues on which they are meant to hinge. It fails because it is conceived according to James's implicit trust in the picture-making matrix of the imagination. By contrast *The Bostonians* is a product, arguably unique in James's work, of the dialectical process whereby the 'body and pressure of time' and the artist's free but responsible creativity engage with each other, a response to, rather than an appropriation of, reality which wins as its prize the 'air' of that elusive but indispensable commodity.

NOTES

1. From 'Turgenev', *Library of the World's Best Literature*, XXV, reprinted as 'Turgenev and Tolstoy' in Henry James (1956a) *The Future of the novel*, ed. L. Edel, New York: Vintage Books.

2. Two editions of James's letters—one edited by Edel and one by Percy Lubbock—have been used.

3. The devotion of James's New England associates may be judged by the excited reaction of Howells upon being told by Hjalmar Boyesen that Turgenev wished to convey both his greetings and his praise of Howells's *Venetian Life* and *A Chance Acquaintaance*. See Howells's letter to Boyesen of 10 June 1874 in W. D. Howells (1979) *Selected Letters of W. D. Howells*, Twain, Boston: vol. 2, p. 61.

4. Unless otherwise indicated, all subsequent references to James's fiction are to the New York edition published by Scribner's Sons.

5. See Turgenev's letters to A. M. Zhemchuznikov of 17 March 1877, and to M. M. Stasulevich of 19 March 1877, in *Letters*, XII, ii, 113–14 and 115–16.

6. See 'Russia and Nihilism in the Novels of M. Tourgenief', *Blackwood's Magazine*, 1890, 127: 623–47 and 'Russian Revolutionary Literature', *Nineteenth Century*, 1877, 1: 397–416. Both articles recommend Turgenev as a source of information on a subject 'shrouded in so much darkness' (*Blackwood's Magazine*, 1890, 127: 647).

7. There may be several reasons for the failure of Insarov as a character study. One might be the difficulty Turgenev experienced in giving sympathetic embodiment to a nationalist cause not his own. Another may be that Insarov is too deliberatly an experimental attempt to create a 'Quixotic' character, undertaken to counterbalance the many 'Hamletic' types already drawn by Turgenev. Most likely cause of all is that Insarov was taken from an extraneous source—the Karatev diaries—and not originally conceived. For information on this last point, see the foreward to the 1880 edition of Turgenev's works reprinted in I. S. Turgenev, *Polnoe Sobranie Sochinenii* (*PSS*), XII.

DENNIS WALDER, GLYN TURTON,
AND PAM MORRIS

Reading
Fathers and Sons

INTRODUCTION
BY DENNIS WALDER

So far in this book we have been concentrating on novels written in English. However, many people feel that the realist novel reached the peak of its achievement outside Britain, and in particular in mid-nineteenth-century France and Russia. The writings of Honoré de Balzac, Stendhal, Gustave Flaubert, Fyodor Dostoevsky, Leo Tolstoy and Ivan Turgenev, to name but a few of the most widely read, deserve attention in any serious account of the genre. In terms of our overall strategy of using detailed 'readings' of a few significant texts to raise the important issues, it seemed a good idea to take as a European text a novel by Turgenev, the first Russian writer to enjoy an international reputation. Turgenev was honoured even more in France, England and America to begin with than in his homeland. Henry James called him 'the novelist's novelist'. As James went on to suggest, Turgenev's achievement was above all as a creator of character, 'character expressed and exposed' ('Turgenev', in Kettle, *The Nineteenth Century Novel*, 1981, p.173). What better text to look at than *Fathers and Sons* (1862)—or

From *The Realist Novel*, edited by Dennis Walder. © 1995 by The Open University.

Fathers and Children, as it is sometimes translated—the novel containing Turgenev's most famous character, Bazarov the nihilist.

The alternative titles raise the issue of translation. The fact that many English novelists influenced by Balzac, Turgenev and other European authors have been unable to read French or Russian (or German, Spanish or Italian) does not seem to have presented a problem. Nor do we as readers need to be limited by purist objections to reading novels other than in the originals. Of course, something of the original is lost when a literary work is read in translation. Novels, like plays or poems, are made up of deliberately chosen words in a particular order, and to alter any of this will alter the meaning. However, as Ian Watt and others have suggested, realist novels as a genre tend to use language in a way that is typically more referential or 'transparent' than poems, and perhaps plays as well, so that translation may produce less alteration. At the same time, we should not forget that what we are reading *is* a translation, and that some adjustment has been made to it.

To a degree, this is true even of novels written in English: they are written in the language of their own time, and we sometimes have to be especially sensitive to this. We should check the notes, for example, when we come across an odd or unexpected usage. The danger is always that we will not notice words that have a familiar meaning but carry a different nuance. An example of this is the reference to Covent Garden in volume II, chapter XV of *Great Expectations*. This would have signified an area of ill-repute and prostitution to contemporaries, although now it might seem a quite innocent place for Pip and his companions to have visited.

As Richard Freeborn, translator of the 1991 edition of *Fathers and Sons* cited throughout this chapter,[1] points out on p.xxviii, there have been many translations of this book, 'but the first worthy translator of Turgenev into English was Constance Garnett', in the 1890s. Freeborn's own translation into a more modern idiom contains some surprising and perhaps clumsy usages. The first of these appears on the first page, where he has the servant Peter sound like an old black retainer from the American South, addressing the landowner Kirsanov as 'sah', rather than 'sir', as in earlier translations. Freeborn is one of the first translators to have had the good fortune to look at Turgenev's working manuscript, presumed lost until recently, as an aid to producing his version. Whilst the Garnett translation sounds to anyone who is not a Russian specialist more authentic nineteenth-century prose, it is inevitably less accurate, which is why we have chosen the Freeborn version. In the discussion that follows, the issue of translation is not referred to, but you should not forget it, especially when considering any quotations from the text of the novel.

The first part of the chapter, taking up the thread of this book so far, offers a 'reading' of *Fathers and Sons* that considers what makes Turgenev a realist writer. There is no single, straightforward answer to this question, but the importance of character, and especially the idea of character as 'type', is central to both the aim and the effect of his fiction. This emphasis produces a kind of realism that raises its obvious historical connection 'to the level of universal human concerns'. The difficulty about finding universality in a novel so obviously engaged, from the first sentence onwards, with contemporary reality—or, to be more precise, with a representation of contemporary reality—is that it may lead us to accept as true and permanent what is actually socially determined, and therefore may be changed.

The chapter goes on to look at what struck the first readers as highly topical—the account of new intellectual movements of the time. This too, through Turgenev's ability to excite our sympathy for his people and their problems, leads us to face a 'realistic' vision of life, in which the capacity for self-knowledge is tragically contradicted by the capacity for error.

Finally, the last part of the chapter explores one of the most interesting ways in which *Fathers and Sons* can be seen to be vigorously involved in contemporary issues, that is, in the link between the representation of women in the novel and the turmoil of 1860s Russia. Most readers find Turgenev's depiction of women remarkably effective, even if they seem more static, more 'symbolic', than his male characters. The question is: how does this function in relation to the overall impact of the novel? Does the apparent 'break' in surface realism—for instance in the rather strange yet suggestive depiction of Anna Odintsova—operate in any way like the characterization of, say, Estella in *Great Expectations*, telling us something on a deeper level about the society in the novel? The relative openness of the Russian novelist about sexuality is striking when compared with contemporary English fiction, as is the sense of debate about serious issues. Both features enable us to see a larger horizon for the genre of realist fiction than was perhaps apparent before.

TURGENEV AS A REALIST WRITER
BY GLYN TURTON

Fathers and Sons, now generally regarded as one of the greatest of nineteenth-century Russian novels, was, in its own time, highly controversial. It could hardly have been otherwise, since the arguments and conflicts enacted in the book stem from the profound political crisis that characterized nineteenth-century Russian society (about which I will have more to say in a moment).

The depiction of fictional character in Russian literature at this time almost always made an ideological statement about a whole society. It is useful to compare English literature of the same period. In this country, the 'condition of England' question as it was called was debated by Thomas Carlyle, Charles Dickens, Mrs Gaskell and others of their generation with no less passion than Turgenev and his contemporaries brought to the issue of Russia's destiny. However, the English literary debate about the state of the nation was articulated in terms of social improvement and reform, whilst the nature of the Russian political system was so reactionary that any imaginative critique of Russian society was potentially revolutionary. It is not difficult to see how the character of the iconoclastic country doctor, Bazarov, committed to denial and destruction as prerequisites of progress, could become a focus of heated ideological dispute.

I want first to relate the figures created by Turgenev in *Fathers and Sons* to certain general questions of character and type in realist fiction. As noted in Chapter One, 'character is difficult to talk about technically or critically' (p.13). In recent discussion about character in fiction, the prevailing tendency has been to question 'naïve' assumptions of a direct correspondence between actual human beings and imaginary ones. This has been part of a wider trend in modern literary theory, which has questioned the straightforward notion of the fictional text directly referring to real life. Such an approach may have its value: by abstracting the text from its context, it is possible to bring to light ambiguities or contradictions never intended by the author and which may even conflict with his or her position. However, this trend also has its limitations, particularly when you try and apply it to a text so historically specific as *Fathers and Sons*. One way of overcoming this is to argue, as the critic A.D. Nuttall has argued, that we should think of texts not as directly transcribing reality but as offering 'hypothetical cases', or versions of, reality that seem probable by comparison with reality (*A New Mimesis: Shakespeare and the Representation of Reality*, 1983).

The construction of hypothetical cases which may be subject to the test of comparison with contemporary reality suggests precisely the process in which Turgenev apparently felt himself engaged in his writing. In the foreword to the 1880 collected edition of his work, he declared his principal purpose as a writer to be 'consciously and impartially to depict and embody in suitable types both what Shakespeare calls "the body and pressure of time" and that rapidly changing physiognomy of Russians of the cultured stratum, which has been preeminently the object of my observations' (*Polnoe sobranie sochinenii i pisem*, 1960–88 edn, vol. XII, p.303). This highlights the nature of

Turgenev's realist conception of fictional art: he speaks of his objective being to embody the spirit of the age in 'types'.

In one sense, Turgenev is simply articulating what must be the aim of any realist writer in any culture. We all of us bear the imprint of the society in which we live, so that a writer who wants to give an account of 'things as they are' must balance the individuality of characters against their social identities. Henry James took his lead from Turgenev when he insisted in 'The art of fiction' (1884) that the realist writer must select from reality but ensure that the selection made is 'typical'. In constructing individuals who were also representative of classes, groups and attitudes, Turgenev was greatly assisted by the rigidly stratified and relatively undiversified nature of nineteenth-century Russian society. The strict division of the greater part of the population into landowners and serfs—the owners and their human property—and the moral problem that this division posed are issues that permeate the themes of *Fathers and Sons*. Thus, it is worth noting that the first thing we learn about the first character to appear in the novel (Nikolai Petrovich Kirsanov) is that he is a landowner who is speaking to a servant.

One of the most impressive features of *Fathers and Sons* is the way in which Turgenev integrates questions of far-reaching social importance with the delineation of individual human personalities. The scope of the issues covered is extremely wide; the sense I am left with after reading *Fathers and Sons* is of an extraordinary inclusiveness, of specific historical events raised to the level of universal human concerns. The key to his approach is *concentration*. This novel, like his others—and in sharp contrast to those of many of his contemporaries in Russia and abroad—is limited in scale. At the outset of his career as a novelist, Turgenev experienced some anxiety about his predilection for the short novel form, wondering whether his apparent inability to compose a novel on the grand scale might be considered a weakness in his repertoire as a writer. Such fears were groundless: Turgenev made the short novel form his own, relying essentially upon a dramatic technique that gives his fiction, at its best, both immediacy and credibility.

However, the dramatic force of *Fathers and Sons* comes not just from the restricted scale of the fiction, but from the combined effect of concentration at several levels. Let me explain what I mean by this. First, the number of principal characters is limited, affording maximum narrative control and the ability, even within a short book, to shape a sense of the individuality of each figure presented. Second, the predominant setting, that of the provincial country house, acts to confine and so to heighten the emotional and intellectual tensions of the novel. Third, the critical interplay of character, upon which most novels rely for their interest, largely derives in

Fathers and Sons from the extensive use of dialogue. A good example of the importance of dialogue is to be found in chapter 10, where the exchanges between 'the fathers' and 'the sons' encapsulate the fundamental conflicts of temperament and ideology that shape the narrative as a whole. Turgenev's use of dialogue intensifies the reader's sense of the human dynamics that the fiction describes, giving the impression that the characters, once visualized by their creator, have assumed a momentum of their own. This is something that Turgenev repeatedly insisted *was* the case, whenever he was accused by the representatives in real life of either 'the fathers' or 'the sons' of travestying their generation.

Later in this part of the chapter I shall examine the relationship between characters in *Fathers and Sons* and their multiple significance—as individual persons, as social types and as human archetypes. First, though, it will be helpful to consider a specific example of Turgenev's method of presenting character.

In the short first chapter of the novel (pp.3–6), how does the author seek to establish the authenticity of the figure he is introducing, Nikolai Petrovich Kirsanov? What realist strategies are evident in the narrative account of Kirsanov?

Discussion

None of the techniques that Turgenev uses to establish a sense of Kirsanov and his background could in itself be called sophisticated. However, the method overall is effective. The narrative uses a moment of enforced inactivity in the present life of Kirsanov as a kind of fulcrum on which to balance the character's significant past and his immediate future. This establishment of a 'life perspective'—the conferring upon a fictional figure of a described past, a briefly dramatized present and a future latent in the narrative about to unfold—is the opening move in what we realize is the realist transaction between writer and reader.

The voice of the third person narrator in the narrative ('We will acquaint the reader with him', p.3) is open acknowledgement of its fictiveness. However, this is counterbalanced by the provision of the social history in which Kirsanov's personal life is embedded as well as by an indication of the key to his individual nature. You will have noticed that time and place are carefully specified, current social and political change alluded to (the newly emancipated house-serf, Peter; the recent reform of the estate) and that the whole way of life of the gentry class is encapsulated in the brief history of Kirsanov. Within these historical and biographical frames, Turgenev intimates Kirsanov's dominant characteristic—his strongly emotional nature and his capacity for attachment to loved ones. Emphasis upon this trait is in turn used to implant in the reader's mind the novel's central theme—the relationship between fathers and sons. The intense fondness of Kirsanov for his son is in implied contrast to the remote, spartan attitude of his own father towards him.

In analysing the realist strategies of the chapter, we might note, as well as this use of historical and personal detail, the positioning of characters' inner emotional lives in relation to an indifferent external world, which gives compelling depth to the narrative. The poignant truth that human and animal life goes on regardless of the sufferer in its midst is suggested by the feeling of the whole of chapter 1, and in particular as Kirsanov experiences the commingled emotions of pride in his son and sorrow that his wife is not there to share it with him. Hope and regret meet in Kirsanov's thoughts of his young son and his dead wife, reinforcing the strong sense of the opening chapter as a moment suspended between past and future. The pathos generated by Turgenev's account of this moment is intensified by the keenly observed details of the physical and animal phenomena around Kirsanov, all of them heedless of the intensity of his experience. As throughout Turgenev's work, nature appears to remain impassive, and impervious to the inner life of human beings.

At one level it is simply the isolating discontinuity between human feeling and the non-human world that registers; at another it is the consonance of the character's emotional state with the images of oppressive heat and listless torpor, creating a mood of languid melancholy, which affects us. This reminds us, perhaps, of our human capacity to see our subjective state mirrored in the world around us. In any case, the distillation of distinct, powerful moods is a notable feature of nineteenth-century Russian writing; it occurs particularly commonly in the stories and novels of Turgenev and in the stories and plays of Anton Chekov. I think that we should take Turgenev's frequent recourse to mood as a fictional device as a mark of his realism, since it is in mood, or atmosphere, that we may be said to experience in potent form a sense of our own reality in relation to the world.

CHARACTER AND TYPE IN *FATHERS AND SONS*

In order to understand fully what Turgenev achieved in *Fathers and Sons*, it is necessary to know that it represents the culmination of his project of depicting 'the rapidly changing physiognomy of Russians of the cultured stratum'. It was preceded by three short novels—*Rudin, A Nest of the Gentry* and *On the Eve*. In all of these, written between 1856 and 1860, Turgenev explored the same question: what effect does Russia have upon educated men and women of exceptional abilities—and what effect can they hope to have on Russia? In working through this question, Turgenev adopted for himself definite forms of classification or hypothetical 'case study' (to adapt Nuttall) in relation to which his characters might be understood. One such 'case' was gender; another was age-group or generation; yet another was the crucial distinction among Russia's intellectual community between westernizers and Slavophils, that is to say, between those who believed in western European solutions to Russia's problems and those who believed in Russian ones. To this list may be added Turgenev's half-literary, half-psychological theory of the essential polarities within human personality, what he used to call the Hamletic and the Quixotic. He understood these terms to refer to the predominance in the personality either of a person's own ego (Hamletic) or of some received ideal or principle (Quixotic). It is in *Fathers and Sons* that these forms of classification are interwoven most subtly to create a sense of the complexity of human individuality in society and the world.

As a result, conflict and affinity, similarity and difference may be seen occurring in different patterns between the characters, depending on the forms of classification Turgenev is considering. These varying patterns lend variety and depth to the central group of characters. For example, looked at in the light of their ideological beliefs, declared interests and age difference, Pavel Petrovich Kirsanov and Bazarov are diametrically opposed. Yet, if we consider them in the light of Turgenev's distinction between the Hamletic and Quixotic principles at work in human life, the two seem strikingly alike. Both claim adherence to firm principles—Bazarov to uncompromising materialism and Kirsanov to 'civilized' virtue—but both are also driven by a powerful sense of self. In other words, there is between them a temperamental affinity. This is strongly hinted at when the critical point in their stormy relationship, the duel, is over.

We may accept that the function of mainstream realist fiction, from Jane Austen onwards, is critical and educative, that is, it aims to teach a moral by dramatizing the lives of human beings who are in the process of (often painful) learning about themselves and others. At the same time, in any mature work of realism there are limits to the extent to which both the fictional character and the reader can be educated, since human behaviour may be considered as much a matter of compulsion as it is of control, of irrationality as of reason. One of the strengths of Turgenev's way of writing is that it embodies and projects knowledge of this view in its delineation of character. As the nineteenth-century realist novel developed, plot tended to be replaced by the drama of consciousness. *Fathers and Sons*, with its minimal plot, proceeds in terms of the conflict of ideas, the clash of temperaments and the consequent shifts in perception, or re-evaluations, that the characters undergo. In this sense, it may be thought of as defining a stage on the route from conventional 'plotting' to the interaction of characters' consciousnesses more obvious in late, even modern fiction. What examples can you find in the novel of changes in, or increased perception, as experienced by characters in the course of their development?

Discussion

There are numerous points at which one or other of the central characters experiences an illumination, an enforced reappraisal of themselves in relation to others or vice versa. One such that occurs to me takes place in chapter 11 when Nikolai Petrovich Kirsanov, an inveterate day-dreamer, is seated alone in the garden, attempting to restore his conception of the world as a place fit for beauty and sentiment, a conception that has been undermined by Bazarov. He does so by entering the bitter-sweet world of his memories, only to be jolted out of it by the voice of Fenechka, his mistress; his attitude towards her reminds him sharply and unavoidably of Bazarov's strictures against class-consciousness (p.69).

What such unasked for moments of insight do (and they are quite frequent, occurring with other figures in the novel) is allow the reader to experience, vicariously, the intensity of altered consciousness. Another example is provided when Arkady is suddenly made aware of 'the entire limitless depth of Bazarov's conceit' (p.129) by the latter's expression of contempt for Sitnikov and his kind. This is surely a milestone on the way of Arkady's withdrawal from Bazarov, a withdrawal that quickens after the violent argument between the two in chapter 21. It remains then for the degree of their separation to be highlighted by Katya (p.201), when she characterizes Bazarov as untamed and Arkady and herself as hand-reared.

Another illumination occurs in one of the most poignant moments in the novel. When Anna Sergeyevna Odintsova visits Bazarov on his death-bed, she is horrified by the sight of his disease-wracked body, and the horror is compounded by the sudden, piercing realization that 'she would not have felt such terror if she had really loved him' (p.236). This moment of realization does more than just set the seal on Odintsova's feelings for

Bazarov; it also powerfully reinforces the dominant (and limiting) trait of her character, namely her ultimate inability to allow her composure to suffer disturbance.

The instincts of both the dramatist and the chronicler were strong in Turgenev and his work illustrates particularly well the way in which 'showing' and 'telling', that is, forwarding the story by means of dialogue or by means of narration, combine in the novelist's art. The conjunction of dialogue and narration occurs most obviously in such moments of revelation, in which characters are made to experience insight, and we as readers to experience a corresponding insight into character.

BAZAROV

It requires little justification to devote a separate section of this chapter to Bazarov, since he is so dominant in the text and so crucial to our understanding of its scope and purposes. More than that, the case of Bazarov vividly illustrates one of the most important aspects of the development of literary realism in the mid to late nineteenth century, already hinted at: the shift in emphasis from plot to character. Character came to be conceived before, and to take precedence during writing over, plot. However, the idea of 'character as destiny' that developed raises questions about the extent to which individual lives can really be thought of as governed by material and ideological factors, by the nature of the historical 'type'.

I discuss Bazarov in the context of history later in this chapter. For the moment, it should be noted that Turgenev's account of the way in which he was conceived conforms exactly to the process outlined above (pp.169–70) of basing fictional type on character derived from observation. Some years after the publication of *Fathers and Sons*, Turgenev, in his essay 'Apropos of *Fathers and Sons*', wrote that he

> never attempted to 'create a figure' unless I had a living character
> rather than an idea, to whom appropriate elements were gradually
> added and mixed in. Since I do not possess a great deal of free
> invention, I always needed solid ground on which I could step firmly.
> That is precisely what occurred with *Fathers and Sons*.
>   (*Fathers and Sons*, 1989 edn, p.169)

Turgenev went on to speak of the real-life model for Bazarov as being a young provincial country doctor who had impressed him, although we should note that three individuals were also named as the basis for Bazarov in the author's preliminary sketches (see *Fathers and Sons*, 1991 edn, p.248).

The historical and cultural significance of Bazarov is most often related to the character's self-proclaimed nihilism, the denial of all received values and a belief only in the liberating potential of scientific materialism. The fact that Bazarov's name has become synonymous with nihilism may have lessened the appreciation of his complexity as a figure. Whilst at one level of the fiction he is the advocate and exponent of a single, uncompromising, revolutionary doctrine, at another he represents a cluster of ambiguities and contradictions in which are combined some of the essential strands of both Russian and European cultural history in the modern period. Yet we may agree that Bazarov is a convincing product of imaginative realism as a result of the author's successful layering of type and archetype, the local and the universal, in the construction of his character.

When the novel was first published, it was easy for Russian readers to see in Bazarov a familiar two-faced model of Russia's history, with its conflicting yet combining forces of modern western enlightenment and medieval, Asiatic savagery. Russia's unstable oscillation between a sense of superiority and one of inferiority towards the West was an unresolved tension, which Turgenev was attempting to work through in the central figure of *Fathers and Sons*, who brings together a mission to educate and an impulse to negate and destroy.

In addition to a purely national crisis of identity and purpose, there are quite elemental and perhaps even universal issues played out in the representation of Bazarov. First, there is the question of sexuality and sexual politics. The portrayal of women in *Fathers and Sons* is dealt with in more detail later in this chapter, but it is worth noting at this point the striking modernity of Turgenev's treatment of the relationship between Odintsova and Bazarov. Odintsova, whose name derives from the Russian word for 'single' or 'alone', is characterized as a privileged, intelligent and independent woman, whom circumstance and disposition ultimately inhibit from a committed sexual relationship with Bazarov. He is a self-proclaimed, upstart sensualist, whose disdain for sentimental entanglement is betrayed by powerful emotion. The novel's handling of sexual attraction in terms of personal and social power relations, force of circumstance and the complication of love by temperament seems to me notably realistic, in the sense that it is I believe of general human application—and ahead of its time.

The complex significance of Bazarov is further enriched if we 'read' him in the light of certain archetypes. One such—which it is intriguing to find in a novel so manifestly realist in conception—is that of the romantic rebel. From the late eighteenth century onwards, the isolated individual in revolt against social and political orthodoxies was a familiar figure in European literature. Typically, the rebellion was undertaken in the name of a higher ideal, such as imagination, individual liberty or the popular will. Bazarov's materialistic nihilism and his denunciation of romanticism as a form of illusion represents a partial inversion of this established pattern; he is a rebel whose belief in the need to annihilate is the cause to end all causes.

It is possible to enlarge the meaning of Bazarov's form of rebelliousness to fit a still wider frame—that of philosophical and moral absolutes—and his kinship with a much more disturbing variant of the romantic rebel, the Man-God, then becomes apparent. In place of the concept of rule by God, the scientific materialism and philosophical and religious scepticism of the nineteenth century left a vacuum. Arguably this could only be filled either by self-restraint on the one hand, or by the assumption of God-like powers of arbitrary self-assertion on the other. The struggle between reasoned restraint and the will to seize power is acted out in European literature from Mary Shelley's *Frankenstein* at the start of the nineteenth century through to the works of Fyodor Dostoevsky, Friedrich Nietzsche and George Bernard Shaw later in the nineteenth century and in the early twentieth century. It gave rise to a denial of moral constraint and compassion and to the exploration, by imaginative means, of acts of calculated amorality. Bazarov's sense of human insignificance in the cosmic order combined with his violent intellectual bullying of Arkady in chapter 21 place him precisely at this problematical intersection of science, philosophy and morality in imaginative art. The conjunction of rational enquiry and willed destruction leads us to another paradox that Bazarov embodies—the coexistence of the roles of messianic liberator and demonic destroyer. I will discuss this dimension of Turgenev's most powerfully realized figure in the course of locating *Fathers and Sons* more specifically in its historical context.

THE HISTORICAL CONTEXT OF FATHERS AND SONS
BY GLYN TURTON

In speaking of the realism of Turgenev's novel, I have tended to emphasize its universality, the sense in which *Fathers and Sons* vividly illuminates the perennial concerns of all men and women. This is why the book has proved so enduringly popular. However, what struck its Russian readers at the time of its publication was its topicality, the way in which it focused, partly explicitly and partly by implication, on the burning issues of the day.

Fathers and Sons was published in 1862, just one year after the most momentous event in the history of nineteenth-century Russia, the emancipation of the serfs. At a stroke, the imperial decree liberating the peasantry from the gentry, whose lands they were obliged to till, loosened the entire structure of Russian society. The system of serfdom, which had developed gradually since the seventeenth century, rested on a strict pyramidic principle. The serfs laboured for the landed gentry and the gentry in turn served the omnipotent Tsar as bureaucrats, soldiers and (most important of all) agents of social control. It took Russia's calamitous defeat in the Crimean War and the accession of a more liberal Tsar, Alexander II, in 1856 to drive home the inevitability of reforming a semi-feudal system which had retarded Russia's economic development and corrupted the nation morally.

The events in Turgenev's novel take place just before the emancipation, at a point when landowners such as Nikolai Petrovich Kirsanov were being encouraged by the government to conduct experiments in economic partnership with their serfs in order to prepare the ground—literally—for wholesale reform (see pp.5, 11 and *passim*). However, this economic and social change did not carry with it any equivalent political reform; emancipation did not mean enfranchisement, either for the peasantry or, in any true sense, for the gentry class that had hitherto owned them. Master and servant alike remained 'children of the Tsar', with nothing remotely resembling the western European notion of civil liberties.

Before concentrating on how this historical situation pervades *Fathers and Sons*, it may be helpful briefly to consider the question of the relationship between realism and history in both its wider and its specifically Russian aspects. Politically repressive regimes bring with them censorship, and censorship, while it restricts artistic freedom, also confers on art enormous potential power. If a single version of the truth is affirmed by the state and all contrary accounts of reality are denied, a writer who persists in dissenting from the authorized ideology becomes a realist in a very special and important sense.

Turgenev's view of these matters had been formed during a literary apprenticeship which was served under the intensely reactionary regime of Alexander II's father, Tsar Nicholas I, whose censors imprisoned him briefly in 1852 for writing a eulogy upon the death of the great Russian novelist Nikolai Gogol. By the time Turgenev wrote his major works—the late 1850s and early 1860s—truth bearing had come to be seen as part of the mission of Russian literature, particularly prose fiction. In all that he said about his writing—and about *Fathers and Sons* in particular—Turgenev insisted that 'to reproduce the truth, the reality of life accurately and powerfully, is the literary man's highest joy, even if that truth does not correspond to his own sympathies' ('Apropos of *Fathers and Sons*', in *Fathers and Sons*, 1989 edn, p.171). This lofty commitment to truth derives partly from the influence of his friend and literary mentor, the critic Vissarion Belinsky, whose role in making Russian literature socially conscious in orientation was all important. It also stems from the way in which Turgenev's own temperament affected his view of the function of art. He was sometimes accused of lacking fire in his convictions, but he cherished one ideal to the point of passion—that of dispassionateness.

If to incur the annoyance of the most partial commentators at both ends of the political spectrum indicates impartiality, Turgenev's aim 'to reproduce the truth' may be regarded as fulfilled in *Fathers and Sons*. The novel divided critical opinion, and in particular the figure of Bazarov did so in a way that no fictional character in Russian literature has done before or since. The book acted as a 'lightning conductor' for all the pent-up political energies that began to circulate once Alexander II's social reforms—modest by western standards but in Russian terms dramatic—were under way. Young radical progressives, whose spirit Turgenev had sought to capture, varied in their response, but in general they accused him of travestying their zealotry in his portrayal of the curmudgeonly, sensual Bazarov. Conversely, conservative critics took the view that Turgenev had been too sympathetic to the forces of revolution in making his nihilist hero attractively superior to the other characters in the novel.[2]

These polarized reactions illustrate both how powerful and how problematical a self-proclaimed realist text can be in the highly charged political conditions of historic change. The years 1861–2 were just such a moment: the emancipation of the serfs was accompanied by serious student unrest in St Petersburg, the first signs of nationalist revolt against Russian rule in Poland and the circulation of revolutionary pamphlets in the capital. These events mark the beginning of the process of political disintegration that was to lead to the revolution of 1917. The impact at such a time of a novel whose central figure is committed to no other principle than that of denial and destruction can easily be imagined. The ability of realist fiction to engage with contemporary life, as opposed to the past, came to be seen as one of its most powerful attributes. In a potentially revolutionary situation, that power was intensely magnified. Writing of the early 1860s, Richard Freeborn observed that '[t]he role of the Russian nineteenth century novel as a chronicle and criticism of its time acquired at this point—on the eve of the emancipation of the serfs—a revolutionary dimension' (*The Russian Revolutionary Novel*, 1982, p.11).

This takes us to the heart of the question of how realist fiction relates to history. Realism in literature, when it deals with contemporaneity, is both documentary and critical. It gives an account of the norms of the time, but it also stands above them. Most realist texts simultaneously communicate a knowledge of the present as the present, and an understanding of the present as it may seem when viewed from the future. I want to try and illustrate this from *Fathers and Sons*.

The novel shows what is actual and intimates what is potential in a number of ways. One of these is in its handling of the question of political change in relation to social class. I referred earlier to the rigid stratification of mid-nineteenth-century Russian society into the vast mass of the dispossessed—the peasantry—and the landowners with their vested interest in the perpetuation of privilege. Few stood outside these categories, but those few were significant beyond their numbers. Bazarov belongs to that narrow layer of educated men and women whose fathers were not landowners but existed on the margins of the social structure, typically in occupations such as priest or doctor. Their absence of a stake in the existing system left such men—and, increasingly, women in the years that followed—free to act as the carriers, first, of explosive ideas and subsequently of explosives themselves. Turgenev's portrayal of Bazarov owes much to his observation of the ardent young intellectuals of the 1850s and 1860s, the successors to his own more liberal, reformist circle of contemporaries (see pp.xi-xii). At a more profound level, in focusing on Bazarov, who is without social affiliation, and his disturbing effect on 'the gentry', the author is dramatizing in microcosm the way in which the whole rigid, flawed edifice of Tsarist Russia might be brought down by the actions of a relatively few single-minded individuals. The prophetic force of this in relation to the Bolshevik Revolution of 1917 is clear.

Most remarkably, this intimation of what the intellectual might ultimately bring about in Russian history is combined in *Fathers and Sons* with a penetrating insight into the difficulties that type of individual would encounter in the short term. One of the things that distinguishes Bazarov from the gentry around him is his ability to talk to and win the trust of the common people (see p.53). He is proud of the fact that his grandfather ploughed the land, but claims to harbour few illusions about the peasantry. This ability to relate to peasants without idealizing them might seem to suggest that Bazarov's gifts of leadership could stir 'the dark people', as the educated called them, into political action. Yet, in chapter 27, when Bazarov attempts political dialogue with the peasants of his father's village, the result is an *impasse*, in which each side contemptuously gives up on the other. At this point, the narrator makes a significant narrative intervention:

> Alas, the contemptuously shrugging Bazarov, who knew how to talk to the peasants (as he had boasted in his quarrel with Pavel Petrovich), this self-assured Bazarov didn't even suspect that in their eyes he had something of the look of a village idiot.
>
> (pp. 224–5)

One way of reading this is to see it as Turgenev, the privileged author–landowner, notwithstanding his claims to impartiality, betraying personal views on the undesirability of educating the peasant. Another is to see it as a remarkable piece of historical foresight. A decade and a half after the events related in *Fathers and Sons*, when the young men and women of the Russian intelligentsia went out into the villages and fields to educate the peasantry to the idea of their own revolutionary potential, the profoundly conservative peasants did one of two things: ignored them or turned them over to the Tsarist gendarmes. The peasantry was not fertile ground for revolution. It was to take the development of an industrial proletariat—which not even Turgenev foresaw—to provide the vital ingredient for political upheaval. What he did foresee was the over-whelming difficulty of radicalizing an illiterate, superstitious and deeply patriarchal peasantry.

Before we leave the topic of realism and history in relation to *Fathers and Sons*, one point remains to be emphasized. Bazarov is a would-be fighter and destroyer (see his conversation with Arkady, p.219), but he is also a scientist, a doctor and an educator. In this respect his case illustrates one of the most important stimuli to the development of nineteenth-century realism as a literary movement: the ideal of science as the key to progress and enlightenment. If science means knowledge (which it literally does), knowledge understanding and understanding progress, then through science human society might be steered towards an enlightened future. The popularity of this line of reasoning among European intellectuals in the mid nineteenth century led to science as an instrument of progress providing a model for novelists committed to realism.

However, the scientific account of the phenomenon of human life has its limits. Ironically, given its indebtedness to the paradigm of science, it was realist fiction that highlighted those limits. Imaginative literature displays not only our capacity for self-knowledge and self-control but also the facts of our irrationality, our proneness to error and our mortality. The fate of

Bazarov, who is undone by love and the inner contradictions of his nature, illustrates this.

Pathos, the quality in literature that excites pity or sadness, can be understood as a form of realism in the strict sense that it compels the reader to confront ultimate, unpalatable realities. It was the great achievement of the nineteenth-century realist novel that it could render faithfully the facts of social existence and explore the claims of human reason, while ultimately measuring them against the immeasurable—the contradictions of human behaviour and the extremes of suffering, which are neither amenable to reason nor changeable through time.

THE REPRESENTATION OF WOMEN IN FATHERS AND SONS
BY PAM MORRIS

The realist novel is one of the great achievements of Russian art, but Russian women writers do not figure prominently in that achievement. This is in contrast to the development of the realist narrative form in England. There are no Russian counterparts of Jane Austen, the Brontës or George Eliot, even though women poets have won the highest praise in Russia. The representation of female characters in Russian literature thus presents us with something of a paradox, since it is the male-authored Russian realist novel that has produced some of the most remarkable and complex female characters in the whole of the novel genre. Turgenev's women are frequently seen as the prototypes of this tradition and Russian readers are as familiar with their names and personalities as with real-life female acquaintances.[3] They are written about in Russian criticism—and elsewhere—as if they were portrayals of real women.

One important underlying question for this section is how 'true' or authentic is Turgenev's representation of women. You may recall that the section on 'Women and the novel' in Chapter Four outlined the feminist critical strategy of rereading canonical texts to reveal the pervasive misrepresentation of women within the literary tradition. In particular, feminist critics have alerted us to the way in which women are frequently constructed as 'other' to a male norm. Instead of being perceived as identities in their own right, women characters tend to function as locations for male desires, fears and anxieties about the female. The representation of women in literature is comprised largely of variations upon the stereotypical images of virgin and whore, wicked witch and child-like innocent, Eve and Magdalene, wife, mother and mistress. It was suggested that when you came to read *Great Expectations* and *Fathers and Sons* you might like to consider how relevant this perception is to Dickens's and Turgenev's treatment of female characters.

How do we estimate Turgenev's women? What are the positive achievements of his imaginative construction of feminine experience and personality?

Discussion

Perhaps what strikes most readers coming to Turgenev from the English tradition of the novel in the nineteenth century is the fullness and maturity of his approach. By comparison, there seems so much English writers leave out of their representation of female characters. In Elizabeth Bennet, Austen offers us a sense of a shrewd and lively intelligence, but a woman with Odintsova's intellectual concern with the latest thinking in science, politics and the arts is surely unimaginable in an English novel? Of course, this has as much to do with more general cultural and historical differences as with narrowly gender issues; male characters in English novels rarely engage in intellectual discourse either. Still, it is noteworthy that even Katya, who in many ways represents opposing values to those of her sister, is quite capable of discussing the merits of Heine's writings with Arkady (p.200). This provides a stark contrast to Mary Shelley's *Frankenstein*, where only the male characters are represented as active intellects.

What is more, in contrast to Nikolai Petrovich Kirsanov, Odintsova is shown to be highly efficient in managing a large estate and in ordering the daily life of the household so that it seems to glide 'along rails' in the manner that so irritates Bazarov even though he enjoys the ease provided. In *Fathers and Sons* it seems taken for granted by the male characters that women can manage their own lives, property and fortunes, even if some disapproval of this is suggested—a point I will come to presently.

What is most striking in the comparison with English writing of the same period is Turgenev's relative freedom in writing about the sexual relationships between the characters, and about their sexual feelings, attitudes and experiences. It is refreshing to find a woman who is sexually mature, who has already been married, and who is not innocently youthful, considered interesting enough to be the heroine of the work. In most English texts marriage marks the end of the heroine's story and any evidence of active sexuality in a female character unsanctioned by a firm attachment to the man she is destined to marry carries ominous moral implications.

Whereas Odintsova is permitted to go on to a second marriage, which promises her the possibility of happiness and even love, it seems unlikely that any English heroine who behaved with the freedom she does with Bazarov would have escaped punishment, unhappiness, even death within the moral unfolding of the plot. In all these ways, Turgenev seems to be concerned to represent his main female character as an interesting identity in her own right. We might also note in passing that although in many ways the Fenichka—Kirsanov relationship is very similar to that of Joe and Biddy in *Great Expectations*, Turgenev's representation seems so much more 'grown-up' in its perceptions.

However, although in this respect Russian nineteenth-century realism appears able to offer more authentic women characters than the English tradition,[4] Turgenev has not escaped criticism in terms of stereotypical representation. It has been argued that women in his novels invariably fall into one of three recurrent types, of which the most important aspect and indicator is their physical beauty or lack of it (Heldt, *Terrible Perfection: Women and Russian Literature*, 1987, p.18). The first two polarized types are beautiful in very different ways: there is the pure young heroine just emerging from youthful awkwardness into shy sexual awareness and the older *femme fatale* who seeks to attract men by her mature sexuality but is not herself passionate, indeed is often coldly incapable of love. The third type is the unattractive or ugly woman who is presented as ridiculous, especially should she presume to try to attract men. Can we recognize these types of women in *Fathers and Sons*?

Discussion

It is not very difficult! Clearly, many of the aspects of the characterization of Odintsova conform to the *femme fatale* type. Although she deliberately sets out to attract Bazarov, asking Arkady to bring him to visit her and when he comes attempting to provoke his interest and actively encouraging him to reveal his emotions, she is shown to be without strong feelings herself. This sense of her lack of passion is reinforced by the image of her in bed, thinking in an intrigued way about Bazarov, yet quickly falling asleep over 'a silly French novel ... all clean and cool in clean and fragrant bed linen' (p.106). The implication is that she seeks out Bazarov from motives of curiosity and *ennui* rather than desire, as he recognizes when he tells her she is probably incapable of love. Although the actual cause of his death is a typhus infection, almost self-inflicted, the text implies that it is Odintsova who has fatally destroyed the force of life in Bazarov. He leaves her house having not slept or eaten for several days, his 'lean profile' almost like a death's head and he tells Arkady the 'machinery's come unstuck' (pp.131–2).

Read in this light we might begin to sense something repressively sterile in the rigid routine Odintsova imposes on her household, excluding all traces of spontaneity or vitality. The 'little speech' with which she greets Arkady and Bazarov on their arrival at her house is delivered 'in a particularly precise way as if she had learned it by heart' (p.98). We might even want to consider whether the white linen and drapery so often associated with her ('She looked paler by the light of the single lamp ... A full white dress covered her whole figure in soft folds. The tips of her feet ... were scarcely to be seen', pp.113–14) hints at death almost as surely as the more obvious symbolism of Miss Havisham's bridal decay in *Great Expectations*. There is certainly a sinister element in the way she seems suddenly prepared to turn her attractions upon Arkady after Bazarov has suggested that the former is in love with her: 'You say he's not indifferent to me and I've always thought he liked me. I know I could pass for his aunt, but I don't want to hide from you that I've begun to think of him more and more. In that kind of youthful and fresh feeling there is a certain charm' (p.215).

Equally clearly, Katya is represented as fresh, young and virginal. As with this type generally in Turgenev's novels, she is given to blushing and tears as indicative of her spontaneous emotional responsiveness. She is apparently demure and quiet but reveals intuitive wisdom and insight; Katya understands Bazarov's nature from the beginning. In opposition to her sister, Katya functions in the text as an image of new life. She '*adored*' nature and is given to arranging flowers. Turgenev's association of this type of woman with life as opposed to death is even more obvious in his representation of Fenichka with her baby. The two women are described in very similar terms; it is not surprising that Fenichka comes to love Katya next to her husband and child. However, despite this there are some oddly sinister connections between them and the character of Odintsova. What is the implication of Fenichka's relations with Bazarov, do you think? Is it being suggested that there is a part of the feminine nature that cannot resist flirtation and has a need for male admiration? After Arkady's declaration of love to Katya, we are told: 'He was already beginning to submit to her and Katya sensed this and was not surprised' (p.220). Earlier she has admitted to herself that she will have him kneeling at her feet (p.206). Is Turgenev implying that even women as apparently guileless as Katya and Fenichka inevitably seek to overpower men, that the female is sinister and deadly to the male?

It seems to me undeniable that there are elements of some such negative or fearful perception of women in the text. However, Turgenev's representation of his female characters is both more interesting and more complex than this implies. Certainly looking at the characters in *Fathers and Sons* as a whole we must be struck by the beauty, mystery and strength of the women and the weakness and failure of the men. To demonstrate the complexity of the women characters we need to situate the novel once again in its historical context, but this time in terms of its engagement with a passionate debate ensuing in Russia at the time upon 'the woman question' (as it was called).

FATHERS AND SONS AND 'THE WOMAN QUESTION'

The long reign of Catherine the Great (1762–96) marked the beginning of a slow process of improving the social position of women in Russia by removing some of the traditional discriminations against them in education, law and the family. However, especially towards the end of the eighteenth century, Russian political life was characterized by intrigue and rivalries fermented in Catherine's court and in the fashionable salons presided over by powerful aristocratic women. This fuelled traditional male prejudice against the dangerous influence of feminine guile and treachery and provoked hostility to what was seen as its origin: the corrupting influence of western culture and political fashions upon the traditional values of Russian life.

Nevertheless, women's position continued to improve into the nineteenth century. During the 1830s and 1840s Russian male intellectuals began actively supporting women's claims to greater equality. Much of the impetus for this was due to the impact in Russia of French political ideas, particularly in the form of romantic aspirations articulating the 'freedom of the heart' and a generalized belief in the emancipation of the human soul. The cult female figure during this phase of romantic political thinking in early-nineteenth-century Russia was the French novelist George Sand, who had separated from her husband to lead an independent—somewhat notorious—life of her own in Paris. It is to this generation that the brothers Kirsanov belong.

The next generation, that of the 1850s and 1860s, was to be more radical in its political views, especially after the failure and defeat of Russia in the Crimean War (1856). These were the sons determined to overthrow the worn-out values and traditions of their fathers, which they believed were suffocating progress in Russia. It was this generation that began actively formulating 'the woman question' in association with the issue of the emancipation of the serfs (1861). Laws were passed forbidding husbands to beat or mutilate their wives, although the habit of wife beating among the peasants was still sanctioned by customary law—a point Bazarov comments upon scathingly in the novel. The rights of women were linked to the emancipation of the serfs in a more material sense than that of a common political ideal. The impoverishment or feared impoverishment of large numbers of the gentry by the return of land to the peasants created a very real need among many women to find a means of economic support, which their fathers or brothers were no longer able to guarantee. In 1859 women were granted permission to attend university lectures with male students, but in 1861 this privilege was removed by government order. However, in the larger cities, and especially in Moscow and St Petersburg, numerous young male intellectuals and radicals offered free tuition and lessons to their female relatives, friends and neighbours. Fictitious marriages became popular, whereby aspiring young women who felt trapped within the provincial familial home were rescued by young men who offered to marry them so that they could acquire the necessary documents and permission to move to Moscow or St Petersburg or to Zurich, Paris or Heidleberg to study the new ideas. Doubtless some of these young women were betrayed, but there is not a great deal of evidence to suggest that Bazarov's sexual cynicism was the prevailing attitude among the male radicals of the 1860s.

Out of the debate upon 'the woman question' came Nikolai Chernyshevsky's novel *What Is To Be Done?* (1863). Chernyshevsky was a leading spokesman for the radical intellectuals during the 1850s and 1860s and his novel became one of the most famous and influential in Russian literature. It was read by Lenin, who declared it 'can fire one's energies for a lifetime' (quoted in Andrews, *Women in Russian Literature*, 1988, p.155) and he used its title for one of his own political works. The main character of *What Is To Be Done?* is the heroine, Vera Pavlovna, who breaks away from all the traditional roles and preconceptions about a woman's life and needs. The plot does not end traditionally with her marriage. Instead, she marries twice and establishes relationships of comradeship and respect with her husbands. More importantly, she pursues a series of active careers, setting up a model sewing co-operative which not only supports herself but allows her to liberate other women into an independent life. Eventually Pavlovna trains as a doctor, finding a fulfilling professional life for herself. The book came to be called 'the bible' for all Russian women with aspirations towards independence, and it inspired many women to leave their parents, husbands, even children and move into the cities to join a circle, co-operative or commune of like-minded women. The more politically radical of these young women became known as *nigilistki* (female nihilists). It is striking that, in the decades leading up to the overthrow of the Tzar and the revolution of 1917, women in Russia were more numerous in and took a far more active and significant part in the many subversive political movements than women anywhere else in Europe.[5]

Chernyshevsky's novel became the focus of an intensifying conservative reaction against demands for women's emancipation. At the centre of conservative views was a belief in the traditional sanctity of motherhood as women's natural sphere and creative fulfilment. In 1850 a writer on the position of women in Russian society declared: 'The family is the kingdom of woman—her life' (Atkinson, 'Society and the sexes in the Russian past', 1978, p.34). However, in the same year a woman writer complained: 'Sometimes it seemed that God created the world for men only.... For them there is fame and art and learning; for them there is freedom and all the joy of life.... But if a woman does not achieve happiness in family life, what is left for her?' (ibid.). Conservatives blamed such disaffection upon the destructive influence of western ideas on the sanctities of the Russian traditional family. In particular, vitriolic attacks were made upon Chernyshevsky's novel and more especially upon those who attempted to put its ideas into practice. Nihilists were caricatured as dirty, sexually immoral and politically dangerous and deceitful. All those involved in radical movements were denounced as 'un-Russian' or as seduced by the destructive allurement of foreign influence; the linking of political subversion with sexual seduction became an obsessive theme in anti-feminist writing.

Turgenev's *Fathers and Sons* can only be fully understood if it is seen as vigorously involved in these passionate issues. Indeed, Chernyshevsky's novel is in many ways a response to Turgenev's work, especially *On the Eve* (1860), the novel that had preceded *Fathers and Sons*. However, where precisely should we situate Turgenev's work within the Russian political spectrum of the 1860s? What attitudes towards 'the woman question' are expressed in *Fathers and Sons?* The most useful starting-point for considering this would be the representation of the liberated woman, Yevdoxia Kukshina, in chapters 13 and 14, and you might then go on to contrast this with the depiction of Bazarov's mother in chapter 20.

Discussion

Kukshina is clearly meant to be representative of the radicalism of the late 1850s to 1860s. She has 'vowed' to defend the rights of women 'to the last drop of my blood', and is scornful of Sand, 'an out-of-date woman' who was the heroine of the earlier romantic generation (pp.83, 80). She has separated from her husband and plans to go abroad to study in Paris and Heidelberg (p.81). The description of her person and household repeats some of the stereotyping of radical women found in most conservative writing. She is dirty and slovenly in her habits and person: her room is scattered and dusty, her hair dishevelled and her dress crumpled. Moreover, her conversation and behaviour is presented to 'show' us that her radicalism is shallow and affected. While she considers herself 'good-natured and simple' (p.79), nothing about her is simple or spontaneous. The narrator 'tells' us that she greets her guests with a string of questions upon topical issues 'with excessively feminine casualness, without waiting for answers' (p.80). It is important to notice the narrator's generalization here, which would seem to impute lack of serious concern ('feminine casualness') to all women as part of their feminine nature, not just to Kukshina as an individual. The narrator draws repeated attention to Kukshina's unattractive physical appearance almost as if that were partly her fault. Kukshina is unfortunate enough to show her gums above her top teeth when she laughs (p.79) and her piano playing reveals 'her flat-cut fingernails' (p.84). However, what is most significant in terms of the dominant patriarchal ideology of mid-nineteenth-century Russia is her declaration 'I'm free, I've no children' (p.81). From a conservative perspective, this would count as a near-sacrilegious statement.

Arina Vlassyevna, Bazarov's mother, and 'a real Russian noblewoman of former times' (p.145) is constructed as Kukshina's opposite in almost every detail. She is represented as superstitiously religious and spontaneously emotional. She has never read a book and, although married against her will, she has devoted herself to her husband's well-being, allowing him the complete management of her estate. Beyond all this she worships her son, finding her entire identity and fulfilment in this maternal role. The rhetorical form of the narrator's comment: 'Such ladies are already few and far between. God knows whether one should be glad of that fact!' (p.146), implies a certain open-mindedness, but in fact the representation contrasting the new and the old schools of women leaves little doubt as to where the text places its values.

The use of polarized characters to confirm the underlying values of the text is a device frequently used by writers. Austen, for example, always has opposing pairs of characters in her novels. In a similar way, writers often construct parallels between characters as a way of unobtrusively guiding the reader's sympathies and judgements in line with the text's value system. In *Fathers and Sons* telling similarities link the characters of Kukshina,

Odintsova and Bazarov. The introduction of Odintsova in the text is carefully positioned immediately after the description of Kukshina. Despite the apparent contrast between the two women in terms of beauty, dignity and intelligence, there are significant common features. Both women despised their husbands and are childless. Odintsova was educated in St Petersburg at the centre of new thinking, her 'reprobate' father treating her as a friend and equal, which suggests that she has acquired little sense of the value of traditional authority. Like Kukshina, she engages in intellectual debates with men, and her discussions with Bazarov imply that, like him, she regards nature from a materialist and scientific point of view, but has no feeling for it as source of life. Even more significantly, she shares Bazarov's nihilism. The narrator tells us that she has 'no prejudices, not even having any strong beliefs ... Her mind was keenly enquiring and indifferent at one and the same time' (p.105). It would seem that she spoke the truth when she told Bazarov that there was 'too much that was the same about us' (p.215).

However, her sense of an unsatisfied desire at the centre of her life also links her to the enigmatic Princess R., who destroys the life of Pavel Petrovich Kirsanov. The princess is also childless, encumbered with a husband she despises, apparently a frivolous coquette, yet she finds 'no peace in anything', laughing by day but spending her nights in anguish and weeping. The most sustained irony of the novel lies in the similarity of the fates of Kirsanov and Bazarov, which both utterly fail to recognize. The enigmatic beauty of the princess bites so deeply into Kirsanov's soul that 'Like someone who's taken poison, he couldn't settle' (p.37). In effect, Kirsanov is dead emotionally from the year 1848, the year in which revolutionary movements all over Europe toppled old authorities and *ancien regimes*. We might say that Bazarov is the luckier of the two in that his poison kills him off quickly, thus sparing him Kirsanov's lingering hopelessness.

This parallelism between two of the main male characters helps to highlight another criticism made of Turgenev's artistic treatment of female characters. In his novels, apart from *On the Eve*, women tend to function merely as episodes in a plot structure, which is intent upon tracing the development of the young male hero into maturity (Heldt, *Terrible Perfection: Women and Russian Literature*, 1987, p.13). In this sense Turgenev's novels are male *bildungsroman*, in which the women are important only in terms of the effect they have upon the hero's life. Within the stories the women do not develop as people and the complex processes of their feelings and intellectual growth are not represented. We can certainly see this pattern in the representation of Princess R. and Kirsanov, but what of Odintsova and Bazarov? Could this criticism be applied to Turgenev's representation of their characters? I suggest you think about this first in terms of plot structure. Does Odintsova simply function as part of the unfolding of Bazarov's story or does she have a story in her own right?

Discussion

It seems to me that Odintsova's main importance in the novel is the fatal effect she has upon Bazarov. Her function is to produce the ironic parallel between the young nihilist and his apparent enemy, the romantic aristocrat Kirsanov. You might feel that Turgenev provides Odintsova with her own story after Bazarov's death, with her later marriage and its possibilities. However, this is surely too perfunctory to count as a story? On the other hand, the fact that he includes it might suggest that Turgenev was more involved imaginatively with Odintsova than he realized. I will return to this point shortly.

In addition to women's position and function within the structure of the plot, it is important to consider in relation to the women characters the effect of the novelistic devices of focalization, 'showing' and 'telling', which are crucial to the way a writer shapes the reader's understanding of and response to characters. The space devoted to Odintsova's own story within the text of *Fathers and Sons*, which is largely confined to chapters 16–18, is certainly quite short in comparison with that allocated to the two main male characters. What is the balance of focalization used for the male and female characters? Are we offered the same insight into Odintsova's feelings and perceptions as into those of Bazarov? How does the alternation of 'showing' and 'telling' function in relation to these two characters? Read pages 105–25, carefully analysing the effect of these three novelistic devices.

Discussion

These are some of the most intensely imagined and written pages of the novel and I have only space here to make a few points, so you may well pick out other important aspects. The narrator 'tells' quite a lot about both characters but I am struck by a difference in the quality of the 'telling'. On pages 105–6 the general character of Odintsova is summarized for us; the narrator's authoritative tone and form of words seem to be offering us a comprehensive understanding of her vague mixture of desires with timid conformism which goes well beyond any self-awareness the character herself might possess. This authoritative knowledge even seems to encompass women as a whole, as if the fact that they are *women* makes such generalized truths about their characters possible: 'Like all women who had not succeeded in falling in love, she sought for something without knowing precisely what' (p. 105). Bazarov, on the other hand, is not offered for us to understand in terms of generalizations about male psychology. In the prolonged passage of 'telling' on pages 110–12 we do not get a summarized knowledge of his personality generally but an account of his feelings at a particular time. The insight into these feelings does not belong to the privileged perception of narrator and reader. Bazarov is shown as self-aware and the passage is largely his focalization.

As with 'telling', 'showing' in the form of the characters' own speech is distributed reasonably evenly between Odintsova and Bazarov, but again I think there is a difference. On the whole Odintsova expresses puzzlement about her feelings and turns to Bazarov for explanations of herself and of life, which, by and large, he feels able to supply. Although we are given Odintsova's words on these pages, we rarely have any sense of her feelings, whereas the struggle of Bazarov's emotions below the surface of his speech is frequently indicated. For example, when Odintsova asks him from what personal experience he speaks when he tells her she is probably incapable of love, he replies to himself: " 'You're bored and you're having a bit of fun with me out of boredom, while I ..." His heart was actually on the point of breaking' (p. 118). The effect of this kind of representation is somewhat paradoxical. Despite the narrator's implied claim to full knowledge of Odintsova, her impulses and character remain to the reader, like those of the Princess R. to Kirsanov, something of an enigma. Whilst utilization of 'showing', 'telling' and focalization directs the reader's sympathy and understanding towards the hero, it is the mysterious image of a woman that haunts the text.

I am arguing that Turgenev's representation of female characters does indeed differ in form and content from his representation of male characters. Whilst his heroes are constructed as developing individual histories, his women are depicted as static images and in the main they function metaphorically or symbolically in the text. However, I certainly do not want to imply this is a wholly critical or negative judgement of Turgenev's women characters. As I suggested above, I think they often exert an immensely powerful effect upon the reader's imagination, often far more than that of the male characters. In *Fathers and Sons* the female characters, Katya, Fenichka and most especially Odintsova, do function to suggest a mysterious 'otherness' in contrast to the 'everydayness' associated with the male characters. For Turgenev, this feminine unknowability may be said to suggest fears and desires that cannot otherwise easily or at all be articulated within the conventions of realism, insofar as such conventions aim to remain true to the 'here-and-now', material reality of life. In a time of great social change and uncertainty, like the 1860s in Russia, when demands were being made that would overturn all the long-held values of a way of life, it is not surprising to find fictional female characters functioning metaphorically to suggest male disempowerment, and even death. However, Turgenev's representation is even more richly ambivalent than this—and more courageous.

Odintsova's need to marry for financial reasons after the death of her irresponsible father is made clear in realist terms. What Turgenev is also honest about is the effect of such a marriage of necessity upon a woman's sexual sensibilities: 'She had hardly been able to stand [her late husband] ... and had acquired a secret aversion to all men, whom she regarded as nothing more than untidy, ponderous and flabby, feebly importunate creatures' (pp.105–6). The sense, represented here, of women's unfulfilment within the present social arrangement, of an unnameable emptiness or desire at the centre of feminine life can be read as suggesting a mysterious unknown force for change or the impending pressure of the future. This is most strongly felt in the image of the window that lets in 'the vexing freshness of the night and its mysterious whisperings' (p.116). Eventually Odintsova retreats from this opening, rejecting the possibility that it offers, even though she has been forced to look back on her life and sees 'no more than emptiness ... or sheer ugliness' (p.125). However, it is significant that it is through the woman character that this opening is revealed, not through the ostensible revolutionary Bazarov.[6] It seems to me that, because aspects of Odintsova are left unexplained, the rend in the fabric of realism is never completely closed up again. The power of the characterization of Odintsova in *Fathers and Sons* and of Estella in *Great Expectations* derives largely from the use of metaphor to intensify the language by which they are represented. In this they may be said to fail one of the requirements of the realist genre: they are not entirely convincing or authentic constructions of women as specific individualized characters. More positively, it might be said that they produce points at which the text exceeds the limits of its representational possibilities as realism. Images of women in male-authored texts very often supply the 'novelness' that has been seen as the defining quality of the novel as a genre. The woman in the text often provides the moment when we catch a glimpse of future possibilities.

Further Readings

Freeborn, R. (1960) *Turgenev: The Novelist's Novelist*, Oxford University Press.

Gifford, H. (1964) *The Novel in Russia*, Hutchinson.

Seton-Watson, H. (1967) *The Russian Empire 1801–1917*, Oxford University Press.

Turton, G. (1992) *Turgenev and the Context of English Literature, 1850–1900*, Routledge.

Notes

1. Unless otherwise stated subsequent references to *Fathers and Sons* are to this edition and pages numbers only are given.

2. For a fuller account of contemporary reactions, see Berlin, '*Fathers and Children*', 1994, pp.280–5.

3. Throughout this section I am indebted to Heldt, *Terrible Perfection: Women and Russian Literature*, 1987; p.13.

4. They are authentic in realist terms, but not, of course, necessarily more powerful or 'true'. Charles Dickens's representation of Miss Havisham in her withered bridal gown and decaying house seems to me one of literature's most unforgettable images of wasted and repressed sexuality.

5. For an account of this see Porter, *Fathers and Daughters: Russian Women in Revolution*, 1976; Stites, 'Women and the Russian intelligentsia', 1978.

6. Porter describes a short prose poem by Turgenev (found posthumously) called *At the Threshold*, in which a young girl stands outside a great door. A voice warns that those who pass through will face cold, hunger, hatred, mockery, contempt, shame, prison, illness, death. 'I know,' the girl says, 'I am ready.' The voice then insists that she will perish and no one will even know whose memory to revere. The girl says 'I need neither gratitude nor pity. I do not need a name' and she crosses the threshold (*Fathers and Daughters*, 1976, p.153). The heroine Elena in *On the Eve* makes a similar declaration before she crosses into the unknown world of historical change and vanishes into a void.

RICHARD GREGG

Turgenev and Hawthorne: The Life-Giving Satyr and the Fallen Faun

I

In temperament, background and—in the loosest sense—philosophy Nathaniel Hawthorne and Ivan Turgenev might seem to stand at the antipodes. True, the fiction of both writers reflects a largely pessimistic view of the human condition. But if in his most characteristic works the reclusive New Englander avoided realistic modes of representation, turned to the haunts of his ancestors for inspiration, and explored such "morbid" themes as sin, guilt, remorse and retribution, Turgenev *as novelist* hewed to the canons of realism,[1] depicted a wide variety of contemporary settings and— true to his liberal, secular and essentially rationalistic view of life—shunned the mysterious, the uncanny corners of human experience. To generalize and simplify somewhat: whereas Hawthorne's fictional world bears, in the Arnoldian and Auerbachian sense, a distinctly "Hebraic" stamp, the broader, brighter and more varied novelistic canvases of Turgenev exhibit a more "Hellenistic" coloration.[2]

In view of these differences it might seem unlikely that Turgenev would show a lively or sustained interest in the American regionalist. Such an interest is nonetheless a fact. Interviewing the novelist in his later years, the Norwegian-American man of letters, H. H. Boyesen recorded that

From *Slavic and East European Journal*, vol. 41, no. 2. © 1997 by American Association of Teachers of Slavic and East European Languages.

Of all our [i.e., American] authors [Turgenev] loved Hawthorne
the most. In him he hailed the first literary representative of the
New World; in *The Scarlet Letter* and the *Twice-told Tales* he had
found that true flavor of the soil which proved them to be the
products of a new civilization. *The Marble Faun* and *The House of
the Seven Gables* bore the same impress of a great and powerfully
original genius (460).

These views could of course be simply the expression of Turgenev's
disinterested appreciation of Hawthorne's genius. Closer inspection of the
Turgenevan oeuvre, however, suggests that extraliterary factors may also
have been involved. For a relatively small body of shorter fiction written
towards the end of Turgenev's life[3] testifies to an increasing interest in
precisely those uncanny zones of human experience which held an abiding
fascination for Hawthorne, but which Turgenev as a realistically oriented
novelist had never explored.[4] Thus, in an odd, half-humorous story entitled
"The Dog" (1866) the narrator recalls how a sinister canine spectre had to
be exorcised for him to recover his peace of mind. In "A Strange Story"
(1869) a hypnotist turned *iurodivyj* makes a near slave of an intensely
religious young woman, who, when she is forcibly separated by her family
from her "master," perishes for want of a cause to serve. In "A Dream" (1876)
the mysterious appearance of the oneiric (and biological) father of an
adolescent culminates—after a series of macabre, hallucinatory episodes—in
the permanent estrangement of mother and son. In "Father Aleksej" (1877)
Evil in the form of an old green mannikin appears to the ten year old son of
a priest and casts a spell which blights the boy's life and causes his eventual
death. In "Song of Triumphant Love" (1881) the serenity of a happily
married but childless young couple is shattered by the sudden materialization
of the wife's former sutor, who, now in the possession of black-magical
powers oneirically seduces and impregnates her before being struck down by
the infuriated husband. Finally, in "Klara Milič (After Death)," published less
than a year before Turgenev's own death in 1883, the ghost of a gifted
actress, rejected in "real life" by the hero, returns to haunt him and cause—
so the mysterious circumstances of his final illness suggest—his untimely
death.[5] All of which is to say that two years after Hawthorne's death (in 1864)
the motif of the malediction so crucial to his fictional vision began to appear
regularly in the works of his Russian admirerer and continued to do so until
his death seventeen years later.[6]

This juxtaposition could of course be a matter of mere coincidence.
The use of occult, mysterious or fantastic motifs in fiction is, after all, as old

as fiction itself. And the large number of contemporary writers who dabbled in the supernatural (e.g., Tieck, Hoffman, Puškin, Gogol, Poe, Balzac—to mention only the most prominent) might seem to make the mediation of the relatively obscure Hawthorne both gratuitous and implausible. But the trio of factors just alluded to, namely, the exceptional esteem in which Hawthorne was held by Turgenev, the common motif which their "mysterious" stories shared (the uncanny spell, curse or blight), and Turgenev's explicit admiration for those works of Hawthorne where that motif is to be found, plainly attest to a bond of sympathy between the two writers. And while consanguinity is one thing and a proven literary influence is quite another, the striking similarities which Hawthorne's last major fictional work shares with the penultimate member of T.'s "mysterious" cycle of tales, namely, "Song of Triumphant Love," leaves little doubt that Hawthorne must be counted among those writers who left a direct and definable imprint on that cycle.

In view of Turgenev's close familiarity with 19th-century fiction in four languages it is not surprising that a number of specific works have been identified as possible sources for "Song of Triumphant Love." Thus, parallels have been drawn between that story and Gogol's *povest'* "A Terrible Vengeance," Flaubert's *Trois Contes*, *Salambo* and *La Tentation de St. Antoine*, "The Case of M. Valdemar" (Poe), "Djoumane" (Merimée), the so-called "Italian Stories" of Stendhal, and Bulwer-Lytton's *A Strange Story*.[7] With the exception of the last of these, however, none can be said to have had a seminal influence on the narrative structure of Turgenev's story. And none, with the same proviso, can, I believe, lay so strong a claim to having influenced Turgenev's tale as a work to which scholarship has yet to draw attention, namely, *The Marble Faun*.

It would be otiose to enumerate the difference which distinguish Hawthorne's rambling, novel-length romance, replete with episodic scenes and travelogue-like descriptions, from Turgenev's compressed, lapidary fable less than a twentieth the length of its predecessor. Nor is there any need to demonstrate that, although Hawthorne's quartet of young lovers (Miriam, Donatello, Hilda and Kenyon) and Turgenev's basic trio (Mutsij, Fabij and Valerija) share certain important features (beauty, artistic inclinations, an Italian setting, an allegorically colored mode of depiction), the specifics of their situation diverge widely. These differences are nonetheless worth noting, for they help explain why, buried (as it were) under a mass of heterogeneous particulars, the resemblances which mark the two groupings have heretofore escaped notice. Exhumed, so to speak, they may be examined under four rubrics: *narrative nucleus, symbolic development, ethical ambivalence* and *incidental detail*. I shall consider them in that order.

The narrative nucleus of *The Marble Faun* can be summed up as follows. Emerging from the troubled past of Miriam, the heroine, is a nameless, swarthy, satyr-like creature (the "model"), who, having once shared with her an undisclosed, but intimate and, critics have surmised, erotic relationship,[8] subsequently exiled himself to the catacombs of Rome, where he had for years been mysteriously roaming. It is in these subterranean surroundings that he meets up with his quondam partner, whom he then proceeds to stalk, blackmail, persecute and in effect, enslave. Miriam's hateful yet, paradoxically, voluntary thralldom ends only when, in a jealous frenzy her "legitimate" suitor, the pure and innocent Donatello, attacks his rival and, under the cover of night and with Miriam's connivance, hurls him to his death from, appropriately enough, the Tarpeian Rock.

Mysterious, melodramatic and so implausible as to seem almost supernatural, these events invite—precisely because of their fantastic coloration—comparison with the homologous core of Turgenev's tale, which may be summarized thus. Emerging from the past of Valerija, the heroine, is a dark-complected, vaguely sinister looking man of—it soon transpires—satyr-like sexual appetites (Mutsij). Once romantically linked to Valerija (he had courted her but was, after some hesitation, rejected for a more conventional lover) he subsequently exiled himself to the Middle East, where for years he has wandered, exploring its sinister mysteries. On returning to his native city, he meets up with the happily married but (unhappily) childless Valerija, whom he proceeds to ensorcel, oneirically seduce and, in effect, enslave. Valerija's bondage is ended only when her virtuous husband, Fabij, in a fit of jealous rage, sallies forth by night and plunges a dagger into the body of his rival, whom he leaves for dead.

That the nucleus of Turgenev's tale shares striking similarities with its Hawthornean forbear needs, I think, no demonstration. Less immediately obvious is the three-tiered moral symbolism which marks the evolution of each narrative viewed as a whole. For, as Roy Male has noted (159), Hawthorne's romance falls into three distinct "theological" parts: a prelapsarian phase where Donatello represents pure, child-like innocence; the Fall, signaled by his murder of Miriam's persecutor; and a postlapsarian phase, marked by a sense of sin and, ensuing therefrom, the promise (no more) of resurrection. Near the end of the work this pattern becomes explicit when Hawthorne ascribes to the creation of a statue three phases: Life, associated with the clay model, Death ("the wages of sin")—with the plaster cast, and Resurrection—with the final marble product (380). That these (somewhat fanciful) ascriptions are made apropos of a sculptured bust of Donatello (himself so often compared to Praxiteles' statue) is clearly not coincidental.

The three moral stages traced by Turgenev's allegorically colored tale are even more sharply delineated. Chapters I–II, describing the courtship of the chaste and virtuous Valerija by "two noble kinsmen," Mutsij and Fabij, paints an idyl of unmixed innocence and goodwill. This prelapsarian state is shattered when, in Chapters III–XII, Mutsij, corrupted by the necromancers of the East, seduces Valerija and is struck down by Fabij. Then, with the departure of the corpse-like Mutsij (XIII–XIV), the third, redemptive stage is reached. Their nightmare lifted, the young couple recover their peace of mind and their hopes for parenthood are fulfilled when the heretofore barren Valerija feels a "new life" stirring within her.

Turning now to the third of our rubrics, as even the truncated precis offered above makes clear, contained in both narratives is the same ethical paradox, namely, that *evil is capable of engendering a potential good*. In Hawthorne's romance this "truth" is of course exemplified by Donatello himself, whose crime has transformed an innocent, childlike "simpleton" into a man of maturity and understanding. Nor is this transformation without quasi-theological glosses. Soon after the murder Miriam finds that a "higher innocence" and "tragic dignity" now invest her friend (283, 284)— an improvement which she later compares to the alleged beneficent consequences of the Fall in Genesis (434). And in the final chapter Kenyon goes even further, declaring that the crime seems to have "awakened [Donatello's] soul" and "developed in him a thousand high capabilities" (460). Indeed, extrapolating on this theory, he even wonders if Adam himself did not fall in order "that we might ultimately rise to a far loftier paradise" (460).

Such forthright speculation notwithstanding it would be a serious mistake to take these 19th century versions of *felix culpa* at face value. The guilt-stained Miriam (who, after all, has a vested interest in claiming a salvific function for sin) is scarcely an infallible witness to the Truth. Kenyon's "Adamic" theory is couched in the form of a question which is so vehemently rejected by Hilda that he himself must backtrack. What is more—and perhaps more important—the ultimate novelistic fate of both culprits (about which I shall have more to say later) offers no evidence at all to suggest that, in this sublunary world at least, crime can improve the spiritual condition of anyone.

"Song of Triumphant Love" is, by way of contrast, wholly devoid of philosophizing. But if, unlike Miriam and Kenyon, Turgenev's characters nowhere articulate the ethical ambivalence of *felix culpa*, the "Adamic," i.e., optimistic, nucleus of the plot, though not without ambiguities, is easy to discern. Unable to have the child which she and her husband have long wanted, Valerija succumbs to the sorcery of a suitor of former years and conceives. The seducer departs and Valerija, her troubled mind now at rest, discovers, while playing the "triumphant song" which had once signaled her "fall," her changed condition. *Felix culpa* indeed!

"Incidental detail," the last of our categories, defies orderly presentation. Less salient than those larger communalities noted above (e.g., an Italian setting, a cast composed mostly of artists, and an allegorical coloration), they present rather a jumble of small particulars. But it is a jumble which deserves examination.

One such detail involves the confessional. For an emotionally troubled young woman to unburden herself to a priest of the Church is not, in Catholic cultures at least, an extraordinary occurrence. Nor is its literary counterpart—the fictional image of the female penitent kneeling before the stern Servant of God having more than its share of popular (not to say mawkish) appeal. It is nonetheless worth noting that near the end of *The Marble Faun* Hilda, "heretic" though she is, finding herself in a Catholic church and unable to live with her terrible secret (she was an accidental witness to the murder), seeks out an old priest to whom she confesses all and feels immense relief thereafter. Likewise two-thirds the way through Turgenev's tale Valerija, profoundly oppressed by her ensorcelment by Mutsij, goes to an old priest to confess her "sin" and receives absolution. Coincidentally or not, the Puritan American and the agnostic Russian have put their "guiltlessly guilty" (*bez viny vinovatye*) heroines through similar penetential paces.

Another point in common involves the symbolic use of *the wordless song*. No reader of "Song of Triumphant Love" needs to be reminded of the eponymous "song," which resounds at three pivotal moments in the story: "snakelike" and portending evil, when played by Mutsij at the outset; gloating when he celebrates his seduction of Valerija; triumphant when at the end she realizes that she is with child. What makes this device worthy of note is its prior appearance in *The Marble Faun*: first when the unhappy Miriam, approaching the Tarpeian Rock gives vent to her foreboding with an overpowering "gush" of sound (163–64); later when the "fallen" Donatello, returned to his native haunts, tries to charm the creatures of the forest with his wild" yet "harmonious" song and attracts only a venomous reptile (247–49); thirdly, when Kenyon and Donatello, standing on the battlements of the "Owl Tower," hear Miriam give voice to her profound melancholy

(268–69). Nor should the trajectory of these threefold sequences be overlooked. For if in both works the first song is a prophecy and the second a ratification, the annunciatory song played by Valerija at the end of Turgenev's tale stands in significant contrast to Miriam's doleful lament. About that "divergence," too, I shall have more to say later.

An altogether different similarity shared by the two stories is the macabre detail of *the villain's indestructible body*. In *The Marble Faun* this phenomenon is symbolically forecast when, the day after the murder, blood—in defiance of all physiological laws—starts to ooze from the victim's corpse (189), an augury which is confirmed when we learn that his mortal remains will be placed on permanent display for the edification (!) of the faithful. Using the same grisly details (a purplish, waxen cadaver, protruding eyeballs, etc.) Turgenev gives this motif an unequivocally supernatural twist by turning his villain into a kind of zombie: although Mutsij is seemingly dead (his unbreathing body is speechless, sightless and without intelligence), he continues, at the command of his sinister Malay "servant," to move his limbs mechanically and even locomote. Possible moral: in Turgenev, as in Hawthorne, Evil can be overcome but not extinguished entirely.

A third feature common to both narratives involves the peculiar appurtenances of a room where hero (or villain) and heroine meet. In *The Marble Faun* this "room" is the richly, exotically appointed "marble saloon," where Donatello encounters the unhappy Miriam, and which, replete with marble floors, walls with deep niches, alabaster pillars supporting a vaulted ceiling and an eerie light, which, in lieu of windows, "magically" emanates from the ubiquitous marble, gives its name to the chapter as a whole (277–87). How attentively Turgenev read "The Marble Saloon" we have, of course, no way of knowing. What is certain is that his description of the chamber in which the unhappy Valerija in her first dream confronts Mutsij replicates certain details of its predecessor with remarkable fidelity. For here, too, we find ourselves in a windowless but luxuriously and exotically furnished room replete with smooth marble-like floors, alabaster pillars supporting a vaulted marble ceiling, walls with niches and, most striking of all, light "mysteriously" issuing from its marble surfaces (60).

Less concrete, but much closer to the thematic core of both works is— to turn to the penultimate similarity—the impingement of sin (or its knowledge) on the creative act of the artist. In *The Marble Faun* all three of its "artist heroes" undergo such an experience. Thus, the reappearance of the loathsome model in Miriam's life is not only a source of continuing torment but threatens, we are told, to inhibit her attainment of "excellence" in her art (32). Similarly, near the end of the novel Hilda, a skillful and fluent copyist

of the old masters, loses, because of her guilty knowledge, that gift—
indispensible to her metier—of appreciating great works of art (335). But it
is Kenyon, the sculptor, whose creative crisis receives the most detailed
treatment. Bent on capturing the boyish beauty of Donatello in a clay bust,
he finds that his now corrupted subject defies his powers of faithful
representation, and he must be content with a "wretched" facsimile of his
friend (270–71).

The analogous episode in Turgenev's tale enjoys even greater
prominence. A day after Valerija's seduction Fabij, unaware of the contents
of her terrible dream, resumes his portrait of his wife, who had been posing
as St. Cecilia. Alas, he is now unable to capture that "pure" and "holy"
expression, which she had earlier worn, and, frustrated, he is forced to
abandon the project (62–61). Quite like Hawthorne's sculptor, Turgenev's
painter finds, momentrily at least, his creative faculties paralyzed by the
fallen condition of his subject.

Prefacing—and foreshadowing—this episode is a sculptural image
which provides the last and most complex of our incidental parallels.
Resolved to finish his portrait, and finding Valerija neither in his studio nor
elsewhere in the house, Fabij goes out into the garden, where, in one of its
remoter corners, he spies his wife sitting on a bench

а за ней, выделяясь из темной зелени кипариса, мраморный сатир, с
искаженным злорадной усмешкой липом, прикладывая к свирели свои
заостренные губы (63).

The obvious symbolism of Valerija's escape from her sterile (impotent?)
husband followed by her rapprochement to a demigod noted for his lustful
ways needs no elaboration. But only a reader well versed in Hawthorne's
fiction will recognize in Turgenev's satyr a conflation of two motifs which
recur repeatedly in *The Marble Faun*. For if this marble statue representing a
faun-like creature playing on his pipes recalls, self-evidently, the statue
which—pipes and all—introduces, gives its name to, and plays such a crucial
symbolic role in Hawthorne's romance, the twisted, malevolent expression
which plays on its lips points to a very different Hawthornean model, namely
the "model" himself, that ugly, malignant, explicitly satyrlike creature (30),
whose sexually linked harrassment of Miriam parallels, as earlier noted,
Valerija's persecution by the man whose marble emblem in the garden
presides over, as it were, her bondage.

There is, I think, no need to itemize and recapitulate. Taken together the diverse evidence adduced here, major and minor, extrinsic and intrinsic, indicates a kinship between the two narratives which is more than coincidental.

II

Quellenforschung is seldom so interesting as when it transcends the enumeration of similarities and asks how the writer in question has made the "borrowed" material characteristically his own; how, in other words, the adaption reflects the adapter. In the given case, moreover, such a pursuit can also move in the "opposite" direction: it can show how the "borrower," by uncovering and highlighting half-hidden aspects of his sources is, in effect, interpreting, or at least reevaluating that source. The relationship between host and parasite, between donor and recipient can thus be mutually illuminating.

At the outset, it will be recalled, a broad distinction was drawn between Hawthorne's "Hebraic" vision (puritanical, relatively narrow, guilt-ridden, hermetic) and Turgenev's more "Hellenistic" outlook: more realistic, capacious, varied and "fully externalized" (6). It was further noted that, breaching this distinction is a small cycle of sombre, supernaturally tinged tales—never novels—to which "Song of Triumphant Love" has traditionally been assigned. I should now like to add that the "breach" is by no means complete; that certain "hellenizing" tendencies in this tale persist, and that even as they betray a "Hawthornean" coloration, they can, paradoxically, underscore and refine our understanding of the differences which separate the two writers. These differences fall under the related rubrics of sex, sin, and the quality of pessimism which the fictional projection of these key concepts involves.

It is not new, of course, to propose that some obscure, illicit sexual act underlies that sense of guilt which pervades much of Hawthorne's fiction. Melville, a brief but close friend, intimated as much.[9] D. H. Lawrence was somewhat more explicit on the subject (83–100). Later critics have followed in their footsteps. Only relatively recently however have scholars—most notably Frederic Crews (49–60, 202–28) and Philip Young (*passim*)—citing ancestral lore, biographical fact, and the recurrence of certain fictional motifs, proposed that incest was the transgression in question.

The voluminous evidence adduced by these scholars to support their theory needs no repetition here. For us it will suffice to note that the vocabulary of horror and revulsion which attaches to Hawthorne's model and his crime (e.g., "Demon," "fiendish malignity," "unspeakable evil"), plus the total blackout imposed by the narrator-censor on the *nature* of that crime, suggest perversion as well as wrong-doing. When, moreover, we recall Miriam's near fixation on Beatrice Cenci, renowned in history for being raped by her father and murdering him in revenge,[10] the parallels between the historical murderess and the novelistic one are inescapable, and the assertion of Leslie Fiedler (49), Crews (228) and Young (56) that an aura of incest surrounds Miriam's thralldom seems almost self-evident.

What makes these findings worth mentioning here is that almost a century before modern hermeneuticists probed the depths of Hawthorne's romance for its secrets, Turgenev the artist had embodied them in his art. For if, as I have tried to show, *The Marble Faun* left a discernible imprint on "Song of Triumphant Love," one can only admire how the latter externalizes what the former had been so careful to hide. For not only is the putative sexuality of the model's crime against Miriam made vividly explicit in Mutsij's rape of Valerija, but that "shadow of incest" imputed by Fiedler et al. has in Turgenev's story a concrete source. Not of course that Mutsij and Valerija are brother and sister. But the fact that Mutsij and Fabij, once "inseparable friends," are also next of kin (*blizskie rodstvenniki*) ensures that Valerija, in sexually submitting to the former, enters into an endogzmous relationship that verges (see *Leviticus* 20.20)[11] on the taboo. All of which of course is to say that Turgenev was the first to have lifted, if only partially, "the minister's black veil," which (so Melville) had "all his life" concealed Hawthorne's "great secret."[12]

We may best take the measure of the second of our categories, namely, a sense of sin, by examining more closely the role which statuary plays in each work. Externally viewed, fauns and satyrs are all but identical. Both are goat-like humanoids, endowed with furry legs, hooves, pointed ears and horns; both are traditionally depicted playing on a set of musical pipes. An important ethical difference nonetheless distinguishes the two: whereas a satyr is wantonly, wickedly lustful, the faun is not. In the given context this fact might, at first glance, seem to reverse our expectations. Should not an innocent faun rather than a wicked satyr have been the favored emblem of Turgenev, whose interest in the sexual aspect of love was small,[13] and whose fiction abounds in the motif of youthful male innocence.[14] Conversely—and perhaps even more to the point—should not the malevolent satyr who lurks in the depths of Fabij's garden be an apt symbol for those sexual demons which—so Young and others—Hawthorne, the troubled Christian,[15] repeatedly sought to exorcise in his fiction?

To grasp the full teleological thrust of our two narratives is not only to perceive the rightness of their symbolism as it stands, but to gain a sharper understanding of the moral vision of both authors. I have earlier noted that the three-tiered spiritual evolution expounded in *The Marble Faun*, namely, from innocence through criminal transgression to final redemption by virtue of a higher knowledge is undercut by the character and/or equivocations of those who expound it. Even more to the point: this optimistic view of human error is contradicted by what the narrative itself enacts. For few readers would deny that high hopes for an "awakened soul" and confidence in a "loftier paradise" are *not* the regnant emotions which mark the last pages of *The Marble Faun*. Anguish and foreboding are. True, the betrothal of Kenyon and Hilda promises a happy ending for the American "half" of the cast. But Kenyon and Hilda are not the chief actors in the unfolding moral drama. Miriam and Donatello are. As instigator and perpetrator, respectively, of the central, defining act in that drama, namely, the murder, they must bear the full blame and suffer the consequences. And no amount of talk about a "fortunate fall" can conceal the fact that, humanly speaking, Donatello's fall is profoundly *un*fortunate. Through it a carefree youth becomes a gloomy and guilt-tormented man, destined to spend years, perhaps a lifetime, in prison. As for Miriam, having compounded her first sin (her mystery-shrouded compact with the model) with the second (her complicity in the murder), she stands at the end of the story a doubly tainted and deeply troubled woman. All of which is to say that the last and "gloomiest" of Hawthorne's romances (Baym 248) shares with the greatest of his short stories ("Young Goodman Brown," "My Kinsman, Major Molyneux," "Ethan Brand," "The Minister's Black Veil") that Calvinistic vision of prepotent evil (c.f. the "power of blackness," which Melville discerned in his friend's fiction)[16] which a theologically questionable notion can in no way erase. In figural terms: when the model plunged to his death from the Tarpeian Rock, his assailant, too, fell—permanently.

Despite the many similarities which connect "Song of Triumphant Love" to *The Marble Faun* the moral trajectory of Turgenev's tale tends to move, as we have seen, in the opposite direction. Like the model, Mutsij represents Evil; like the model, his persecutions are cruel and their effects lasting; like the model, he is ultimately destroyed. But by substituting a potentially "life-creating" transgression (seduction/rape) for murder, "Song of Triumphant Love" changes the moral complexion of its antecedent and alters thereby the quality of its pessimism. For, even as Turgenev augments the villainy of the crime itself, he introduces at the end notes of purgation (Mutsij has sunk into oblivion), reconciliation (the rift between Fabij and Valerija is closed) and hope (the child which Valerija is carrying). To be sure, important uncertainties shadow the ending of this explicitly *incomplete* tale. How can we be sure that the wicked Malay, still alive and armed with supernatural powers, will not return to avenge his master's "death"? Will it be possible for Valerija to recover fully from the horror of her violation? What legacy will the biological—and criminal—father bequeath to his child? It cannot be gainsaid, however, that a violent storm has been weathered; something has been salvaged; life goes on. Compared with the Christian gloom which shrouds Hawthorne's doomed pair the terminal ambiguities of Turgenev's tale are painted in chiaroscuro.

None of which of course can explain the (perhaps unexplainable) paradox that an egregious act of wickedness has produced a potential good. But if the epigraph of the story offers no ethical solution to that paradox, at least it confronts its pagan, amoral essence squarely. Taken from Schiller's poem "Thekla," it reads: "Wage du zu irren und zu träumen." To whom, we are entitled to ask, does this provocative advice apply? Not, plainly, to the conventional law-abiding Fabij, nor yet—on a conscious level at least—to his pious wife. If this triple imperative is relevant to any person in the story, it can only be to Mutsij, who, exploiting Valerija's *unconscious*, i.e., amoral, libidinous self, has indeed dared, dreamed and erred—and has thereby produced precisely what his "victims" had so long desired. Not unlike Mephistopheles (whose iconclastic spirit Turgenev had echoed elsewhere)[17] he is "Ein Teil von jener Kraft / Die stets das Böse willt / Und stets has Gute schafft" (64).

Although the buoyant, amoral optimism expressed in these lines is, it needs no saying, atypical of Turgenev's fiction taken as a whole, an attenuated, residual hope nonetheless marks the denouement of a large number of his narratives. Indeed, for all their allegedly "wanton melancholy" (Henry James 317) none of Turgenev's novels end in unmixed gloom.[18] And while a poignant sense of loss or defeat regularly marks the endings of his *povesti*, some of the most famous of these (e.g., "Spring Torrents," "First Love," "Asia") evoke a moment in the hero's with such freshness and lyrical intensity that a kind of Pushkinian *svetlaja pecal'* hangs over the whole. Viewed in this fictional context Mutsij's "serpentine" song, at once "frightening" and "triumphant," enigmatic and hopeful, may be seen as paradigmatic; and the seed which he has planted in Valerija—a not-too-distant avatar of that *life-giving drop*, which the boy-hero of a fairy tale once told by Turgenev, rescues from a dark cave filled with deadly reptiles and offers as a balm to his stricken parents.[19]

Notes

1. In a recent book-length study Elizabeth Cheresh Allen has challenged the traditional view of Turgenev as a realist. Arguing that an authentically realistic narrative takes as its subject society as Gemeinschaft (22–31), and claiming (further) that such a narrative depicts life in "Dionysian" terms, she sees Turgenev, whose vision is allegedly "Apollonian," and whose subject is society as Gesellschaft, as falling beyond the pale of realism. Since a detailed rebuttal of Ms. Allen's—to me—highly questionable criteria lies beyond the scope of this article, I will simply note that I am content to ally myself with such eminent critics of Turgenev as H. James, Mirskij, Grandjard, Wilson and Freeborn—all of whom find the term "realism" an apt and accurate description of Turgenev's narrative method. The fact that Turgenev himself repeatedly endorsed this view of his fiction is also worth noting.

2. Auerbach's distinction between the Homeric and Old Testament modes of narration (3–23) is not of course the same as Arnold's famous polarity. But the two dichotomies, the cultural and the literary, share—above and beyond their ethnic labels—much in common and can, I believe, be meaningfully yoked. Compare, for instance, the "radiancy" and "light" which Arnold attributes to Hellenism with the "brightly illuminated" world of Homer perceived by Auerbach (3); or the "clearness" of the Hellenistic vision (Arnold) with the "clearly outlined" images in Homer (Auerbach 3); or the Hellenes, who "saw things as they actually are" (Arnold) with Homer, who made things "visible and palpable in all their parts" (Auerbach 6); or "the whole play of the universal order," which the Hellenistic vision included (Arnold) with the "perfect fullness" of Homer's manner of presentation (Auerbach 6).

3. It could be claimed, perhaps, that the relatively early *povest'* "Faust" (1856) is an exception to this generalization. In point of fact, however, the only incident in the story which might be construed as supernatural in nature, namely, the cry of the dying heroine which the narrator imagines he hears, is open to a realistic interpretation. It could, he admits, have been no more than the nocturnal cry of an owl.

4. Marina Ledkovsky (69–70) has called attention to the fact that already as a young man Turgenev had shown an interest in parapsychological phenomena.

5. I have omitted the fantasy "Phantoms" (1863), because as a pure exercise in the oneiric mode (it actually derived from a dream Turgenev had), it lacks the impingement of the supernatural on the "real" which marks all the other stories.

6. The most important studies of Turgenev's "mysterious" cycle of tales are Marina Ledkovsky (see "Works Cited"); James Woodward, "Typical Images in the Late Tales of Turgenev," *SEEJ* 17 (1973): 18–32; Eva Kagan Kans, "Fate and Fantasy: A Study of Turgenev's Fantastic Short Stories," *Slavic Review* 28 (1969): 543–560; Nadezhda Natova, "O misticeskix povestjax Turgeneva," *Transactions of the Association of Russian-American Scholars* (1983): 113–49; and A. B. Muratov, *Turgenev-novellist (1870–1880 gody)* (Leningrad: Izdatel'stvo Leningradskogo Universiteta, 1980), 65–106.

7. See M. Gabel' (202–225) and A. B. Muratov (65–106) for a summary of these alleged influences. For a detailed—and more persuasive—discussion of the likely influence of Bulwer-Lytton's novel on "Song of Triumphant Love" see Ger?enzon (98–110).

8. See *infra* and Notes #9, #11 and #12 for a more detailed discussion of, and bibliographical information on, this subject.

9. In Melville's long narrative poem, *Clarel: A Poem and Pilgrimage to the Holy Land*, Vine a character based on Hawthorne, wears in an unguarded moment an expression reminiscent of the "Cenci portrait." The reference is of course to the famous painting, attributed to Guido, of Beatrice Cenci, accused of incest. (See Philip Young 98–102).

10. The fact that some modern historians doubt if Cenci ever actually committed incest in no way invalidates the course the significance of the widespread nineteenth century belief that she had.

11. "If a man takes his brother's wife, it is impurity." It is, perhaps, worth noting that Edmund Wilson, unconsciously influenced, one surmises, by the incestuous aura of the relationship, uncharacteristically gets his facts wrong and claims that Mutsij rapes his *sister-in-law* (125).

12. Quoted by Young (99). Here I am conflating Melville's statement to Julian Hawthorne, given in quotes, with the title of one of Hawthorne's most famous and patently guilt-ridden stories.

13. To a woman friend Turgenev once confided that "The physical side of my relationships with women have always mattered less than the spiritual." (Quoted by Leonard Schapiro, *Turgenev: His Life and Times* [Cambridge: Harvard UP, 1982], 72).

14. E. g., the narrator in "Andrej Kolosov," Kister in "The Bully," Rogačëv in "Three Portraits," Arkadij in *Fathers and Sons*, and Aleksej in "The Watch." For a detailed discussion of this type see Richard Gregg, "The Wimp, the Maiden and the Mensch: Turgenev's Bermuda Triangle," *Russian Literature* 38 (1995), 51–82.

16. See Young (7).

17. "Je préfère Prométhée, je préfère Satan, le type de la révolte et de l'individualité" (*Pisma*, No. 73, 279).

18. *On the Eve* is the only possible exception to this generalization. But even here Elena's resolve to serve as a nurse in the Balkans after Insarov's death may be seen as not only heroic but "life-affirming."

19. This story was paraphrased by Edmund Wilson (81–83), who used the expression "life-giving drop" as the title of his well-known essay on Turgenev.

WORKS CITED

Allen, Elizabeth Cheresh. *Beyond Realism: Turgenev's Poetics of Secular Salvation*. Stanford: Stanford UP, 1992.

Auerbach, Erich. *Mimesis: The Representation of Reality in Western Literature*. Princeton: Princeton UP, 1953.

Baym, Nina. *The Shape of Hawthorne's Career*. Ithaca: Cornell UP, 1976.

Boyesen, H. H. "A Visit to Tourgeneff." *The Galaxy* 17 (1874): 456–66.

Crews, Frederick. *The Sins of the Fathers: Hawthorne's Psychological Themes*. Berkeley: U of California P, 1964.

Fiedler, Leslie. *Love and Death in the American Novel*, New York: Stein and Day, 1973.

Gabel', M. "Pesn' toržestvuiščej ljubvi: Opyt analiza." *Tvorčeskij put' Turgeneva*. Ed. by NL. Brodskij. Petrograd: Knigoizdatel'stvo "Sejatel'", 202–23.

Geršenzon, M. *Mečta i mysl' Turgeneva*. Moskva: 1919, 98–110.

Goethe, Johan von. *Samtliche Werke*. Ed. A. Shone. Vol. 7. Frankfort: Deutscher Klassiker Verlag, 1994.

Hawthorne, Nathaniel. *The Marble Faun: Or the Romance of Monte Beni*. Vol. 2. The Century Edition of the Works of Nathaniel Hawthorne, 20 vols. Columbus: Ohio State UP, 1968.

James, Henry. *French Poets and Novelists*. London: Macmillan, 1878.

Lawrence, D. H. *Studies in Classical American Literature*. New York: Viking P, 1971.

Ledkovsky, Marina. *The Other Turgenev: From Romanticism to Symbolism*. Wurzburg: Jalverlag, 1973.

Male, Roy R. *Hawthorne's Tragic Vision*. Austin: U of Texas P, 1957.

Muratov. A. B. *Turgenev-novellist*. Leningrad: Izdatel'stvo Leningradskogo Universiteta, 1985, 65–106.

Turgenev, I. S. *Polnoe sobranie sočinenij*, Vol. 13. 30 vols. Moskva-Leningrad: Izdatel'stvo akademii nauk SSSR, 1961.

Wilson, Edmund. *A Window on Russia*. New York: Farrar, Straus and Giroux, 1972.

Young, Philip. *Hawthorne's Secret: An Un-told Tale*. Boston: David R. Godine, 1984.

PAUL W. MILLER

Willa Cather, Sherwood Anderson— and Ivan Turgenev

As oblique and evasive as their comments on this influence sometimes were, it is clear that Midwestern writers such as Cather and Anderson, like their literary predecessor Howells and their successor Hemingway, often admired, praised and emulated nineteenth-century Russian writers, especially Tolstoy and Turgenev. But the nature and extent of Russian influence on Cather and Anderson, the authors under discussion here, were very different. Whereas Cather in the early 1900s turned away from Turgenev and Tolstoy to James and Wharton as models, only to return to the Russians as models about 1912, Anderson felt a particular kinship with the Russians from the time he first read them, about 1911, to the end of his life. He especially admired Turgenev's *A Sportsman's Sketches*, consisting of loosely bound but closely related vignettes told from the viewpoint of a hunter in the Russian countryside. But if we ignore for a moment the striking parallel in structure between *Winesburg, Ohio* and the *Sketches*, it would be fair to say that his sympathy and admiration for the Russians was based more on the shared intensity of feeling they generated in him than on their usefulness to him as models. Both Cather and Anderson were slow if not reluctant to acknowledge the influence of the Russians on their writing. Cather's long silence on this subject is puzzling. Anderson's repeated denials that he had read the Russians before writing his early stories, including

From *MidAmerica* 24. © 1997 by the Society for the Study of Midwestern Literature.

Windy McPherson's Son (1915), may have been based on his fear that he would be written off as derivative if he admitted the fact that he had not only read them but profited from their inspiration and example, as his critics surmised.

In the first place, although both Cather and Anderson paid tribute to the power of Tolstoy, both seem to have found Turgenev's *Sketches* more useful to their craft of writing than the formidable, gigantic *War and Peace*. And although the influence of Turgenev's work on the conception and development of *Winesburg, Ohio* is apparent, the *Sketches'* influence on *O Pioneers!* and its successors is much more pervasive and complex, involving Cather's abandonment of the plot-driven, Jamesian drawing-room novel in favor of a novel of character resembling Turgenev's, developed for the most part by carefully juxtaposed characters in a predominately rural landscape.

Secondly, although *O Pioneers!* is a novel of character, its characters are limited in their development by poverty, drought, and lack of educational opportunity. In portraying Alexandra Bergson and her contrasting brothers Lou and Oscar as shaped in very different ways by their restrictive, sometimes apparently hostile environment; Cather again shows the influence of Turgenev rather than James, whose novels of transcendent freedom for the artist and somewhat less freedom for his international heroes had provided the inspiration for a very different, more powerful, though flawed hero in her first novel, about the never-taming bridge engineer Bartley Alexander. In making the difficult transition from what was literally her first novel, the Jamesian *Alexander's Bridge* she deprecated, to *O Pioneers!*, the first novel of which she was proud, Cather deserves credit for critical insight as well as creativity. Unlike James himself, who regarded Turgenev's work "as the absolute epitome of his own esthetic," she must have gradually come to realize that in their conception of reality James and Turgenev were poles apart. As Glyn Turton has recently phrased the issue, "James believed that the artist enjoys an absolute freedom to reconstitute the facts of reality in a formal order that transcends life itself. By contrast, Turgenev possessed a strong sense of the historical determinants of culture" (35). The apparent changes in Cather's philosophical assumptions from the composition of *Alexander's Bridge* to *O Pioneers!* signifies that she was rejecting the Jamesian approach to fiction as the transcendence of imagination over reality in favor of Turgenev's more historical, deterministic view.

Finally, the language of *O Pioneers!*, perhaps anticipating Cather's denunciation some years later of what she called the "over-furnished novel," suggests that as early as 1912 she may have already been moving away from the elaborate, well turned periods of James toward the objective, minimalist style of Turgenev. Consider with what apt simplicity Cather's oft-quoted opening sentence of *O Pioneers!* strips winter life on the frontier to its essentials: "One January day, thirty years ago, the little town of Hanover, anchored on a windy Nebraska table-land, was trying not to be blown away" (11). Clearly this sentence, inviting comparison with Turgenev's bare descriptions of the Russian steppes, is a far cry from James's urban refinement and complexity of language, which Cather had earlier praised.

Before exploring further the influence of the Russians, especially Turgenev, on Cather and Anderson, it would be useful to establish the context of this influence, which was much stronger in United States than in England, perhaps because it was easier for Americans to identity with what James called "the sense of wide Russian horizons" (293). According to Royal Gettmann, author of a fine, older study of the influence of Turgenev in England and America, Westerners admired the Russians because they had exalted the novel as a literary form and "unveiled a new and precious vision of life" (9). From about 1890 to 1940, the period of greatest Russian influence, Tolstoy, Dostoyevsky, and Chekhov were in the forefront of admiration, with Turgenev also being praised by an elite minority that included William Dean Howells in America, and in England, Henry James, Arnold Bennett, Virginia Woolf, and Ford Madox Ford, the last of whom pronounced Turgenev greater than Shakespeare (44-77, 165). On Bennett's list of the world's twelve best novels, all were Russian, with six of them by Turgenev (Gettmann 156). From 1871 on, Howells in his *Atlantic Monthly* reviews and elsewhere had praised Turgenev for his objectivity and detachment, for painting character and custom "without a word of comment" (Gettmann 55). Turgenev's reputation in America peaked about 1874, with 16 translations having appeared in the U.S. from 1867 to 1873, six of them in the form of books. But by the 1890s his limited popularity if not his reputation had been overtaken by Tolstoy, and later by Chekhov and Dostoyevsky, in spite of a cult revival of interest in Turgenev early in the twentieth century. Both Cather and Anderson seem to have been swept along on this new wave of enthusiasm for Turgenev, as was Hemingway, under Anderson's influence, in the second decade of the century. Let us turn back now to what may be the three main manifestations of Turgenev's influence on Cather: her development of the novel of character in place of the plot-driven novel, her portrayal of characters realistically limited by their time and place in history, and finally, her development of an objective, minimalist style freed from the intrusive author.

Elizabeth Sergeant's account of how *O Pioneers!* came into being, sheds light on Cather's approach to her first novel of character, involving the mysterious fusion of two stories she had meant to write separately, "The

White Mulberry Tree" and "Alexandra." "She [Cather] said she could only describe this coming together of the two elements ... as a sudden inner explosion and enlightenment. She had experienced it before only in the conception of a poem. Now she would always hope for similar experience in creating a novel, for the explosion seemed to bring with it the inevitable shape that is not plotted but designs itself" (Woodress 231-32). The two heroines of "The Mulberry Tree" and "Alexandra," Marie Shabata and Alexandra Bergson, are the most fully developed among numerous contrasting characters in the novel that came out of this fusion. And this fused story consciously or unconsciously follows the method of development illustrated by Turgenev in *A Sportsman's Sketches*, as described by James in *Partial Portraits*: "the germ of a story, with him, was never an affair of plot— that was the last thing he thought of: it was the representation of certain persons. The first form in which a tale appeared to him was as the figure of an individual, or a combination of individuals, whom he wished to see in action" (314). Contributing to the development of theme as well as plot in the works of Turgenev and Cather is the deliberate juxtaposition of characters, as Richard Harris has recently noted: "The importance of both Turgenev's and Cather's characters generally depends not on their development as psychologically complex characters but rather on the representation of qualities they possess relative to other characters, both major and minor. It is by means of the juxtaposition of characters that much of the thematic material in the fiction of both authors is presented" (176). By the time she was writing *One of Ours* in 1921, her use of juxtaposition had extended to things as well as people and was quite deliberate, as she stated in an interview:

> In this new novel *One of Ours* I'm trying to cut out all analysis, observation, description, even the picture-making quality, in order to make things and people tell their own story simply by juxtaposition, without any persuasion or explanation on my part. Just as if I were to put here on this table a green vase, and beside it a yellow orange Side by side, they produce a reaction which neither of them will produce alone.... I want the reader to see the orange and the vase—beyond that, I am out of it. Mere cleverness must go. (Harris 175-76)

Though Cather had frequently praised Turgenev as a master of the novel's finish, even as she had praised Tolstoy for the power of his writing, she admits no explicit debt to the Russians in the text of *O Pioneers!*. And though David Stouck has pointed out several of her artistic borrowings from Turgenev's stories in this novel, there are only two possible hints of her indebtedness to Russia in its introductory apparatus: in the epigraph chosen from an epic poem of the Polish exile to Russia, Adam Mickiewicz—"those fields, colored by various grain!"—and in her dedication of *O Pioneers!* to the memory of Sarah Orne Jewett, her recent model of artistic perfection, whose *Country of the Pointed Firs* Cather had once heard compared to Turgenev's *Sketches* (Stouck 2- 5; Woodress 209). Cather's published tribute to *The Firs* might also be applied to Turgenev's *Sketches*, or to *O Pioneers!* itself. The sketches in *The Firs*, she wrote, were "living things caught in the open, with light and freedom and air-space about them. They melt into the land and the life of the land until they are not stories at all, but life itself" (Woodress 241). In a presentation copy of *O Pioneers!*, she made clear her abandonment of James as a model, but ignored the new influences on her writing: "This was the first time I walked off on my own feet—everything before was half real and half an imitation of writers whom I admired. In this one I hit the home pasture and found that I was Yance Sorgeson [a prosperous but traditional Norwegian farmer] and not Henry James" (Woodress 239-40). Not until 1922, in a letter to H. L. Mencken, did she confess that as a young woman she had begun her long apprenticeship with James and Wharton in order to escape from the pervasive influence of the Russians, especially Tolstoy, on her view of America. But in writing *O Pioneers!* she wonders if she has really recovered from the Russian influence (Stouck 2). Indeed she had not, but for reasons hard to fathom, about which one can only speculate, she was chary of admitting this influence on her characterization, her conception of the artist's role in society, or her increasingly objective, minimalist style.

In order to understand Cather's changing conception of the artist's role in society, one must turn to her comments on *O Pioneers!* and to her statements on the role of the Russian writers in the development of the American novel. Underlying these comments is her belief, derived from Turgenev and the Russians, that the novelist must subordinate her imagination to the earth about which she is writing. If she can do this, then and then only can she portray truthfully and sensitively the characters which spring not from her imagination only, but from the earth itself in a particular time and place. Thus in an undated letter to Elizabeth Sergeant she wrote that in *O Pioneers!* the country insisted on being the hero and she did not interfere; her story came out of the long grasses like the *New World Symphony* of Dvorak, who had visited Nebraska in the 1880s (Stouck 9). Then in 1921 she contrasted *Alexander's Bridge* with *O Pioneers!*. The former was written when the drawing room was considered the proper setting for a novel, when only smart or clever people were deemed worth writing about, and when the younger writers were all imitating Henry James or Mrs. Wharton, "without having their qualifications." Then she began writing *O Pioneers!*, before "the novel of the soil" became popular in this country. Though it was a story without a hero, concerned "entirely with heavy farming people, with cornfields and pasture lands and pig yards,—set in Nebraska of all places," writing it not only pleased her immensely but put her on the road to writing *My Antonia*, that archetypal "novel of the soil" which was to assure her recognition as a major writer (*Willa Cather on Writing* 92-94). In a speech made in 1933, Cather once again returned to the great impact of the Russians on the American novel, associating Turgenev among others with the "novel of the soil" that had shaped her development as a novelist: "The great group of Russian novelists who flashed out in the north like a new constellation at about the middle of the last century did more for the future than they knew. They had no benumbing literary traditions behind them. They had a glorious language, new to literature.... Horse racing and dog racing and hunting are almost the best of Tolstoy. In Gogol, Turgenev, Lermontov, the earth speaks louder than the people" (*Willa Cather in Person* 170). In sum, it is the concept of the earth as the shaping force of the novel that Cather derived from the Russians, especially Turgenev, and that she also found in the modern American novel.

Let us turn now from Turgenev's probable influence on Cather's novel of character and on her choice of subject matter to his possible reinforcement of her objectivist, minimalist bent, already apparent in *O Pioneers!*, but not rationalized in print till the 1920s. Extending her method in *O Pioneers!* of developing the novel by juxtaposition of characters more than by analysis, observation, or description, she wrote in 1920: "Art, it seems to me, should simplify. That, indeed, is very nearly the whole of the higher artistic process; finding what conventions of form and what detail one can do without and yet preserve the spirit of the whole—so that all that one has suppressed and cut away is there to the reader's consciousness as much as if it were in type on the page" (*Willa Cather on Writing* 102). And in 1922 she wrote: "Whatever is felt upon the page without being specifically named there—that, one might say, is created. It is the inexplicable presence of the thing not named, of the overtone divined by the ear but not heard by it, the verbal mood, the emotional aura of the fact or the thing or the deed, that gives high quality to the novel or the drama, as well as to poetry itself" (*Willa Cather on Writing* 41-42). Though she may also have found this objectivist-minimalist practice and theory in other writers she admired, such as Gogol, Merimee and Jewett, one notes an almost uncanny resemblance between her literary practice and

Turgenev's, leading one to suspect his influence here also. One of his best interpreters, Avrahm Yarmolinsky, has summed up Turgenev's literary practice as follows: The writer "must maintain close contact with life. To represent it truthfully and fairly, without philosophizing about it or trying to improve it—that was the greatest happiness for the artist. But since reality 'teemed' with adventitious matter, the novelist's gift, [Turgenev] insisted, lay in the ability to eliminate all superficialities, so as to render only that which, in the light of his knowledge and understanding, appeared significant" (252).

Turgenev's practice was clearly consistent with his literary theory, which appears in two of his letters to anticipate Cather's insistence on the presence in literature of "the thing not named" as the mark of its excellence: A writer, he said, "must be a psychologist—but a secret one; he must know and feel the roots of phenomena, but only present the phenomena themselves." And in another letter he said that the writer must have a complete knowledge of his characters in order to avoid overloading the page with unnecessary detail (Stouck 6). To build up this secret knowledge, he kept "dossiers" on his characters, as though they were criminals who needed to be thoroughly and systematically investigated (James 315). Though this third possible influence of Turgenev on Cather cannot be finally demonstrated, its likelihood exists, just as there is a likelihood that Hemingway, despite his consistently disparaging remarks about Cather, was influenced by her as well as Turgenev when he first came out with his supposedly original iceberg theory, articulated in various forms from 1923 to 1932 and later. According to this now all too familiar bromide, the greatness of literature depends at least in part on the deliberate omission of material that the writer knows well and the reader nevertheless feels, just as the "dignity of movement of an ice-berg" depends on its being seven-eighths under water (Smith 271-73). Hemingway's recurrent comparisons between writing and painting, particularly the painting of Cezanne, tend to confirm this influence. They may echo Cather's comparison of her writing method in a published interview of 1921 to the painterly juxtaposition of a green vase and a yellow orange, as in a still life by Cezanne (though he preferred to paint apples). Hemingway may well have read this *Bookman* interview, even as he read the Pulitzer Prize winning book Cather was discussing in the interview (Smith 271, 284; Hemingway 105).

Compared to Turgenev's influence on Cather, his influence on Anderson amounts to no more than an appendix to a book, or a codicil to a will, but a very interesting codicil all the same. For despite his frequent praise of the intensity of such Russians as Gorki, Tolstoy, Dostoyevsky, and Chekhov, Anderson seems not to have found their genius compatible with his own, except for Turgenev in the *Sketches*. One of his early references to the Russian writers is in a letter to Marietta Finley of December 21, 1916. It dwells on parallels Anderson has observed between American life and the Russian life described by these writers, and laments the failure of the Americans to write with the intensity of the Russians: "There is no reason at all why Americanism should not be seen with the same intensity of feeling so characteristic of Russian Artists when they write of Russian life. Our life is as provincial. It is as full of strange and illuminating side lights. Because we have not written intensely is no reason why we should not begin" (Sutton 301). But though he admired their intensity, he claimed he did not want to write like them. Although as late as 1939 in a letter to Rosenfeld he denied that he had read the Russians before writing his first stories, elsewhere he told a different tale, as befits a story teller. Thus in 1924 in a letter to Roger Sergel he wrote that he had been fumbling around as a story teller till he read the Russians. Then, in a tribute that recalls Keats' great tribute to Chapman in the sonnet "On First Looking into Chapman's Homer," he recalls the epiphany of his first reading Turgenev's *Sketches*, the work that was to encourage and guide him like a beacon light, an ideal through life, whenever he stooped, as he often did, to money-grubbing: "I was perhaps 35 years old [roughly 1911] when I first found the Russian prose writers. One day I picked up Turgenev's 'Annals of a Sportsman.' I remember how my hands trembled as I read the book. I raced through the pages like a drunken man" (Sutton 301). In 1924, in *A Story Teller's Story*, he evasively said that the Russian impulse behind his stories was plausible (Sutton 301). But of the influence of Turgenev on *Winesburg, Ohio*, which cries out for comparison with *A Sportsman's Sketches*, Anderson remains discreetly silent.

All one can say without detailed comparison of the texts, is that each consists of twenty-five loosely bound but closely related sketches, depending less on dramatic impact than lyrical insight. Each is also told from the apparently detached viewpoint of an observer, in one case George Willard, in the other a sportsman devoted to hunting. Although differences between the two works abound, the most obvious may have to do with their narrators. Willard is a struggling youth of the town, becoming acquainted in his reporter's capacity with the elite as well as the common folk of Winesburg. The well-to-do, aristocratic Russian, on the other hand, devoted to hunting, pursues his sport everywhere in the Russian countryside, which is vividly conjured up for the reader by a few deft strokes of the artist's pen. In the process the narrator, like the reader, meets serfs and noblemen alike, the former at their back-breaking, penurious work, and the latter enjoying or feverishly managing their lavish but often decaying estates. Another key difference is that although *Winesburg, Ohio* is in one sense a developmental work, focused on George Willard's maturing, *The Sketches* has the viewpoint of a mature man, unchanged from beginning to end, even though a reader's sense of outrage at the aristocrats' exploitation and abuse of the serfs may increase as one reads the sketches.

In retrospect one can see that though the Russian novelists, especially Turgenev, exerted a powerful influence on both Cather and Anderson. Turgenev's influence on Cather was much more extensive and complex, extending to her development of the novel of character, to what she later called the "novel of the soil," and probably to the objectivist-minimalist style to which she became increasingly dedicated after experimenting with *O Pioneers!* For Anderson, the Russian novelists chiefly provided inspiration based on their passionate intensity, which he may have emulated in his own writing, but in an environment he perceived to be radically different from theirs. For both American authors, *A Sportsman's Sketches* seems to have been Turgenev's seminal work, which may have contributed importantly to the radical change in Cather's art that begins about 1912, and which in the same decade may have inspired Anderson to compose *Winesburg, Ohio*, that remarkable fusion, like Turgenev's *Sketches*, of the short story and novel form

WORKS CITED

Cather, Willa. *O Pioneers!* Ed. Susan J. Rosowski and Others. Lincoln: U of Nebraska P, 1992.

_____. *Willa Cather in Person*. Ed. Brent Bohlke. Lincoln: U of Nebraska P, 1986.

_____. *Willa Cather on Writing*. Lincoln: U of Nebraska P, 1988.

Gettmann, Royal A. "Turgenev in England and America." Illinois *Studies in Language and Literature* 27, No. 2. Urbana: U of Illinois P, 1940:1-196.

Harris, Richard. "Willa Cather, Ivan Turgenev, and the Novel of Character," *Cather Studies* 1. Lincoln: U of Nebraska P, 1990:172-79.

Hemingway, Ernest. *Selected Letters 1917-1961*. Ed. Carlos Baker. New York: Scribner's, 1981.

James, Henry. "Ivan Turgenieff." *Partial Portraits*. Westport, CT: Greenwood, 1970 [1888]:291-323.

Smith, Paul. "Hemingway's Early Manuscripts: The Theory and Practice of Omission." *Journal of Modern Literature* 10 (1983):268-88.

Stouck, David. "Willa Cather and the Russians." *Cather Studies* 1. Lincoln: U of Nebraska P, 1990:1-19.

Sutton, William A. *The Road to Winesburg*. Metuchen, NJ: Scarecrow, 1972.

Turton, Glyn. *Turgenev and the Context of English Literature 1850-1900*. London: Routledge, 1992.

Woodress, James. Willa Cather: *A Literary Life*. Lincoln: U of Nebraska P, 1987.

Yarmolinsky, Avrahm. "Fathers and Children." *Fathers and Sons*. Ed. Ralph Matlaw. New York: Norton, 1989: 251-57.

Chronology

1818	Born on October 28 in the provincial town of Orel, the second son of Varvara Petrona (nee Lutovinova) and Sergei Nikolaevich Turgenev, a handsome cavalry officer. His mother is well-read, especially in late eighteenth century French literature, and has an extensive library. His father had some literary contacts, such as the poet, Vasilii Andreevich Zhukovsky and the historical novelist, Mikhail Nikolaevich Zagoskin.
1821	Sergei Nikolaevich retires from active duty and the family moves to Spasskoe, a place which would be important throughout Turgenev's life.
1822	In May the family embarks on a journey through Western Europe for about a year.
1824	In February, the Turgenev family moves to Moscow.
1827	Turgenev begins his formal schooling, alternating between local schools and private tutors. He receives a broad education with an emphasis on languages—French, German, Latin, Greek, and Russian.
1833	Ivan's father petitions Moscow University to allow his son, who had not yet reached the minimum age of seventeen, to take the requisite exams for entrance to the Philology Faculty. An exemption is finally granted, thanks to the intervention of the Minister of Education. During the

summer of that year, Ivan's family lives in a dacha outside Moscow. Ivan meets and falls for Ekaterina Shakhovskoy. He soon learns that she has several suitors, including his own father, an incident that would later inspire the short story, "Pervaia liubov" ("First Love") published in 1860. Ivan begins his university studies in the fall.

1834   Ivan Turgenev transfers to St. Petersburg University and lives with his elder brother, Nikolai, and his father. Sergei Nikolaevich dies on October 30, 1834. By this time, Ivan is already writing poetry, imitating Byron in his poem *Steno* (later published in 1913). While at St. Petersburg, he reads and encounters many contemporary writers, among them Gogol (who briefly served as his professor of history) and Pushkin (whom he met twice within days of Pushkin's fatal duel in 1837).

1836   Turgenev successfully completes the Philological Faculty. In October, his name appears in print for the first time, under a review of a travelogue to Russian holy places.

1837   Turgenev returns to St. Petersburg University to obtain the degree of Candidate, which would enable him to continue his studies.

1838   In January, he publishes a lyric poem, "Vecher" in *Souvremennik* (*The Contemporary*). In May, he leaves for Germany on the steamer, *Nicholas I*, with the intention of studying philosophy at Berlin University. The steamer catches fire, an incident that he will later record in a sketch, "Une incendie en mer" ("Fire at Sea") which documents his panic and fear of death at nineteen years of age.

1840   In Berlin, Turgenev becomes close to fellow Russians such as Mikhail Aleksandrovich Bakunin and Timofei Nikolaevich Granovsky. Nikolai Vladimirovich Stankevich became a model for many of Turgenev's noblest of characters (including Pokrovsky in *Rudin* and hero of the story, "Iakov Pasynkov." He also becomes a habitué at the Frolov family salon, where he meets such prominent Germans as Karl Werder, the student of and successor to Georg Wilhelm Friedrich Hegel as Professor of Philosophy at Berlin University; the explorer Alexander von Humboldt; the critic and essayist Karl Varnhagen von Ense; and

| | Bettina von Arnim, known for her memoirs of Johann Wolfgang von Goethe, an author whom, along with Shakespeare, Ivan cherished. |

1841   In May, Turgenev returns to Russia, stopping first at the Bakunin family estate, where he becomes romantically involved with Bakunin's sister Tat'iana. At Spasskoe, he studies for his comprehensive exams.

1842   In April-May, he takes his exams at St. Petersburg University. On April 26, Turgenev's daugher, Pelageia is born, the product of an affair with Avdot'ia Ermolaevna Ivanova, one of his mother's seamstresses at Spasskoe.

1843   In February, Turgenev becomes a member of Belinsky's intellectual circle and meets Pavel Vasil'evich Annenkov, who will become a close friend and literary advisor. In April he publishes a narrative poem, *Parasha*, which marks the official start of his literary career. In June, Turgenev is appointed to a minor post at the Ministry of Internal Affairs in the office of Vladimir Ivanovich Dal', the famous lexicographer and collector of folk sayings and proverbs. In October, St. Petersburg is captivated with the French diva Pauline Viardot-Garcia. On his twenty-fifth birthday, Turgenev meets her husband, Louis Viardot, a political writer, journalist, and translator of *Don Quixote* into French. Turgenev's relationship with Pauline influenced much of his later life. Their relationship has been the subject of much speculation, particularly as to whether it was a "platonic" one. Ironically, Turgenev's relationship with Louis Viardot never suffered from the gossip.

1844   In February, Turgenev meets Alexsandr Ivanovich Herzen who would later become the editor of the émigré journal *Kolokol* (*The Bell*) and in April he meets some of the founding members of the Slavophile circle, including Iurii Fedorovich Samarin and Konstantin Sergeevich Aksakov. The first of his short stories, "Andrei Kolosov," appears in the November issue of *Otechestvennye zapiski* (*Notes of the Fatherland*). Also begins a series of literary collaborations with Louis Viardot with a French translation of Gogol, later to be followed with translations of Pushkin, Lermontov, and Turgenev into French.

1845	In April, with increased literary activities, Turgenev leaves his post at the Ministry of Internal Affairs and leaves Russia in early May and joins the Viardots at Courtavenel, their estate south of Paris. It is here that he also meets George Sand, who has become a mentor to Pauline. In November, he returns to Russia for Pauline's third consecutive season of engagements in both Russian capitals and becomes involved in the literary world of St. Petersburg and makes a commitment to assist in the publication of a journal, *Sovremennik*.
1847	In January, the first issues of *Sovremennik* are published and include Turgenev's cycle of nine lyric poems under the title "Derevnia"—establishing him as a major international writer. *Zapiski okhotnika* occupies Turgenev's literary efforts for the next few years. In mid January, he returns to Berlin. In May, Berlinsky arrives with the futile expectation of curing his tuberculosis at the spa town of Salzbrunn.
1848	Publishes the play, *Gde tonko, tam i rvetsia* (*The Weakest Link*) in the November issue of *Sovremennik*. Makes short visit to Brussels when he learns of the start of the 1848 Revolution in Paris and rushes back to Paris to observe the events in which many of his friends were involved.
1849	Publishes a comedy, *Kholostiak* (*The Bachelor*) in the September issue of *Otechestvennye zapiski* which is soon performed for the first time at the Aleksandrinskii Theater in St. Petersburg.
1850	Turgenev ends his stay abroad and arrives in St. Petersburg on June 20 and quickly moves on to Moscow. In the summer, while in the country, Turgenev begins the final set of sketches of *Zapiski okhotrika*, each devoted to particularly striking individuals from among the peasants.

Turgenev sees his eight-year-old daughter, Pelageia. Pauline Viardot offers to raise Pelageia in her own family to which Turgenev assents as a way of sparing the child from all legal and social problems in Russia associated with her illegitimacy. In October Pelageia is dispatched to Paris, but the decision is a source of difficulties and friction for many years.

Turgenev is still at odds with his mother—he and his

brother break ties with her and repair to the small estate they had inherited from their father. In November, his mother falls seriously ill and Turgenev arrives in Moscow just after her funeral. Her death leaves Ivan a wealthy landowner and he inherits his beloved Spasskoe.

1851   Publishes *Provintsialka* (*A Provincial Lady*) in September 1849 in *Otechestvennye zapiski*. In October, Tugenev meets Gogol again, this time as a young writer whose works Gogol had noted with appreciation.

1852   Gogol dies on February 21. His socially conscious work had been a source of inspiration for Turgenev and others. Turgenev writes a short obituary that was banned by the St. Petersburg censors. Following this, he sends his obituary to Moscow where it is published on March 13 in the newspaper *Moskovski vedomost* (*Moscow News*) which precipitates a storm upon Turgenev's head. As a result, Nicholas I orders Turgenev's arrest and imprisonment at a local police station on April 16, followed by exile to his estate at Spasskoe, where he is permitted to travel within the provice of Orel, visit with neighbors, and go hunting. He writes "Mumu," a touching story of a deaf serf and the dog his mistress forces him to drown because it disturbed her. Many believe that his punishment was for *Zapiski okhotrika*, which were published in early August 1852. August Viedert translates some of the sketches into German.

1853   In March, he travels secretly with a false passport to Moscow to meet with Pauline Viardot. In November, through the efforts of his friends, Tugenev is reprieved and granted permission to return to St. Petersburg. He completes the first part of his novel, "Dva pokoleniia" ("Two Generations") in March, although only a short extract is ever published, the remainder being lost. Turgenev also assumes an active role in the literary and intellectual life of the capital, attending theatre and concerts. He establishes a primarily platonic relationship with a distant relative, Ol'gra Aleksandrovna Turgeneva. Ol'gra served as a model for the much-suffering heroine, Tat'iana Shestova in Turgenev's novel, *Dym*.

1854   *Zapiski okhotrika* is beginning to make its way through
            Europe. A French translation is done by a former private
            tutor in Russia, Ernest Charrière, which appears in Paris in
            April 1854, after the start of the Crimean War. Viedert
            arranges for half of the stories to appear in a volume one of
            Aus dem Tagebuch eines Jägers (*From the Diary of a Hunter*)
            published in Berlin in October. Charrière's translation
            establishes Turgenev's name among the European reading
            public.

1855   Publishes *Mesiats v derevne* (previously titled, *The Student*) is
            finally published, after years of censorship, in January.
            August Boltz translates and publishes the second volume of
            Aus dem Tagebuch eines Jägers. *Zapiski okhotrika* is published
            in Edinburgh in 1855 under the title *Russian Life in the
            Interior, or The Experiences of a Sportsman* in a translation by
            James D. Meiklejohn. Turgenev spends considerable time
            in bringing the poetry of Tiutchev and Baratynsky as well
            as Afansaii Afans'evich Fet's translation of the odes of
            Horace to the public awareness. Most of the summer is
            spent writing *Rudin*, his first published novel. He returns to
            St. Petersburg in 1855 and reads his new work to friends
            and colleagues from the *Sovremennik* circle. Leo Tolstoy
            arrives in St. Petersburg in mid-November and moves in
            with Turgenev. Their relationship is turbulent although
            they admire each other's work.

1856   In January and February, *Rudin* appears in two issues of
            Sovremennik. The eponymous hero, modeled in part on
            Bakunin, is concerned with the bifurcation of idealistic
            ideas and their practical implementation and the novel is
            generally considered to be an important milestone in
            Turgenev's writing career. Also publishes, in January,
            "Perepiska" ("A Correspondence"), a story which he had
            labored over for nearly a decade. On July 21, Turgenev
            leaves for Europe to be reunited with Pauline Viardot and
            his daughter, whom he hardly knew. In November, the
            corpus of his works is made available in a collected edition,
            Povesti i rasskay I.S. Turgeneva (*The Novellas and Stories of I.S.
            Turgenev*).

1857   In May, Turgenev travels to England for an extended visit.
            Here he meets many prominent British figures, including

Thomas Carlyle, Williame Makepeace Thackeray, Thomas Macaulay, Benjamin Disraeli and Florence Nightingale. Spends the summer visiting various spas and doctors in an attempt to rid himself of a mysterious illness. He begins the story "Asia" while at the spa in Sinzig, a small town on the Rhine. In late September he leaves for Rome.

1858   "Asia" is published in the January issue of *Sovermennik*, a work which in some ways marks a significant change in Russian intellectual life, the break between Turgenev's 1840s liberals and the radical generation which followed in the 1860s. In January, a leading radical, Chernyshevsky, publishes an article in Atenei which uses "Asia" as a pretext for criticizing liberal indecisiveness. This attack is soon followed by another reviewer, Dobroliubov, criticizing the split between duty and personal happiness in Turgenev's *Faust*.

1859   In early June, he returns to Russia, immediately leaving St. Petersburg for his beloved Spasskoe. He spends the summer and autumn hunting and working on his second novel, *Dvorianskoe gnezdo* (*A Nest of the Gentry*). While on his estate, he begins to work on a settlement with his peasants in anticipation of the emancipation process in Russia, and is a member of the Society for Aid to Needy Authors and Academics. He returns to St. Petersburg in mid November. Annenkov reads the novel to a circle of friends and colleagues. *Dvorianskoe gnezdo* appears in the January 1859 issue of *Sovremennik*. Its influence on Russian intellectual life is unprecedented. Turgenev makes his final separation from *Sovermennik*.

1860   In January, he reads his essay, "*Gamlet i Don Kikhot*" ("Hamlet and Don Quixote") at a fund-raiser for the literary fund, arguing that these two literary figures are representative of two fundamental and opposing human psychological types, the egotistical paralyzed by excessive self-absorption and the selfless personality given over to selfless waste and inappropriate causes. His new novel, *Nakanune*, appears in February in a double issue of *Russkii vestnik* (*The Russian Herald*). It is not well-received, in particular by Countess Lambert. Charged with plagiarism by Osnovsky, an informal arbitration hearing is held on March 29 at which the judges, Annenko, Druzhinin and Dudyshkin, find Turgenev not guilty.

1861   While in Paris on March 6, Turgenev hears of the Emancipation of the Serfs. In May he returns to Spasskoe and visits with his neighbor, the poet Afanasii Afanas'evich Fet, and Tolstoy. He and Tolstoy have a heated argument on the issue of charity, Tolstoy being opposed to anything "compulsory." On August 29, Turgenev leaves the manuscript for *Ottsy i deti* (*Fathers and Sons*) with the editor of *Russkii vestnik*, Mikhail Katkov, and returns to Paris.

1862   *Fathers and Sons* appears in the February issue of *Russkii vestni*, with generally favorable reactions. The word nihilist that he had introduced in the novel began to be identified with young radicals and, when Turgenev was in St. Petersburg that year, he was accused by an acquaintance of having caused the civil unrest that brought with it wide-spread arson.

1863   Pauline Viardot officially retires from her operatice career in the summer, citing among various reasons her opposition to Napoleon III of France, and takes up residence at the cosmopolitan spa town of Baden-Baden near the German Black Forest. Turgenev begins to gravitate towards this town.

1864   From Baden, Turgenev set out in early January to St. Petersburg to face a Senate Commission of Enquiry into this contacts with London émigrés. "Prizraki" ("Apparitions") is published in Dostoyevsky's journal, *Epokha* (*Epoch*) and "Sobaka" ("The Dog") is completed, though not published until March 1866.

1865   Turgenev moves to Baden-Baden following his daughter's marriage on February 25, 1865 to Gaston Bruère, the manager of a glass factory in Rougement. He begins his fifth and most ideological novel, *Dym*. The Moscow publisher F. Salaev issued a five-volume collected edition of his work.

1867   After suffering from his first attacks of gout, Turgenev arrives in St. Petersburg in late February, where he reads the story "Istoriia leitenanta Ergunova" ("The Story of

Lieutenant Ergunov") and the first chapters of *Dym* to a group that included Botkin and Annenkov. He also gives public readings from his novel for charity. The critical response to the novel following its appearance in the March 1867 issue of *Russkii vestnik* is not favorable and, among other things, he is criticized for having been absent from Russia, a fact which many believed undermined his ability to understand the people.

1868   Turgenev builds an impressive villa next door to the Viardots' chalet in Baden-Baden. Prior to his occupancy, the villa had been the venue for a series of operettas composed by Pauline Viardot to librettos by Tugenev performed before audiences that often included royalty such as Augusta, Queen of Prussia. Turgenev looked forward to living in peace and harmony here, next to the people he loved the most. That harmony would be broken by the Franco-Prussian War of 1870-1871. The Moscow publisher, F. Salaev publishes a seven-volume edition of his work in 1868-1869.

1871   The defeat of Napoleon III and the occupation of France forced the Viardots to move to London in October. Turgenev followed them and, when they eventually returned to their house in Paris, he was offered the top floor of their house as his residence.

1872   Turgenev publishes *Veshnie vody*, a novella, and begins to think about the narodnik movement which expressed the selfless desire of young Russians to reciprocate the debt they owed to the emancipated serfs (for all the privileges they received in their youth from the serfs).

1874   Publishes "Nashi poslali," a reminiscence of the fighting he observed in the streets of Paris during the 1848 Revolution.

1875   Turgenev builds a villa for himself in Bougival, where he would later die.

1876   Spends the summer at Spasskoe and begins working on his last novel, *Nov'* (*Virgin Soil*). In July, he experiences the first signs of back pain that would later prove to be a symptom of spinal cancer.

1877   *Nov'* finally appears in the first two issues of *Vestnik Europy*. Preliminary reception to the novel is basically negative.

First of the mass *narodnik* trials, the so-called "Trial of 50" are held in February-March.

1878   Turgenev the vice president of the International Literary Congress (devoted to the cruicial issues of authorial rights and copyright), attends an event held in Paris to coincide with the International Exhibition. In April, the economic decline forces him to sell his personal art collection.

1879   Turgenev is lionized and feted wherever he goes in Russia—the younger generation of the 1860s, who had previously vilified him, now welcomed him as a revered writer. Honored with a Doctorate of Civil Laws from Oxford University. He visits Tolstoy at his estate, Iasnaia Poliana.

1881   Publishes "Pesn," ("A Song of Love and Triumph") an historical and exotic story set in sixteenth-century Ferrara. Makes his lat visit to Russia, spending much of the summer at Spasskoe where he is visited by Tolstoy.

1882   Turgenev's health deteriorates rapidly and he spends the remainder of his life in excruciating pain. His daughters marriage breaks down as she flees from her husband in February 1882 with her two children to go into hiding in Switzerland.

1883   Turgenev publishes his final work, the story "Klara Milich" which returns to the theme of the power of love—here, so powerful that it defeats death. On January 14, he is operated on for the removal of a hypogastric protrusion. Bulletins about his health appear regularly in European newspapers. On April 28, he is transported to Bougival. The Viardots give him extraordinary care though Louis Viardot dies on May 5 while Pauline takes dictation for his final stories—the account in French of the fire aboard the *Nicholas I* and "Une fin" ("The End"), a character sketch of the landowner Talagaev. Ivan Turgenev dies on September 3, surrounded by the family he loved. On September 27, his body travels to its final resting place in the Vokov Cemetery, a huge crowd lines the streets of St. Petersburg to pay their respects and salute the massive funeral procession.

Contributors

HAROLD BLOOM is Sterling Professor of the Humanities at Yale University and Henry W. and Albert A. Berg Professor of English at the New York University Graduate School. He is the author of over 20 books, including *Shelley's Mythmaking* (1959), *The Visionary Company* (1961), *Blake's Apocalypse* (1963), *Yeats* (1970), *A Map of Misreading* (1975), *Kabbalah and Criticism* (1975), *Agon: Toward a Theory of Revisionism* (1982), *The American Religion* (1992), *The Western Canon* (1994), and *Omens of Millennium: The Gnosis of Angels, Dreams, and Resurrection* (1996). *The Anxiety of Influence* (1973) sets forth Professor Bloom's provocative theory of the literary relationships between the great writers and their predecessors. His most recent books include *Shakespeare: The Invention of the Human* (1998), a 1998 National Book Award finalist, *How to Read and Why* (2000), and *Genius: A Mosaic of One Hundred Exemplary Creative Minds* (2002). In 1999, Professor Bloom received the prestigious American Academy of Arts and Letters Gold Medal for Criticism, and in 2002 he received the Catalonia International Prize.

RICHARD FREEBORN retired in 1988 as Chair of Russian Literature at London University. He is an editor of *Ideology in Russian Literature* (1990) and the author of *The Rise of the Russian Novel: Studies in the Russian Novel from Eugene Onegin to War and Peace* (1973).

KATHRYN FEUER has been a Professor of Russian Literature at the University of Virginia. She is the author of "Intentional and Emergent

Structures in Dead Souls: Chichikov: A Case for Defense" (1989) and Tolstoy and the Genesis of *War and Peace* (1996).

EDGAR L. FROST teaches in the Modern and Classical Languages Department at the University of Alabama in Tuscaloosa. He is the author of "Characterization Through Time in the Works of Chekhov, with an Emphasis on 'The Cherry Orchard'" (1976) and "Hidden Traits: The Subtle Imagery of Zhivye moshchi" (1992).

ROBERT COLTRANE teaches in the English Department at Lock Haven University in Pennsylvania. He is the author of "Legend, Autobiography, and the Occult in 'The Cap and Bells': A Fusion of Disparate Entities" (1990) and "The Crafting of Dreiser's Twelve Men" (1991).

RICHARD C. HARRIS has been Associate Professor of Humanities at the State University of New York, Maritime College. He is the author of "Willa Cather and Pierre Charron on Wisdom: The Skeptical Philosophy of *Shadows on the Rock*" (1999) and *William Sydney Porter (O. Henry): A Reference Guide* (1980).

HAROLD K. SCHEFSKI is a Professor in the Foreign Language Department at California State University in Long Beach. He is the author of "Tolstoy and Jealousy" (1989) and "Childhood on a Pedestal: Tolstoy's Oasis from Nihilism" (1989).

PATRICK WADDINGTON is Emeritus Professor of Russian Literature, Victoria University of Wellington, New Zealand. Among his publications are *Russian by Subjects: A Classified Vocabulary* (1992); "Russian Variations on an English Theme: The Crying Children of Elizabeth Barrett Browning" (1997); and *Ivan Turgenev and Britain* (1995).

IRENE MASING-DELIC is an associate editor of *The Russian Review* and has been an associate professor of Russian Literature at Ohio State University in Columbus. She is the author of "The Metaphysics of Liberation: Insarov as Tristan" (1989) and a contributing editor to *Solzhenitsyn: A Collection of Critical Essays* (1976).

GLYN TURTON has held the position of Head of Humanities at Chester College of Higher Education.

DENNIS WALDER has been Senior Lecturer of Literature at the Open University. He is the author of *Post-Colonial Literatures in English: History, Language, Theory* (1998) and editor of *The Nineteenth-Century Novel: Identities* (2001).

PAM MORRIS has held the position of Reader in English at Liverpool John Moores University. She is the author of *"Bleak House* and the Struggle for the State Domain" (2001) and "A Taste for Change in *Our Mutual Friend*: Cultivation or Education?" (2000).

RICHARD GREGG has been a Professor of Russian at Vassar College. He is the author of "Gogol's 'Diary of a Madman': The Fallible Scribe and the Sinister Bulge" (1999) and "Pushkin's Novelistic Prose: A Dead End?" (1998).

PAUL W. MILLER is Professor Emeritus at Wittenberg University. He is the editor of *Seven Minor Epics of the English Renaissance, 1596-1624* (1967) and the author of "Sherwood Anderson's Discovery of a Father" (1999) and "Hemingway's Posthumous Fiction: From Brimming Vault to Bare Cupboard" (1994).

Bibliography

Allen, Elizabeth Cheresh. *Beyond Realism: Turgenev's Poetics of Secular Salvation*. Stanford, California: Stanford University Press, 1992.

Atteberry, Phillip D. "Regenerative and Degenerative Forces in Turgenev's *Fathers and Sons. South Central Review*, vol. 5, no. 1 (1988 Spring): 48-60.

Beaumont, Barbara, ed. *Flaubert and Turgenev, A Friendship in Letters: The Complete Correspondence*. London: Athlone Press, 1985.

Kenneth N. Brostrom. "The Journey as Solitary Confinement in *Fathers and Children*." *Canadian-American Slavic Studies* 17, no. 1 (1983): 13-38.

Brouwer, Sander. *Character in the Short Prose of Ivan Sergeevic Turgenev*. Amsterdam and Atlanta, GA: Rodopi, 1996.

Brang, Peter. "Turgenev and the –isms." *Russian Literature* 16, no. 4 (1984): 305-22.

Cockrell, Roger and David Richards, eds. *The Voice of a Giant: Essays on Seven Russian Prose Classics*. Exeter: University of Exeter, 1985. (check publisher details)

Costlow, Jane T. *Worlds Within Worlds: The Novels of Ivan Turgenev*. Princeton, N.J.: Princeton University Press, 1990.

———. "'Oh-là-là and 'No-no-no': Odintsova as Woman Alone in *Fathers and Children*." In Sona Stephan Hoisington, ed. *A Plot of Her Own: The Female Protagonist in Russian Literature*. Evanston, Ill.: Northwestern University Press, 1995: 21-32.

FitLyon, April. "I.S. Turgenev and the 'Woman Question.'" *New Zealand Slavonic Journal* (1983): 161-73.

Friel, Brian. *Fathers and Sons: After the Novel by Ivan Turgenev*. London: Faber, 1987.

Gettemann, Royal Alfred. *Turgenev in England and America*. Westport, Connecticut: Greenwood Press, 1974.

Gottlieb, Nora and Raymond Chapman, eds and trans. *Letters to an Actress: The Story of Ivan Turgenev and Marya Gavrilovna Savina*. London: Allison & Busby, 1973.

Grossman, Joan Delaney. "Transformations of Time in Turgenev's Poetic." *Stanford Slavic Studies*, 4, no. 1 (1991): 382-400.

Ford, Ford Madox. *Portraits from Life: Memories and Criticisms of Henry James, Joseph Conrad, Thomas Hardy, H.G. Wells, Stephen Crane, D.H. Lawrence, John Galsworthy, Ivan Turgenev, W.H. Hudson, Theodore Dreiser, Algernon Charles Swinburne*. New York : Houghton Mifflin Company, 1937.

Freeborn, Richard. "Bazarov as a Portrayal of a Doomed Revolutionary." *New Zealand Slavonic Journal* (1983): 71-83.

———. "Turgenev and Revolution." *Slavonic and East European Review*, 61, no. 4 (1983): 518-27.

Hellgren, Ludmila. *Dialogues in Turgenev's Novels: Speech-Introductory Devices*. Stockholm: Almqvist & Wiksell International, 1980.

Henry, Peter. "I.S. Turgenev: *Fathers and Sons*" (1862). In Williams, David Anthony.*The Monster in the Mirror: Studies in Nineteenth-Century Realism*. Oxford UP for Univ. of Hull, (1978): 40-74

Hershkowitz, Harry. *Democratic Ideas in Turgenev's Works*. New York: Columbia University Press, 1932; New York: AMS Press, 1973.

Hier, Edmund. "Duty and Inclination in Turgenev's 'Faust.'" In John Whiton and Harry Loewen, eds., *Crisis and Commitment: Studies in German and Russian Literature in Honour of J.W. Dyck*. Waterloo, Ontario: University of Waterloo Press, 1983: 78-86.

Holquist, Michael. "Bazarov and Sečenov: The Role of Scientific Metaphor in *Fathers and Sons*." *Russian Literature* 6, no. 4 (1984): 359-74.

Hutchings, S. "Love of Words/Words of Love: Self-Sacrifice, Self-Identity and the Struggle with Dualism in Turgenev's *Rudin*." *The Slavonic & East European Review*, 76, no. 4 (1998): 614-32.

Jahn, Gary R. "Character and Theme in *Fathers and Sons*." *College Literature* 4 (1977): 80-91.

Lowe, David Allan. *Critical Essays on Ivan Turgenev*. Boston, Mass.: G.K. Hall, 1989.

Lowe, David. "Doubling in Fathers and Sons." *Essays in Literature* 9, no. 2 (1982 Fall): 240-250.

Margarshack, David. *Turgenev: A Life*. London: Faber & Faber, 1954.

Masing-Delic, Irene. "The Metaphysics of Liberation: Insarov aas Tristan." *Welt der Slaven*, 32 (N.F. XI) no. 1 (1987): 59-77.

Moser, Charles A. *Ivan Turgenev*. New York: Columbia University Press, 1972.

Peterson, Dale E. "From Russian with Love: Turgenev's Maidens and Howells' Heroines." *Canadian Slavonic Papers*, 26, no. 1 (1984): 24-34.

Pritchett, V.S. *The Gentle Barbarian: The Life and Work of Turgenev*. New York: The Ecco Press, 1977.

Ripp, Victor. *Turgenev's Russia: From Notes of a Hunter to Fathers and Sons*. Ithaca: Cornell University Press, 1980.

Schapiro, L. *Turgenev*. London: Oxford University Press (1978).

Seeley, Frank Friedeberg. *Turgenev: A Reading of His Fiction*. Cambridge and New York: Cambridge University Press, 1991.

Sheidley, William E. "Born in Imitation of Someone Else": Reading Turgenev's 'Hamlet of the Shchigrovsky District' as a Version of Hamlet." Studies in Short Fiction, 27, no. 3 (1990 Summer): 391-98.

Traill, Nancy H. *Possible Worlds of the Fantastic: The Rise of the Paranormal in Fiction*. Toronto and Buffalo: University of Toronto Press, 1996.

Waddington, Patrick, ed. *Ivan Turgenev and Britain*. Oxford, UK: Providence, Rhode Island: Berg Publishers, 1995.

———. *Turgenev and England*. London: Macmillan, 1980.

———. "Turgenev and Pauline Viardot: An Unofficial Marriage." *Canadian Slavonic Papers*, 26, no. 1 (1984): 42-64.

Wasiolek, Edward. *Fathers and Sons: Russia at the Cross-Roads*. New York: Twayne, 1993.

———. "Bazarov and Odintsova." *Canadian-American Slavic Studies*, 17, no. 1 (1983): 39-48.

Wilkinson, Myler. *Hemingway and Turgenev: The Nature of Literary Influence*. Ann Arbor, Michigan: UMI Research Press, 1986.

Woodward, James B. *Metaphysical Conflict: A Study of the Major Novels of Ivan Turgenev*. München: O. Sagner, 1990.

———. *Metaphysical Conflict: A Study of the Major Novels of Ivan Turgenev*. Munich: Verlag Otto Sagner, 1990.

———. "Turgenev's 'New Manner' in His Novel Dym." In his *Form and Meaning: Essays on Russian Literature*. Columbus, Ohio: Slavica Publishers, 1993: 75-93; 337-39.

————. "Turgenev's 'Constancy' in His Final Novel." In Arnold McMillin, ed., *From Pushkin to Palisandriia: Essays on the Russian Novel in Honor of Richard Freeborn*. New York: St. Martin's Press, (1990): 128-48.

Acknowledgments

"The Literary Apprenticeship, Pushkin—*A Sportsman's Sketches*" by Richard Freeborn. From *Turgenev: The Novelist's Novelist*. © 1960 by Richard Freeborn. Reprinted by permission of Oxford University Press.

"*Fathers and Sons*: Fathers and Children" by Kathryn Feuer. From *The Russian Novel from Pushkin to Pasternak*. © 1983 by Yale University Press: New Haven and London. Reprinted by permission.

"Turgenev's 'Mumu' and the Absence of Love" by Edgar L. Frost. From *Slavic and East European Journal*, vol. 31, no. 2. © 1987 by American Association of Teachers of Slavic and East European Languages: Arizona State University: Tempe, Arizona. Reprinted by permission.

"Hemingway and Turgenev: *The Torrents of Spring*" by Robert Coltrane. From *Hemingway's Neglected Short Fiction*, edited by Susan F. Beegel. © 1989 by The University of Alabama Press: Tuscaloosa and London. Reprinted by permission.

"First Loves: Willa Cather's Niel Herbert and Ivan Turgenev's Valdimir Petrovich" by Richard C. Harris. From *Studies in American Fiction*, vol. 17, no. 1. © 1989 by Northeastern University. Reprinted by permission.

"'The Parable of the Prodigal Son' and Turgenev's *Fathers and Sons*" by Harold K. Schefski. From *Literature and Belief*, vol. 10. © 1990 by Harold K. Schefski. Reprinted by permission.

"No Smoke Without Fire: The Genesis of Turgenev's *Dym*" by Patrick Waddington. From *From Pushkin to Palisandriia: Essays on the Russian Novel in Honor of Richard Freeborn.* © 1990 by Arnold McMillin. Reprinted with permission of Palgrave Macmillan.

"Philosophy, Myth, and Art in Turgenev's *Notes of a Hunter*" by Irene Masing-Delic. From *The Russian Review*, vol. 50, no. 4. © 1991 by The Ohio State University Press. Reprinted by permission of the publisher.

"Turgenev in the Critical Outlook of Henry James" by Glyn Turton. From *Turgenev and the Context of English Literature 1850-1900.* © 1992 by Routledge: London and New York. Reprinted by permission.

"*Reading* Fathers and Sons" by Dennis Walder, Glyn Turton and Pam Morris. From *The Realist Novel*, edited by Dennis Walder. © 1995 by The Open University: Routledge: New York and Canada. Reprinted by permission.

"Turgenev and Hawthorne: The Life-Giving Satyr and the Fallen Faun" by Richard Gregg. From *Slavic and East European Journal*, vol. 41, no. 2. © 1997 by American Association of Teachers of Slavic and East European Languages: Arizona State University: Tempe, Arizona. Reprinted by permission.

"Willa Cather, Sherwood Anderson and Ivan Turgenev" by Paul W. Miller. From *MidAmerica* XXIV. © 1997 by the Society for the Study of Midwestern Literature. Reprinted by permission.

Index

her changing conception of an
  artist's role in society, 209–210
the disappointment she had with
  modern American life, 80
on impact the Russians had on the
  American novel, 210
the influence *Sketches* had on her
  writing, 206
her interest in Turgenev, 72
her leaning toward Turgenev's
  historical view, 206
on similarities with Turgenev, 73–75
Chekhov, 19, 151–152, 207, 211
  admired by Turgenev, 207
  on powerful moods in his writing,
  165
Chernyshevsky, 34–35
Coltrane, Robert
  on Hemingway and Turgenev, 57–70
Conversation, The, 11
  on malaise in Turgenev's generation,
  12
Crews, Frederic, 197
Crimean War, 171, 179

Dark Laughter, (Anderson), 57–58
  on Hemingway finding it a failure,
  60–61
  on infidelity, 63
Dead Souls, (Gogol), 20, 122, 128
Death of Lyapunov, (play), Gedeonov, 5
Derzhavin, G. R., 103
Diary of a Superfluous Man, 17, 26
  on an emotional relationship in, 18
Dickens, 21
District Doctor, The, 117–118
Dostoevsky Fydor, 15, 122, 124, 170
  on his admiration of *Fathers and
  Sons*, 35
  the beginning of his career, 21
  on Turgenev's admiring his works,
  207
Double, The, (Dostoyevsky), 21

Duellist, The, 15
Dym, 97, 105, 108
  on hope, 98
  theme of, 97–98
  on title of novel, 103–104
  as a weak novel, 97

Edel, Leon, 131
Eliot, George, 138–139, 157
"End of Something, The,"
  (Hemingway), 65
English Criticism of the Novel, (Graham),
  147
Eugene Onegin, (Pushkin), 6–7, 21, 91
  as documentary record, 20
  on hero in, 7–8
  on heroine in, 7–8
  the law of fate in, 8–9
  on realism in, 9
  on the social and moral dilemma in
  Russian society, 8

Fathers and Sons, 23, 25–26, 30
  on altered consciousness, 167
  on Bazarov, 168
  the conflict between men of
  different times, 23
  on conflict of ideas, 167
  the female characters in, 151–152,
  169, 184–186
  on Hemingway's study of, 59
  the human individuality in, 166
  on the intellectual, 173
  on the prodigal sons theme, 86–94
  on realism and history, 173–174
  religion in, 94
  on science and the future, 174
  strength of women in, 179
  the theme of, 33–34, 165
  truth in, 171–172
Faust, (Goethe), 12–14
Feuer, Kathryn
  on *Fathers and Sons*, 23–37

War and Peace, (Tolstoy), 138, 206
Washington Square, (James), 139
Wellek, Rene
  on interpretation of *Fathers and Sons*,
    24–25
Wharton, 205
What Is To Be Done?, (Chernyshevsky),
    34–35, 180–181
"White Mulberry Tree," (Cather), 208

Who is Guilty?, (Herzen), 21
Woolf, Virginia, 207

Yarmolinsky, Avrahm
  on Turgenev's literary practice, 211
Yermolay and the Miller's Wife, 17
Young, Philip, 197
Youth and the Bright Medusa, (Cather), 80